Authentic PORTUGUESE COOKING

Authentic
PORTUGUESE
COOKING

185 Classic Mediterranean-Style Recipes of the Azores, Madeira and Continental Portugal

Ana Patuleia Ortins

creator of Portuguesecooking.com and author of *Portuguese Homestyle Cooking*

Photography by Ted Axelrod

PAGE STREET
PUBLISHING CO.

PAGE STREET
PUBLISHING CO.

First published in 2015 by
Page Street Publishing Co.
27 Congress Street, Suite 1511
Salem, MA 01970
www.pagestreetpublishing.com

Distributed by Macmillan, sales in Canada by The Canadian Manda Group.

25 24 23 22   4 5 6 7

ISBN-13: 978-1-62414-686-2
ISBN-10: 1-62414-686-4

Library of Congress Control Number: 2018948133

Cover and book design by Page Street Publishing Co.
Photography by Ted Axelrod

Printed and bound in China

Dedication

This book is created in memory of my father, Rufino, who taught me so much; my mother, Filomena, who, like my father, was a strong influence in my cooking; my brother "Rudy" (Rufino Jr.), for his passion and encouragement; and my grandmother Tereza and grandfather José, for their lessons and inspiration. I wish you all were here to enjoy the results of your passion for passing on our great food, and your culinary influence and enthusiasm that pushed me forward.

To my S.N.A.C. team, Sophia, Natalie, Andrew and Colin: This is for you with love from Vóvó, to go forward with your enthusiasm to cook and to keep our traditional recipes alive.

Foreword

What struck me most when I first met Ana in her home was her warm and welcoming nature. I had experienced this, to the extent it was possible, during our many conversations when I was writing my own cookbook. I had approached her for advice on the publishing process. At that time, Ana's first book, *Portuguese Homestyle Cooking*, had already been in print for a decade and was prominently placed in my cookbook library. In the ensuing days of my visit with Ana, her natural warmth was combined with passion and perfectionism that I found very impressive. Ana wanted her food and recipes to be perfect. She wanted her dishes to tell a story. We all do, but Ana took it to another level—one that is perfect for a cookbook writer. Though my copy of Ana's book was dog eared and worn from much use for inspiration and education, I came away with even more appreciation for what was sitting on my shelf.

As with Ana's first book, her latest work is firmly rooted in preserving the traditional dishes. This is hugely important. Many chefs, myself included, attempt to evolve Portuguese cuisine, but one can do that only with deep understanding of the classics. Ana has added a few modern adaptions of her own, which is only natural. Incredible dishes ranging from whole roasted pig to squid are covered in this book. Ana not only shares a wide range of recipes with us, but she also offers thorough and clear instructions so even a novice can produce extraordinary food.

This book you are holding in your hands now is a shining example of Ana's pursuit of perfection and her passion for Portuguese food—and her warmth. Soak it in as I have.

—**Manuel H. Azevedo**, author of *LaSalette Cookbook,* chef and owner of LaSalette Restaurant

Introduction

Authentic Portuguese Cooking, as in my first book, *Portuguese Homestyle Cooking*, continues to preserve the fundamental traditional dishes of my Portuguese heritage and shares its wonderful flavors with those who are eager to try a new cuisine. In addition to preserving these made-from-scratch recipes and hopefully passing on my passion to you, I hope to show you that cooking Portuguese can be flexible "*com gusto*" (to your liking) and erase the opinion that all Portuguese food is salty; after all, it is the cook's hand that adds the salt.

 All around us, food is always evolving from dishes we know and love into new creations fused with ingredients of multiple ethnicities. New ingredients have been making their way into Portuguese cuisine as well. Fusion can be fun only so long as dishes are not portrayed as authentic of one cuisine or another.

It would be an understatement to say I am passionate about preserving good old family recipes. That being said, I feel it is important to hand down these traditional recipes so that cooks, present and future, can experience and understand the traditional flavors of these comfort foods from past generations before embarking on a new style of Portuguese cooking. Then, if they like, they can go forward, build on these flavors, think outside the box and create their own versions as I sometimes have, hopefully without compromising the integral flavor of traditional well-known dishes. They can give their new versions new names or create new and different dishes with clear elements of Portuguese flavors.

I never anticipated writing a second book of the authentic home recipes of my Portuguese upbringing. In *Portuguese Homestyle Cooking*, I included only the most basic recipes, a few of which I have repeated in this book. After the book was published, I was surprised to receive many emails and letters from around the globe requesting this recipe or that recipe, some long lost, others vaguely remembered or simply fondly recalled by those who enjoyed a visit to Portugal's mainland or the Azores. At the same time, I connected with many in the Portuguese community, near and far, who shared old family recipes with me. So in addition to the recipes I left out of the first book, *Authentic Portuguese Cooking* includes recipes sent to me, requested and researched with Portuguese cooks. I also relied on my treasure of Portuguese relatives and friends, their family recipes that have been updated and ones I created.

This book, like *Portuguese Homestyle Cooking*, is *not* meant to be a Portuguese dictionary or a book on Portuguese history. I leave the history to the historians and the language to linguists who can present them better than I can. However, *Authentic Portuguese Cooking*, like *Portuguese Homestyle Cooking*, is a cookbook that is focused not only on preserving traditional dishes before they are lost to fusion or cooks and writers, who continue to offer adulterated versions as authentic, but also on sharing the recipes and food memories of my heritage. It also introduces some contemporary creations that are in keeping with the Portuguese flavors.

Although the Azores, Madeira and the mainland of Portugal are not on the Mediterranean, they may as well be. The flavors in these recipes of our culture are Mediterranean in style. This book is meant to enable adventurous cooks, young and old, novices and professionals alike, who wish to explore the traditional, soul-comforting, everyday culinary fare of the Portugal beyond what tourists find in hotels and sidewalk cafés. Don't get me wrong—that is all good but there is more beyond *bifana*s (marinated pork medallions), Portuguese fried potatoes and sardines. There is still a great variety of traditional Portuguese home cooking that is soothing, exciting and satisfying.

While there are some fabulous five-star restaurants in Portugal's larger cities, the food tends to be contemporary and not a true representation of traditional Portuguese fare. Though I welcome and enjoy a modern twist on some old favorites or a new Portuguese creation (some of which I have included in this book), my main focus of this book is on the traditional dishes you would enjoy in the outskirts of the big cities. There are also a few, which are noted, that I have slightly updated with a shortcut method, different texture or just my way of doing something but getting the same result and flavor. In addition, you will find a few main ingredients for which I have given more than one method of preparation. My cousin Claudia told me that when she is out in Lisbon with her young son or with her friends, they will enjoy modern fare, but at home their hearts and cooking passions are with the traditional recipes. Like Claudia, we all enjoy eating modern dishes, yet few words can describe the enjoyment of cooking and eating traditional favorites. Traditional favorites just bring your soul home.

As you explore the recipes in this book, I hope you will be tempted to cook up a Portuguese feast! Experiment a little. Any questions or comments regarding the recipes can be sent to me at ana@portuguesecooking.com. Visit my website www.portuguesecooking.com for additional recipe information and a resource guide. From my kitchen to yours, *bom apetite!*

Ana Patuleia Ortins

Before You Begin

While teaching classes, I often hear students claim they are not good cooks, or they get nervous cooking if it is too much work. Being prepared will help you avoid mistakes. Here are a few tips for the novice or nervous cook:

Read a recipe through three times.

The first time is to see what is involved, if there is special prep, something you don't understand or something that needs to be done several hours or a day ahead, like soaking beans, marinating and so on.

The second is to make your shopping list, checking your pantry for what you don't have or for a special pan or ingredient.

The third is when you are prepping and cooking. Have everything ready, meaning rinsed, peeled, chopped, measured out and lined up in the order of use according to the recipe; this way, there should be no need to stop the process of cooking because you forgot to purchase or prepare something first. You will find cooking far more enjoyable, less stressful and much easier.

Always taste as you cook and more than once.

Have a separate spoon, and a little dish so you can ladle or place a tidbit of the recipe on it to taste. Frequently taste for salt and other seasonings.

Use the freshest ingredients you can get.

Yes, fresh vegetables, meats, breads. What about spices and herbs? Even while you can get ground spices, make sure they are fresh. Try using whole allspice berries, cumin seeds and peppercorns and crushing them yourself. Just like saffron threads, you can toast these spices in a small fat-free dry skillet for a few minutes, then crush them. For the best flavor, use the freshest green herbs whenever possible. Herbs like parsley, cilantro and basil lose flavor when dried.

Lastly, don't be thrown by the length of any recipe in this book.

Really read the recipe through. In my attempt to give detailed instructions so any novice can understand, I know some recipes are wordy and long to the experienced chef, but I don't like to assume that every cook reading one of my recipes is clear on the method. Long does not mean the recipe is difficult.

Meats and Poultry
Carnes e Aves

Eating off the land is clearly more than consuming vegetables in the garden and fruits off the trees unless you are a vegetarian or vegan. The Portuguese do quite well cooking poultry and meats as well as their beloved seafood. All meats can be sautéed, roasted and braised. However, it is the cut of the meat that determines which method is best used. This chapter features a variety of down-to-earth, homestyle dishes ranging from heart-warming stews to roasts, braises and sautés. The recipes for Valencia Rice and Duck with Rice are really about the resulting flavorful rice that makes the meal, but because they are a main dish with meat, I have placed them in this chapter. Some recipes are quick and easy while others require old-fashioned slow cooking, with mouthwatering results. If a recipe seems long, it is because I am giving step-by-step directions so even the novice can follow. Remember to read the recipes through completely before beginning to see what is needed. Prep ahead and line up ingredients in the order of use. Cooking is so much easier and enjoyable that way.

***

I grew up helping my father cook Sunday dinner while the Portuguese radio station played music. Mostly watching, I hoped I would learn how to make his flavorful one-pot stews and braises. He was particularly fond of making his stove-top and oven braises. Braising cannot be rushed he would say, in between his rendition of a Portuguese song and a few dance steps. Whether it was rabbit, beef short ribs, lamb shanks, shoulder cuts and tougher cuts of meat, they would simmer slowly from 2½ to 4 hours (depending on the cut) in a Dutch oven over medium-low heat with a combination of wine and water along with vegetables, spices and herbs. At the end of cooking, a cornstarch slurry would give body to the braising broth.

When my father wasn't cooking inside, he would be grilling outside at the brick fireplace he built. Back then, you could burn your own rubbish, so with his Portuguese ingenuity he built a two-sided fireplace. The back of the fireplace was for incinerating the rubbish and the front, an open fire pit, was put to good use cooking sardines, lamb or whatever he set his mind to. When weather permitted, he would set up his Motorola record player and cook outdoors for family and friends, listening to the sounds of Amàlia Rodrigues singing fados. Something joyful happens when music and cooking come together; in my kitchen it is like someone turns on a happy switch and the memory of my father dancing and cooking sits on my shoulder.

Evelina's Spicy Azorean-Style Beef Stew
Carne Guisada à Açoreano

SERVES 4

Whatever Cousin Evelina had on hand, she could turn into something very flavorful. Her beef stew wasn't any different. Made in the style of her upbringing on the island of Graciosa, this stew, flavored with garlic, tomato, saffron and a little kick, goes the great distance in satisfying one's hunger.

¼ —— cup/60 ml olive oil

2 —— pounds/908 g beef stew meat, cut into 2- to 3-inch/5- to 7.5-cm cubes, patted dry

1 —— large onion, thinly sliced (about 1 cup/130 g)

4 —— garlic cloves, coarsely chopped

1 —— bay leaf

1 —— tablespoon/15 g tomato paste

1 —— tablespoon/15 ml Chile Pepper Paste (page 365)

1 —— teaspoon/6 g coarse kosher salt or to taste

½ —— teaspoon crushed saffron

Ground black or white pepper to taste

1 —— cup/235 ml white or rosé wine (red will darken the meat)

1. Heat the oil in the bottom of a 4-quart/3.6-L pot over medium-high heat. Blot the meat with paper toweling to remove excess moisture. Work in small batches and brown the meat on all sides. Add the onion and sauté until they are soft and translucent, about 2 to 3 minutes.

2. Mix in the garlic, bay leaf, tomato paste, chile pepper paste, salt, saffron and pepper.

3. Pour in the wine and cover tightly. Place the pot over medium-low heat. When the wine starts to bubble, reduce the heat to low and simmer slowly for 1½ to 2 hours. The meat should be fork-tender. Discard the bay leaf. Serve with boiled potatoes or cooked rice.

Pico Island Pot Roast with Allspice
Carne Assada à Moda do Pico

SERVES 6

Ester Mendonca takes pride in her *carne assada*, and rightly so. Her Pico Island–style pot roast combines cinnamon and allspice, which are complementary to the beef, but not overwhelming. After 4 hours of slow cooking the meat will shrink, but it will almost melt in your mouth.

---

4 ——— pounds/1818 g boneless chuck or bottom round roast

1 ——— large onion, thinly sliced

½ ——— cup/112 g butter, softened

¼ ——— cup/60 ml wine vinegar or juice of 2 oranges

¼ ——— cup/60 ml water

2 ——— garlic cloves, smashed

1½ ——— teaspoons/5 g paprika

1 ——— teaspoon/6 g coarse kosher salt or to taste

3 or 4 — Jamaican allspice berries (about ¼ teaspoon)

1 ——— small chile pepper

1 ——— 2-inch/5-cm piece of cinnamon stick

White wine as needed (you can use red but the meat will be darker)

1. Preheat the oven to 350°F/180°C, or gas mark 4. Place the roast in a large Dutch oven or braising pan.

2. In a bowl, combine the onion, butter, vinegar, water, garlic, paprika, salt, Jamaican allspice and chile pepper. Transfer the ingredients to the pot, dumping them evenly across the top of the roast. Turn the roast to coat. Toss in the cinnamon stick then pour in enough white wine to come three-fourths of the way up the sides of the roast. Cover the pan tightly.

3. Place the roast in the oven for 1 hour. Reduce the heat to 200°F/95°C. Continue to slow roast for 3 more hours. Serve with buttered rice and sautéed greens.

Salted Meats
Carnes Salgadas

On occasion, questions of old methods and recipes are brought up. One such question was that of "salted meats." Besides using oil or rendered fat to preserve meat through the winter months or on long voyages, Portuguese cooks and sailors would pour a thick bottom layer of coarse salt into a large ceramic crock or wooden barrel. Layers of meat would be added with layers of coarse salt in between. To use the salt-dried meat, the desired number of pieces would be washed in fresh water and used in soups. Needless to say, additional salt was not needed.

Holy Ghost Wine and Spice Braised Beef

Sopas

SERVES 6

I have had requests for a recipe called "*sopish*" (*sopas*), a dish that is prepared especially for the feast of the Holy Ghost celebrated on Pentecost Sunday. Certain regions, such as the islands of Terceira and Graciosa of the Azores archipelagos, make Holy Ghost Soup, the recipe given in *Portuguese Homestyle Cooking*. Other Portuguese descendants in the United States described their search for a version that resembles braised beef. The principle is almost the same, but the former is truly a soup where the meat is removed from the soup broth and served separately. The broth with vegetables is ladled over bread and garnished with mint. The latter version of the *sopish* is definitely more of a pot roast. A search brought me to the family recipe of Richard Silva. The meat is also separated from the pan juices. Is it traditional to the Azoreans? I honestly don't know. This could be an adaptation created in the United States. However, depending on the island in the Azores, I found the meal for the feast of the Holy Spirit can be quite lean, as with the soup from the island of Santa Maria, to abundant ones like this.

THE DAY BEFORE

4 —— pounds/1818 g beef chuck roast, bone-in

1½ —— cups/355 ml red wine

4 —— garlic cloves, peeled and smashed

1 —— bay leaf

½ —— teaspoon crushed dried chile pepper

THE NEXT DAY

1 —— cup/235 ml water

1 —— large Vidalia or yellow Spanish onion, thickly sliced

1½ —— cups/270 g finely chopped, peeled, very ripe tomatoes

¼ —— cup/60 g ketchup

2 —— tablespoons/30 g tomato paste

1 —— 2-inch/5-cm piece of cinnamon stick

7 —— whole cloves

7 —— Jamaican allspice berries

¼ —— teaspoon cumin seeds

1 —— bay leaf

½ —— tablespoon/9 g coarse kosher salt or to taste

6 —— thick slices day-old Portuguese, Italian, Spanish, Greek or crusty artisan bread

6 to 12 —— mint leaves

THE DAY BEFORE

1. Place the roast in a non-reactive 5-quart/4.5-L pot with a tight-fitting lid such as a Dutch oven. Pour the wine over and toss in the garlic, bay leaf and crushed dried chile pepper. Cover and marinate for several hours or overnight, turning the meat over occasionally.

THE NEXT DAY

1. Add the water to the pot containing the roast and marinade. Toss in the onion slices. Mix the tomatoes and ketchup with the tomato paste and stir into the pot.

2. Place the cinnamon stick, cloves, Jamaican allspice, cumin and bay leaf in a square of cheesecloth. Tie it up with a piece of kitchen string and place in the pot. Sprinkle the salt over the roast.

3. Make sure the liquid comes halfway up the sides of the roast. If not, add more wine and water in equal amounts.

4. Cover and bring to a boil over medium-high heat. Reduce the heat to medium-low and turning the meat occasionally, simmer slowly until the meat is falling-off-the-bone tender, about 3 hours.

5. To serve, remove the meat and pull it off the bone in pieces. Place a thick slice of crusty Portuguese or artisan bread in each soup plate topped with a mint leaf or two. Ladle a generous amount of broth over the bread to soften. Serve the meat over or beside the moistened bread.

Tomato and Onion Sauced Beef

Bife de Molho

SERVES 4 TO 6

Americans would say this reminds them of Salisbury steak but up a level. You could almost call this *desfeita*, meaning "shredded," because by the time the meat is done, it is so tender, it nearly falls apart as though shredded. Although it is another of Cousin Evelina Cunha's flavorful recipes that she brought from her home on the island of Graciosa, here in the States she used cube steak. I have also used chuck steak for this dish with great results. Serve the meat and onions sauce over sliced Portuguese or artisan bread as an open-faced sandwich, in a bun or serve with bread on the side.

1	tablespoon/14 g butter
3	medium onions, coarsely chopped (about 3 cups/454 g), divided
3	bay leaves
3	garlic cloves, coarsely chopped, divided
1½	cups/270 g coarsely chopped, peeled tomatoes, divided
1½	teaspoons/5 g paprika
1½	teaspoons/9 g coarse kosher salt or to taste
¾	teaspoon ground black pepper
½ to 1	teaspoon Chile Pepper Paste (page 365)
½	teaspoon ground or 6 Jamaican allspice berries
¾	teaspoon cinnamon
2	pounds/908 g (8 pieces) cube steak (bottom round) or beef chuck, cut into ¾-inch/2-cm slices
¾	cup/180 ml white or rosé wine
¼	teaspoon ground cumin or to taste
1	tablespoon/15 g tomato paste

1. Melt the butter in a 5-quart/4.5-L Dutch oven. Working with two layers of beef and three layers of seasoning, excluding the wine, cumin and tomato paste, scatter one-third of the onions, bay leaves, garlic, tomatoes, paprika, salt, black pepper, chile pepper paste, Jamaican allspice and cinnamon over the melted butter.

2. Now add one single layer of beef, arranged on the seasoning. Again, take half of the remaining onions and seasonings and scatter them over the steak. Top that with the second layer of beef, placing them crosswise over the first layer. Finish with the remaining spices and onions on top.

3. Cover tightly and place the pot over medium heat so the ingredients will sweat and form their own juices, about 5 minutes. Reduce the heat to medium-low and simmer slowly for 20 minutes. When the beef juices start to come together in a sauce, combine the wine, cumin and tomato paste together and slowly pour over and around the meat. Recover and continue to simmer over medium-low heat. After simmering for an additional 15 minutes, check to make sure the meat isn't getting dried out. The meat should be just about done. Simmer for about 5 minutes more if need be. Discard the bay leaves. Serve from the pot with boiled potatoes and plenty of bread to soak up the sauce.

Steak with Garlic Mustard Cream Sauce
Bife com Molho de Mostarda e Nata

SERVES 4

Although a popular old recipe, especially on the mainland, this recipe can certainly hold its own against the masses of elegant steak dishes. Creamy smooth with just a light flavor of mustard, the sauce envelops the steak, tantalizing the taste buds. I have replaced the use of dry mustard with prepared mustard. Though this dish is not for those with cholesterol issues, I felt it still warrants a place among the favorite beef dishes of the Portuguese.

---

4 —— rib-eye or sirloin steaks or beef fillets, cut 1½ to 2 inches/3.8 to 5 cm thick, excess visible fat removed

8 —— tablespoons/112 g softened butter, divided

4 —— garlic cloves, finely chopped

Coarse kosher salt, to taste

Fresh ground black pepper, to taste

¼ —— cup/60 ml red wine

1 —— cup/235 ml milk

¼ —— cup/60 ml heavy cream

¼ —— scant cup/60 ml Simple Mustard Cream Sauce (page 374)

2 —— tablespoons/30 ml lemon juice

1. Make sure the steaks are trimmed of excess fat. Pat them with a paper towel to remove excess moisture. In a small bowl, combine 4 tablespoons/56 g of the butter with the chopped garlic, salt and pepper. Divide the garlic butter among the 4 steaks, coating both sides of each one.

2. Heat a large heavy skillet over medium-high heat. Add the steaks, searing them for about 5 minutes. Turn and cook for 5 minutes more, or until desired doneness, turning once. Make a small cut in the middle of the steak to see if it is done to your liking. Transfer to a warm plate and cover tightly.

3. Deglaze the pan with the red wine, scraping up the bits on the bottom. Add the remaining 4 tablespoons/56 g butter and the milk, cream and mustard sauce. Whisk well to blend. Stirring continuously, add the lemon juice and continue to simmer over low heat until it becomes a slightly thickened sauce, about 2 to 3 minutes. Do not allow to boil.

4. Return the steaks to the pan, turning them in the sauce for just 1 minute to heat through. Serve with buttered or plain rice, or boiled or fried thick potato slices.

Note: For a lower-fat alternative, simply use equal parts of regular or even Dijon mustard and white wine and do not use cream. Place in a jar or bottle with a tight-fitting lid. Shake it up really well to emulsify. Stir into the pan drippings and continue with step 4.

Garlic Nailed Steak on a Plate
Prego no Prato

SERVES 2

It is thought that this recipe was transplanted from Mozambique, a former Portuguese colony, to South Africa by holiday travelers who then brought the recipe home to Portugal. Growing up, we referred to this dish as *Bife à Portuguesa*, though it is also known by some as *Prego no Prato* (Garlic Nailed Steak on a Plate). I like to cook the beef this way and toss it in a roll for Saturday lunches. The sauce, which comes from the cooking of the seasoned meat, is what is considered to be the real "Prego sauce," and not to be confused with the Prego pasta sauce in the jar. Some contemporary cooks in South Africa add a touch of tomato paste to the pan sauce. Some also use chicken cutlets in place of beef.

---

2 —— sirloin or rib-eye steaks, ¾ inch/2 cm thick, trimmed of any visible fat

6 —— garlic cloves (or more if you like), thinly sliced

Coarse kosher salt as needed

Ground black pepper as needed

4 —— tablespoons/56 g butter, divided

1 —— large onion, thinly sliced

½ —— cup/120 ml white wine

¼ —— teaspoon crushed dried chile pepper

Pinch of cumin (optional)

1 —— tablespoon/4 g finely chopped parsley

1. Place the steaks on your workspace or cutting board. Lay the slices of garlic on one side of the steaks. Using a tenderizing mallet, "nail" the garlic to the steak by pounding the slices into the meat, then season with some salt and pepper. Repeat on the reverse side of the steaks. Let stand for ½ hour at room temperature.

2. Melt 3 tablespoons/42 g of the butter in a skillet over medium-high heat. Sear the steaks in the butter for barely 5 minutes, turning once and cooking the other side for another 3 to 4 minutes. Make a small cut in the middle of the steak and check the color for your desired doneness. Transfer to a dish and cover.

3. Set the same skillet over medium heat and melt the remaining 1 tablespoon/ 14 g butter. Add the onions and sauté until golden, about 5 minutes. Transfer the onions to the dish holding the steaks. Pour the wine into the same skillet. Using the flat edge of a wooden spatula, scrape up the brown coating on the bottom of the pan. Raise the heat to medium-high and reduce the sauce by half. Once reduced, turn heat to medium-low.

4. Season the wine sauce with the chile pepper, cumin and half the parsley. Taste the sauce for salt and pepper and adjust to your taste. Return the onions and beef to the sauce and heat through for 1 minute. Serve the beef and onions, drizzled with the sauce and a salad on the side for a perfect lunch. Garnish with the remaining parsley.

Beef Fillet with Prosciutto

Bife com Presunto

SERVES 4

One of our favorite restaurants in Lisbon makes this dish the best. The restaurant, Senhor Vinho, well known for its food, service and fado singers, never lets us down. The recipe is adapted from them. You want the prosciutto to be thin enough that you can fold it over. When we had this dish in Portugal, the prosciutto was slightly crispy and there wasn't a lot of sauce. As for the garlic, which has small and large cloves, you have to remember that filet mignon is mild tasting and if you give it too much garlic, it will overpower the meat. After all is said, it is your preference as to the amount of garlic you add, the amount of sauce you want and how crispy you make the prosciutto. Some prosciuttos are also saltier than others. The Portuguese one is definitely saltier. Italian prosciutto is a perfect substitute.

---

8 — large garlic cloves, finely chopped (about 1 teaspoon/10 g per side of each steak)

1 — teaspoon/6 g coarse kosher salt, divided as needed

½ — teaspoon ground black pepper, divided as needed

4 — filets mignons, 1 inch/2.5 cm thick

2½ — tablespoons/35 g butter, or as needed

2½ — tablespoons/37 ml olive oil (equal to butter)

1 — bay leaf, broken in half

4 — slices *presunto*/prosciutto or boiled ham, thinly sliced

1 — teaspoon/3 g cornstarch

3 — tablespoons/45 ml red wine vinegar

½ — cup/120 ml red wine

1 — tablespoon/15 ml lemon juice

2 — tablespoons/8 g finely chopped parsley, divided

1. Using a mortar and pestle, make a paste of the garlic, salt and pepper. Season each side of the steaks with ½ teaspoon of the paste, or to your preference.

2. Heat the butter and olive oil together in a large heavy skillet until hot but not smoking. Add the bay leaf and the steaks, frying the steaks for about 5 minutes on each side or to your desired doneness. Remove the steaks to individual serving dishes and keep warm.

3. Reduce the heat to medium. Using the same pan, lightly and quickly fry the slices of prosciutto (about 30 seconds to 1 minute), but don't let them get too crispy. The slices will shrink a bit, so you want to just pick up flavor and grab a hint of color. Transfer a slice to the top of each steak, folding it over to fit.

4. Mix the cornstarch with the wine vinegar, red wine and lemon juice and add to the pan juices, heating through just until the pan sauce thickens slightly, about 1 minute. Be careful not to reduce the pan sauce. Add half of the parsley and give the sauce a stir. Discard the bay leaf. Spoon some pan juices over each steak. Serve with fried potatoes and a salad. Garnish with the remaining parsley.

St. Michael Island–Style Spicy Beef Steaks
Bife à São Miguel

SERVES 2

Although in the touristy areas the food of the island of São Miguel can be almost on the bland side, the island folk have always been known for their spicy dishes. Just the sauce alone is reason enough to make this dish. The buttery, tangy sauce gives the steak just the right amount of kick. Inspired by the island's traditional food culture, I adapted this beef recipe from my friend Helder Texeira. I suggest adding the hot sauce to taste.

---

2 ——— steaks (like rib eye or T-bone), cut 1 inch/2.5 cm thick

Coarse kosher salt to taste

Ground black pepper to taste

4 ——— tablespoons/56 g butter

4 ——— garlic cloves, finely chopped

1½ ——— teaspoons/4 g flour

½ ——— cup/120 ml red wine

1 ——— tablespoon/15 ml hot sauce or to taste

1. On your workspace, season one side of the steaks with salt and pepper.

2. Melt the butter in a heavy skillet until hot but not burning. Add the steaks, seasoned side down. Season the top with salt and pepper.

3. Sear the steaks for about 5 minutes on each side over medium-high heat, to your preference. Remove the steaks to a platter after they are done and keep warm.

4. Add the garlic to the pan, giving it a turn in the pan drippings. As the garlic becomes slightly aromatic, about 30 seconds, stir in the flour to form a roux. Whisk in the wine and hot sauce, then simmer for a minute over medium-low heat, slightly reducing the sauce by about one-third. Return the steaks to heat through, turning to coat in the sauce, for about 1 minute. Transfer the steaks to serving dishes and drizzle the sauce over them. Serve with vegetables and rice or potatoes and extra hot sauce on the side. Don't forget the bread to dip in the sauce!

Madeiran Wine and Garlic Beef Kabobs

Espetada da Madeira

SERVES 4 TO 6

On the island of Madeira, cooks are known for their *espetada*, chunks of beef skewered on bay laurel branches and cooked over a wood fire. Rosemary branches work well, too. Very little is needed to accompany this dish: a little vegetable, rice, olive, bread, good wine and friends to share with. As an alternative, you can thread whole bay leaves in between the chunks of meat, using wooden skewers. Some might even spritz a little lemon juice over the meat.

---

2 ——— teaspoons/12 g kosher salt or to taste

3 or 4 — garlic cloves, peeled and coarsely chopped

3 or 4 — large bay leaves, crumbled

½ ——— teaspoon fresh ground black pepper

Pinch of crushed dried chile peppers

1 ——— tablespoon/15 ml red wine

1 ——— tablespoon/15 ml red wine vinegar

2 ——— tablespoons/30 ml olive oil

2 ——— pounds/908 g beef sirloin strip, cut into 1½- to 2-inch/3.8- to 5-cm pieces

Wooden skewers soaked in water for ½ hour

1. Using a mortar and pestle, combine the salt and garlic, mashing the two until the garlic becomes a paste. Mix in the crumbed bay leaves, black pepper, chile pepper, wine, wine vinegar and olive oil.

2. Place the meat cubes in a shallow nonreactive bowl. Pour the seasoning paste over the meat and turn the meat to coat thoroughly on all sides. Let stand for 2 to 4 hours or even overnight in the refrigerator.

3. Using water-soaked skewers or even metal ones, thread the meat onto the skewers. Grill, turning on all sides, approximately 5 inches/12.5 cm above the flames until medium, about 10 minutes, or broil to desired doneness.

Pork with Clams Alentejo Style
Carne de Porco à Alentejana

SERVES 6

Succulent sautéed pieces of marinated pork somehow work so well with briny clams. It all comes together in a zesty garlic- and wine-based broth infused with Sweet Pepper Paste (page 367), paprika and most importantly, fresh chopped cilantro, giving it a lemony essence. This version, adapted from my first book, *Portuguese Homestyle Cooking*, does not make the sauce separately. This recipe is actually the one that I knew growing up, served with potatoes simmering in the sauce, which absorbs the flavors of the sauce as they cook. This dish is often served in today's restaurants with fried cubed potatoes. Any addition of chopped, pickled vegetables to this dish, which gives it a vinegary taste that hides the wonderful spices and flavorful sauce, is not traditional nor found in the Alentejo style. This is a great one-pot dish to serve for guests. Read the recipe through and the notes at the end of the recipe before beginning.

A DAY AHEAD

2½	——	pounds/1135 g pork tenderloin, trimmed of silver skin
8	——	garlic cloves, coarsely chopped (adjust amount to your taste)
1	——	tablespoon/8 g paprika
1	——	bay leaf, crumbled
¼	——	teaspoon black pepper
¼	——	cup/15 g finely chopped fresh cilantro
1	——	tablespoon/15 g Sweet Pepper Paste (page 367)
2	——	teaspoons/10 ml hot pepper sauce
1	——	cup/235 ml white wine

TO COOK

½	——	cup/120 ml olive oil or as needed
1	——	medium onion, finely chopped (about 1 cup/160 g)
1	——	cup/180 g peeled, seeded, coarsely chopped tomato
1	——	garlic clove, smashed
1	——	teaspoon/3 g paprika
1	——	tablespoon/15 g tomato paste

A DAY AHEAD

1. Cut the tenderloin into cubes about 2 inches/5 cm in size. Place in a nonreactive bowl.

2. Using a mortar and pestle, make a paste by mashing the garlic while incorporating the paprika, crumbled bay leaf and black pepper. Stir in the cilantro, sweet pepper paste and hot pepper sauce, blending thoroughly.

3. Add the seasoning paste to the bowl of pork and turn the meat, seasoning throughout. Pour the wine over the cubes of meat. Cover and marinate for several hours or overnight in the refrigerator.

TO COOK

1. Remove the meat from the refrigerator about 30 minutes before cooking. Reserving the marinade, drain the pork into a sieve set over a separate bowl. Strain the marinade and set aside.

(continued)

1 —————— cup/235 ml white wine

24————— parboiled baby boiling potatoes like red bliss or creamers

3 —————— pounds/1362 g small littleneck clams, 2 to 3 inches/5 to 7.5 cm in diameter, about 6 per person, scrubbed well in cold water

¼ —————— cup/15 g finely chopped cilantro

1 —————— lemon, cut into wedges

2. Heat the olive oil in a wide, heavy-bottomed pan, cataplana pan, paella pan or braising pan over medium-high heat. Brown the pieces of pork in small batches so that they will brown properly, about 5 to 8 minutes per batch. Transfer the browned meat to a dish and cover.

3. To the same pan, add the onions. Sauté them until lightly golden, about 5 minutes. Stir in the tomatoes, garlic and paprika. Cover and simmer over medium-low heat for 10 minutes until tomatoes are soft and married to the onions. Stir in reserved marinade. Mix tomato paste with the wine and stir into onions and tomatoes. Simmer covered for 1 minute. Add the meat back to the pan. Nestle the parboiled potatoes in between the pieces of meat.

4. Nestle the clams between the meat and potatoes and cover the pan. Continue to cook until the meat is fork-tender, the potatoes have taken on the flavor of the sauce and the clams are opened, about 12 to 15 minutes more, adjusting for the size of the shellfish. Discard any clams that do not open. Set the pan on the table and serve directly from the pan, garnished with the finely chopped cilantro. Serve with bread and olives on the side and squeeze some lemon juice over the dish, if desired.

Alguidar vs. Caçoilo

The definition of meat preparations and the cooking vessel they are cooked in can mean the same thing but not always. So what are an *alguidar* and a *caçoilo*, you ask? Here is the breakdown:

The *alguidar* is an orange-red, flat-bottomed clay pot with flared sides, much like a lampshade turned upside down. It is used specifically for making *alcatra* (recipe in *Portuguese Homestyle Cooking*), a beef rump, or even short ribs, slowly braised in seasoned wine. An *alguidar* can be used as well to make *caçoila*. Like the *alcatra*, the name *caçoila* indicates a slowly cooked stew but with pork. In the Azores, the *caçoila* is often made after the winter slaughter of pigs. The recipe differs depending on whom you ask.

The *caçoilo*, not to be confused with the *caçoila*, is a round black clay pot. The best ones, it is said, come from northern Portugal, in the town of Poiares, where cooks used pots made from the black *molelos* clay for their famous oven-braised goat dish called *chanfana*. Although it is typically made with goat, cooks from nearby towns, like Aveiro, are known to make it with lamb. It is said the black pots of Poiares impart special flavor to the meat, and I would say it is akin to cooking a steak in a stainless steel skillet versus a cast-iron one: the cast-iron one imparts flavor to the meat. That makes a difference to the taste buds. Lastly, we have the *cachola*. This is an Alentejo dish of pork liver and offals made during the winter slaughtering season. People were poor and nothing got wasted. The *cachola* is also made in a black clay pot but not necessarily one from Poiares.

Confused? Are the pots interchangeable? If you have no choice, sure. You can also use a heavy-bottomed stew pot or Dutch oven, but the flavor will be different and less braising liquid will be evaporated.

In summary, *alguidars* are used to cook *alcatras* and *caçoilas*. The *caçoilos* are used for *chanfana* and *cacholas*. Both need to be preseasoned before using. If my grandmother were to say she was going to make an *alcatra* or a *caçoila*, in a word it is understood what it is and how it is cooked. Today it is also understood what will be on the table no matter what type of pot you use, even if it is not the traditional vessel.

Pork Stew with Cinnamon, Wine and Garlic
Caçoila de Porco

SERVES 8 TO 10

When Imelda Silva makes her *caçoila* with pork butt, including the pig's heart, tongue and lungs,
she is utilizing the by-products created during the winter *matança* (slaughtering of pigs). By all means, you can
make the dish with just the pork butt, as I do (due to preference and the availability of by-products in markets).
Although the flavor is slightly different, this stew is very doable in a regular pot.

---

5 —— pounds/2270 g pork butt, trimmed of excess fat

½ —— cup/120 ml olive oil

2 —— onions, finely chopped

1 —— large green pepper, cut into medium pieces (optional)

1 —— head garlic, peeled, coarsely chopped

1 —— bay leaf

2 —— generous tablespoons/30 g tomato paste

2 —— tablespoons/30 g Chile Pepper Paste (page 365)

2 —— cups/470 ml white wine

4 —— red bliss potatoes, peeled, halved or quartered, if large

1 —— 2-inch/5-cm piece of cinnamon stick or 1 teaspoon/3 g ground cinnamon

1 —— teaspoon/6 g coarse kosher salt or to taste

½ —— teaspoon ground black pepper

1. Cut the pork into 2-inch/5-cm pieces and set aside.

2. Heat the oil over medium heat in a heavy 5-quart/4.5-L pot until hot but not smoking. (If you are using a clay pot, prepare the pot as directed and use over a heat diffuser on top of the stove.) Toss in the onions, cooking them until soft and translucent, about 2 to 3 minutes. Add the green pepper, garlic, bay leaf, tomato paste and chile pepper paste. Give it a few stirs to disperse the tomato paste into the onions. Add the pieces of pork and cook for 10 minutes, turning frequently.

3. Pour in the wine and stir. Cover and bring to a boil, about 2 minutes. When the wine starts to boil, add the potatoes, the cinnamon stick or shake ground cinnamon over the meat, and the salt and ground pepper. Reduce the heat and simmer over medium-low heat until the meat is fork-tender and the potatoes are cooked, about 45 minutes. It should be tender and not dried out. Discard the bay leaf.

Pulled Pork Shoulder with Onions and Peppers

Carne de Porco Desfeita

SERVES 8 TO 10

My friend Ezilda Raposo generously shares her father Joaquim Martin's wonderfully simple recipe for smoked pork shoulder. A long-standing family favorite, this works wonderfully as a main course, as a buffet offering or as a stuffing. Based on estimated measurements of her father's creation, I have adapted them with great results. The beauty of this recipe is that you can use whatever size smoked shoulder you want and add less or more of the vegetables. The amounts that follow are for a 5-pound/2270-g smoked shoulder. You can also use a fresh shoulder but the flavor will obviously be different (see Note).

---

1 ——— 5-pound/2270-g smoked shoulder, with bone

1 ——— teaspoon/3 g smoked paprika (optional, if using fresh shoulder)

½ ——— cup/120 ml olive oil

6 ——— large onions, peeled, thinly sliced

2 ——— green peppers, stemmed

4 ——— large garlic cloves, finely chopped

1 ——— generous teaspoon/3 g sweet paprika

Coarse kosher salt to taste

Ground black pepper to taste

1. On your workspace, trim the shoulder of any netting, rind and as much white fat as possible.

2. Place the meat in a large stockpot and cover with cold water. If using fresh shoulder, add the smoked paprika at this time. Cover tightly and bring to a boil. Reduce the heat to medium-low and simmer for 2 to 3 hours, until the meat is falling off the bone.

3. Reserving the broth for a soup base or the variations listed at the end, transfer the cooked meat to a cutting board. Remove and discard the bone. When the meat has cooled a little, cut into large pieces, then use two forks to pull apart the meat. Cover and set aside.

4. Meanwhile, heat the olive oil in a large skillet. Working in batches if your pan isn't too big, add the onions and sauté them until soft and translucent, about 2 to 3 minutes. Add the peppers, garlic and sweet paprika. Continue to sauté the onions and peppers until the onions are richly golden and a bit caramelized, about 5 to 10 minutes.

5. Add the meat to the pan of onions and peppers and stir. Season with salt and pepper if needed, to your taste. Transfer to a serving bowl. Serve with boiled, mashed or roasted potatoes.

Note: If you prefer to use fresh shoulder, side-stepping the preservatives, but like the smokiness, add the smoked paprika to the cooking water or replace the sweet paprika with smoked paprika, or add to the cooked onions and peppers.

Variations: Wondering what to do with leftovers or first overs? See Pulled Pork–Stuffed Kale Rolls, page 189. For a gathering, add a spritz of hot sauce, fill lettuce leaves and serve this on a buffet platter as lettuce wraps for a contemporary touch.

Matança
The Slaughtered Pig

Many ethnic groups practiced the slaughtering of pigs forever. Other than for a special occasion or religious feast day, slaughtering pigs for food was, and still is in some areas, usually done during the winter months because temperatures were cold enough to enable sufficient time to prepare the meat for preservation without spoilage. In the time previous to refrigeration, folks used rudimentary methods, such as salting or heavily coating sausages in lard to preserve meat.

Today there are many people in the world who enjoy eating pork and other meats but don't care to know beyond the supermarket from where and how it came to be on the shelf. I cannot say how it is done commercially; however, through my own experience, I can tell you about how those who carry on the tradition enjoy prepping the pig for food for their family. I must also rave about the undeniable great flavor of fresh pork. My friends Rui Neves and Jose Antonio use the utmost care to prevent the pig from suffering.

It may surprise some folks, but pigs do have hair on their skin. The men use tools to burn and then scrape off the hair. They work quickly, removing every last hair before the pig is bronzed with the torch. The pig's skin is then scrubbed clean of its outer layer, leaving the creamy white skin that one might see in the supermarket package of pig's feet, knuckles and fatback. Jose Antonio uses his skills like a surgeon, taking utmost care to remove reproductive organs and other parts of the body like the bile duct and bladder while the pig is whole, without piercing them, to avoid contaminating the meat. Once the meat is carefully prepped, it is ready to roast whole or is butchered into roasts, chops and the like, packaged and properly stored in the refrigerator or freezer. Nothing is wasted.

During the time of a *matança*, a *cachola*, depending on the region, may be made with the lungs, blood and other offals in addition to some of the pork meat. Other typical dishes include blood sausages, called *morcelas,* and the ever-popular *chouriço* and *linguiça* sausages, to name a few. Future meals that are greatly anticipated include *caçoila*, a pork stew; *sarapatel*, a dish of sweetened chopped liver, scallion and parsley; and *picado de fígado*, chopped cubes of liver mixed with onions, garlic, potatoes and wine. Of course, a hard day's work has its reward of a delicious meal of what else but char-grilled fresh pork belly and accompaniments.

Forno de Lenha
Wood-fired oven

What is a *forno de lenha*, you might ask? It is a dome-shaped stone oven that usually sits on a square concrete base. It is wood fired, and sorry but there isn't a thermostat on this baby. It does have hinged metal doors in the arched opening. Some do not have doors. The size of the stone ovens varies. It goes back a long way and is used to cook *leitões* (suckling pigs), breads and other dishes outside. It takes practice to learn what is a strong heat, moderate heat and low heat; how much wood to burn; how long to wait for the fire to die down to just the right amount and then timing it all. It is done by eye and feel—the amount of wood, height of the flame and amount of heat you feel when you open the doors. Practice makes perfect with a *forno de lenha!*

The Suckling Pig
Leitão

The most well-known *leitão* is in the style of Bairrada in northern Portugal, where roasting a whole suckling pig is an art in itself, not to mention the presentation on the table. The pigs and piglets are raised and fed organically. These piglets are still being fed on their mother's milk, making them lean and very tender. In Bairrada, on the Portuguese mainland, the best piglets are said to come from sows that are usually fed acorns and perhaps truffles. The typical initial preparation for a roasted piglet dinner is similar to that for the larger pig but on a smaller scale because there is virtually no hair to remove. After preparation, the piglet is then rinsed thoroughly inside and out with cold water, drained and readied for the next step.

A seasoning can include garlic, salt and pepper, herbs and, of course, bay leaf and just enough olive oil to bring it lightly together. White wine is basted during the roasting process to keep the skin from cracking open. A wooden or metal rod, longer than the piglet, is placed through the mouth and out the anus to enable ease in turning the piglet over. The piglet can be slowly roasted on a spit or inside a *caixinha* (little box) placed in the stone oven (*lenha*). The method of removing the piglet from the fire or oven—thus forming condensation on the skin so the piglet will *constipar* (catch cold)—then returning it to finish roasting makes for a crisper skin.

Alas, for some of us, home ovens will have to do unless one has a *forno de lenha*. Otherwise, simply place a rack inside a sheet pan large enough to accommodate the piglet. Insert the 1½-inch/3.8-cm diameter wooden or metal dowel for turning the piglet over, place it in the oven, and then remove it from the oven periodically, allowing moisture to escape while roasting. For the leanest and most tender results, use the best-quality piglet you can find and one weighing no more than 10 to 12 pounds/4.5 to 5.4 kg or more than 6 weeks old. After that, once it is weaned from the mother, the piglet starts to accumulate more hair, fat and pronounced flavor. Unless you are acquainted with a humane pig farm and can buy direct, usually through special order, a butcher can obtain one and have it cleaned and ready for your recipe.

Roast Suckling Pig
Leitão no Forno

SERVES 6 TO 8

My method is not the Bairrada style. I like to first brine the piglet overnight, as I do with my turkeys, and use my father's seasoning paste. Some cooks brine and some don't. I then let it air-dry for the next 24 hours. Unless you have a walk-in refrigerator, hang it outside in winter in an enclosed unheated shed or garage, when temperatures are below 40°F/4°C, or do just as I do by draining it well on large kitchen towels, then pat dry, inside and out, with a kitchen towel. Then refrigerate uncovered on a tray until needed.

In order to brine you will need a large food-safe bucket with cover that will accommodate the size of the piglet (available at restaurant supply stores). A 9-gallon/32-L one works very well. There are also food-safe brining bags, which you can look into, but I happen to prefer the bucket. The food-safe buckets are not cheap, but you can use it for brining your turkey at Thanksgiving as well as letting your bread dough rise in it. If you don't want to brine it, just add 1 to 2 tablespoons/18 to 36 g of coarse salt to the seasoning paste. Suckling pigs are mild in flavor, so go easy on the garlic. Some cooks use as much as two heads of garlic but one has to strike a balance so that the buttery-soft texture of the meat is not overseasoned and the delicate flavor is not lost. Depending on the weight of the piglet, if it is a very small head of garlic, then two are okay. Poultry shears come in handy for carving up the meat, especially the ribs and bone joints.

The piglet is basted with seasoning sauce, inside and out. First the belly is basted then trussed closed followed by the tying of the feet and basting all over before roasting.

EQUIPMENT

1 ——— 9-gallon/32-L food-safe bucket with lid

1 ——— 20 x 15–inch/50 x 38-cm sheet pan with 1-inch/2.5-cm sides

Wire rack to fit the sheet pan

Instant-read or oven-safe meat thermometer

Curved (makes it easier) upholstery needle or trussing needle

Strong butcher's twine or kitchen twine

1 ——— 1½-inch/3.8-cm diameter wooden dowel, cut the length of the pig (long enough to extend slightly beyond mouth and butt) or 2 dowels about 10 inches/25 cm long

BRINE (DAY 1)

4 ——— cups/1152 g coarse kosher salt, or 1 cup/288 g coarse kosher salt for every 1 gallon/3.6 L of water to cover piglet completely

4 ——— gallons/14.4 L water as needed to cover piglet

4 ——— oranges, squeezed juice and rinds

3 ——— lemons, squeezed juice and rinds

2 or 3 — whole cloves

1 ——— 10- to 12-pound/4.5- to 5.4-kg fresh suckling pig, cleaned and rinsed

SEASONING PASTE AND ROAST (DAY 3)

1 ——— red bell pepper, stemmed and seeded

½ ——— cup/112 g butter, softened

¼ ——— cup/60 ml olive oil

18 to 20— garlic cloves, peeled, coarsely chopped

2 ——— tablespoons/36 g coarse kosher salt (use only if not brining)

1 ——— tablespoon/8 g ground black pepper

1½ ——— teaspoons/4 g ground white pepper

1 ——— tablespoon/8 g sweet paprika

½ ——— cup/30 g finely chopped parsley, divided

1 ——— bay leaf, crumbled

½ ——— cup/120 ml brandy

3 to 4 — cups/705 to 940 ml semi-dry white wine as needed for basting

2 ——— oranges, cut into wedges

MAKE THE BRINE ON DAY 1

1. Mix the coarse salt with the water in the food-safe bucket so the salt is well distributed and dissolved. Stir in the juice and rinds of the oranges and lemons and add the cloves. Stir well. When you see the salt is nearly dissolved, add the piglet, making sure it is completely covered with the brine solution. Add additional brine water in 1:1 ratio as needed to completely cover the piglet. Mix it up with the previously salted water.

If it is winter in the north, there isn't an issue. You can leave the closed container in an unheated garage or shed provided the temperature is below 40°F/4°C. Unfortunately, in order to keep this in the refrigerator, you would have to put everything else in a cooler with ice and remove the shelves, which isn't practical. It is better to err on the side of caution and keep it cold. Because the piglet is an odd shape, a brining bag would be difficult to work in this case, but since I haven't used one, I can't be sure if it would fit in the refrigerator with the brine water completely covering the piglet. Brining bags are like extra-large plastic zipper lock bags and you must be careful not to puncture them. A piglet in a brining bag might do better covered in ice placed in a large cooler. That way if a leak were to occur, the water would be contained in the cooler.

AIR-DRY THE PIGLET ON DAY 2

1. Early in the day, drain the piglet from the brine and rinse the piglet thoroughly inside and out with cold water. Drain well. Ideally, if you had a clean, cold environment, hanging it to drain is best. Otherwise, dry the inside and out well with paper towels. Let air-dry, uncovered, overnight or for at least several hours, in the refrigerator on a tray, turning it over to air-dry the other side. You might need to wipe the tray and the pig again.

MAKE THE SEASONING PASTE AND ROAST ON DAY 3

1. Preheat the oven to 450°F/230°C, or gas mark 8.

2. One hour before roasting, remove the piglet from the refrigerator and allow it to come to room temperature while you make the seasoning sauce.

3. Add the red pepper to the bowl of a food processor and purée until fairly smooth, about 10 seconds. Set aside.

(continued)

4. In a saucepan, melt butter with the olive oil and set aside. Meanwhile, using a large mortar with pestle, mash the garlic (using salt if you did not brine). Grind in the ground black and white peppers and paprika to the garlic followed by ¼ cup/15 g of the parsley and the crumbled bay leaf. Stir the seasoning paste into the warm butter and olive oil. Mix in the puréed red pepper. Warm over low heat until the garlic is aromatic, about 1 minute, then stir in the brandy, making sure all is thoroughly blended. Set aside.

5. Lay the piglet on your workspace. Prick the skin of the piglet all over with the sharp tines of a roasting fork. With some of the seasoning, generously coat inside the cavity of the belly of the pig, getting it into the crevices. Using heavy cotton kitchen thread and with a sharp trussing needle, or metal turkey trussing pins, close up the belly opening as you would a turkey. With the butcher's twine, tie the feet together front to back as best as you can, bending the legs to fit.

6. Coat one side of the piglet with some of the remaining seasoning and place the seasoned side down on the rack set on the sheet pan, making sure it is centered and not hanging over the pan. Use the remaining seasoning to coat the top of the pig. Make sure you use all of the paste. Cover the ears and tail with foil to prevent burning. Make a ball of foil and stick it in its mouth to hold it open to facilitate turning and enable garnishing with an orange in its mouth. Place the pan in the preheated oven and roast for 15 minutes. Remove the piglet from the oven and discard the ball of foil.

7. Initially, you can turn the piglet by grabbing the legs with a kitchen towel, but as it becomes done, the legs will easily fall off and you will need strong roasting forks or the use of dowels to lift and turn it. To use the dowels for turning, insert the end of the long dowel beneath the tail and wiggle it through so that it comes out its mouth, or use one smaller dowel at each end to lift and turn the piglet over. At this point, lift and turn the piglet over and baste what is now the top with some white wine. Using a branch of the bay leaf plant to baste would be the traditional method, but today we use a long-handled basting brush to baste the piglet with some wine. An extra pair of hands might help here. After basting, you can remove the dowel(s) and return the piglet to the oven, then reinsert it each time you take the pig out to baste. Taking the piglet out of the oven each time helps ensure the crisping of the skin. Reduce the oven temperature to 350°F/180°C, or gas mark 4.

8. Continue roasting, basting the pig and alternating from side to side, as above, every 15 to 25 minutes during the first 2 hours of roasting. Keep lifting by the dowel ends to turn the piglet over for basting the underside. Stop turning and basting with wine after 2 hours and remove the foil. Baste just the ears with wine. If the skin doesn't seem to be getting crispy enough, leave the oven door slightly ajar to let out any moisture and continue to roast for 30 minutes. You can also raise the temperature toward the end, to 500°F/250°C, or gas mark 10, to crisp the skin.

9. Continue to roast until the meat is nearly falling off the bone (fork-tender) and the temperature of the thickest part of the leg, without touching the bone, reaches 150°F/65°C. The skin should be a beautiful mahogany bronze color. Total roasting time is about 2½ to 3 hours, depending on the exact weight. Lift and transfer onto a bed of greens on a platter for presentation or a cutting board for carving and rest 10 to 15 minutes. Remove the wooden dowel. The drippings should have very little fat and can be ladled over the meat. Serve with a wedge of orange in its mouth with the rind showing, if desired, and garnish the greens with orange slices and the remaining ¼ cup/15 g parsley. Serve accompanied by boiled rice and a vegetable like green beans or sautéed leafy greens.

Roast Pig on a Spit
Porco Assado

This is not an exact recipe, but the method is for adventurous cooks with strong equipment for roasting a large pig on a spit and many friends to enjoy it. Less than 100 pounds/45 kg is easiest to handle with two or three strong people for lifting. Over 100 pounds/45 kg, you need at least four strong friends. Pigs can be obtained already cleaned and prepped through butchers and pig farmers and specialty meat markets. I cannot tell you how to weld a half steel barrel with heavy metal rotisserie bars or where to buy or rent one, but this is the recipe for the pig. Make sure you have proper refrigeration available and workspace to handle the pig and refrigerate it. Cover the workspace with plastic tablecloths. After hoisting the pig onto the rotisserie, replace the tablecloths with clean ones. Without the refrigeration, have it delivered, already prepped, early on the day you will need to cook it. Unless you have a chilled walk-in refrigerator, do this in the winter when temperatures are below 40°F/4°C and use a clean unheated shed or garage for sheltering.

Whether you cook a 40-pound/18-kg pig (serves 35 to 40) or a 100-pound/45-kg pig (serves 90), when prepped and ready to cook, the head and lower legs can be removed for ease of handling; otherwise, they need to be secured by tying the ankles together with wire (12 to 14 gauge) so they are not hanging loosely. If the head is attached, cover the ears as well as the tail with foil. According to my friends Rui and Lucy Neves, who were generous in sharing their basting sauce recipe, roasting will take 8 to 9 hours. You will need about 40 pounds/18 kg of charcoal set in a half metal barrel just to get started, and you will use up to another 100 pounds/45 kg of charcoal or ½ cord of wood.

A large mortar and pestle is helpful to make the paste, but you can work in batches with a small one or just finely chop the garlic in a food processor. The amounts for the seasoning paste and basting sauce are approximate as they are usually done by eye. For cooking, it is best to start early, as it can take anywhere from 8 to 9 hours for an 80-pounder/36-kg to 11 to 12 hours for a 100-pound/45-kg pig, depending on the size and the heat of the fire and whether you slice the meat as it becomes done or cook the pig completely before removing it from the rotisserie to carve up. Remember to baste the pig periodically with the basting sauce and keep the pig turning to prevent burning and flare-ups, for which you need to keep a spray bottle of water handy. Make sure the motor of your rotisserie can handle being near the heat. If you don't own one, look for rentals.

EQUIPMENT

Kitchen twine

Upholstery needle

Heavy-duty motorized rotisserie, and set up

100 pounds/45 kg charcoal (about 1 pound/454 g per pound of pig)

Spray bottles of water for flare-ups

Heat and flame-proof mitts

(continued)

SAUCE (DAY 1)

5 ——— quarts/4.5 L white wine

2 ——— 750 ml bottles port wine

1 ——— 750 ml bottle whiskey

2 ——— quarts/1.8 L lemon juice from fresh lemons, set aside rinds

2 ——— tablespoons/16 g paprika

6 ——— heads garlic, peeled, mashed or finely chopped

1 ——— tablespoon/6 g each of ground cloves, cumin, black pepper, white pepper and crushed dried chile pepper

2 ——— pounds/908 g coarse kosher salt

20——— bay leaves

6 ——— whole lemon rinds

2 or 3 ——— branches of rosemary

THE HERB SACK

1 ——— 10-inch/25.4-cm square piece of cheesecloth

1 ——— teaspoon/3 g each of thyme, marjoram, oregano, rosemary and sage

MAKE THE SAUCE

1. In a large container with a lid, combine all the ingredients, except the whole lemon rinds and rosemary branches, forming a well-seasoned sauce. Mix thoroughly and frequently.

MAKE THE HERB SACK

1. In the center of the cheesecloth, place the thyme, marjoram, oregano, rosemary and sage. Tie the cloth up, making a sack and leaving a long tail of thread, about 10 inches/25.4 cm long. Place the sack in the sauce with the tail end hanging out of the container. Cover. Let the sauce stand overnight in the refrigerator.

ROAST ON DAY 2

1. Lay the pig (with help) on your worktable. Use 1½ quarts/1.5 L of the sauce to coat the inside of the belly in every crevice with a couple of branches of rosemary. (If you cannot get the branches, use a basting brush.) Place the rinds of 6 lemons into the belly of the pig. Using butcher or kitchen twine and a sharp upholstery or trussing needle, close the belly up tight. Then place the rotisserie bar through the opening of the butt end until it comes out the mouth or neck end (if you have the head removed).

2. Set up the coals or wood and get the fire going. Once the fire has simmered down, with help, hoist the pig onto the rotisserie and with a long-handled basting brush, coat the entire pig with some of the remaining basting sauce.

3. Hopefully you are using a motorized rotisserie and that the motor is away from the heat so that it doesn't overheat. As the pig turns, periodically baste and be watchful of flare-ups. The basting sauce will cause the flare-ups. Spray the coals lightly with water at the flares, as necessary to prevent burning the pig. With a pig of this size, as the meat cooks, it will reach doneness from the outside in.

4. This is the tricky part. You can carefully, with help, stop the rotisserie and quickly with a long, sharp slicing knife, cut pieces of cracklings and meat from the whole pig as it becomes done. Do not keep the pig from turning too long or you will get burning and flare-ups. Then baste the cut sides with the sauce to prevent the meat from drying out and burning. Return the rotisserie to turning. Keep turning and cooking, then slicing, basting and cooking some more, transferring the meat to a platter, covering to keep hot. The shoulders and legs are where it takes longest to cook. Slow cooking it best, though it is tempting to hurry it up.

Pork Belly Cracklings
Torresmos

One of the earliest dishes is *torresmos*, or "cracklings" in English, which in Portugal originated from the process of rendering pork fat (lard) for preserving and cooking. In addition to preserving meats and sausages in large clay pots with the rendered fat, the pork lard helped the very poor make it through hard times when the meat ran out. It was used to flavor bread as well as vegetables. The most basic version is *Torresmos Brancos* (White Fried Pork Bellies), which is simply salted pork belly fried down in its own fat until golden. The rendered fat is used as lard. Today, there is less lard used. Those in the Azores did not have olive oil as the mainlanders did. What did remain after rendering the fat were crisp bacon-like bits of meat.

I have had many requests with various descriptions for *torresmos*. Some folks were looking for a long-lost family version but had a vague memory of ingredients, and others enjoyed the dish in a particular region of Portugal or the Azores and so on. Some versions have just the fried fatty pork belly, as described above, or include marinated butt end cut into large cubes, baby back ribs or a combination (*Torresmos de Carne*).

One variation of *torresmos* is *Torresmos em Vinho d'Alhos*, the recipe that follows. Cubes of meat and ribs are marinated overnight in seasoned white wine before frying.

Wine and Garlic Marinated Pork

Torresmos em Vinho d'Alhos

SERVES 6 TO 8

This dish, though it can be made anytime, is typically made the day after a pig is slaughtered. Some recipes include the ribs of the pig. The use of red or white wine is the cook's preference. Despite slight variations in additional seasonings from cook to cook, you will taste the constant ingredients of garlic, wine and vinegar. Usually *torresmos* are simply fried, but because it has been marinated there will be a little sauce to dip some bread into. This can also be made alcohol-free by using orange juice in place of wine. The meat can be cut into smaller pieces to serve as a starter on a buffet.

FOUR HOURS AHEAD

4	pounds/1818 g pork butt, trimmed of excess fat, cut into 2-inch/5-cm chunks, or 2 pounds/908 g pork butt and 2 pounds/908 g pork ribs
1	tablespoon/15 g Chile Pepper Paste (page 365) or generous pinch of crushed dried red chile pepper
1	cup/235 ml white wine
½	cup/120 ml red wine vinegar
8	garlic cloves, smashed

TO COOK

½	cup/120 ml olive oil
6	garlic cloves, smashed
¼	cup/32 g paprika
1	tablespoon/15 g Chile Pepper Paste (page 365) or hot sauce to taste
2	teaspoons/12 g coarse kosher salt or to taste
½	teaspoon freshly ground black or white pepper
½	teaspoon ground cumin
½	teaspoon cinnamon
4	Jamaican allspice berries
1	bay leaf
1	cup/235 ml red wine vinegar
2	cups/470 ml water

FOUR HOURS AHEAD

1. Combine the ingredients in a nonreactive baking dish. Marinate for 2 to 3 hours or overnight in the refrigerator.

TO COOK

1. About 1 hour before cooking, drain the marinade from the pork and discard.

2. Heat the oil in a heavy skillet and, working in small batches, brown the chunks of meat on all sides, about 5 to 10 minutes. Transfer to a pot large enough to accommodate all of the meat.

3. When all the meat has been browned, add the remaining seasonings followed by the wine vinegar and water. Add more liquid in the same ratio of 1 part wine vinegar to 2 parts water as needed, until it is halfway up the sides of the meat; cover.

4. Place the pot over medium-high heat. Bring the contents to a boil. Reduce the heat to low and simmer the stew very slowly for about 1½ hours, until the meat is fork-tender. Discard the bay leaf. Serve with boiled sweet potatoes, taro root, white potatoes or rice. Of course, don't forget the bread to sop up the sauce.

Milk-Braised Pork with Garlic and Onion Sauce

Lombo de Porco Assado com Leite

SERVES 6

I have to admit, I was skeptical when my friend Ester Mendonca told me about this very, very old method of cooking pork loin on the Azorean island of Pico, which she stated was one of the oldest recipes of the island. However, since I am open to different methods I gave it a try, and I must say I was not disappointed. Ester's method is so simple. The loin came out extremely moist and very tender. Seeing the milk become subtly infused with the flavor of the meat, I wanted to take advantage of this, so I thickened it with a cornstarch slurry, creating a savory white sauce and giving it a personal touch. This recipe has been adapted from *Portuguese Homestyle Cooking*.

EQUIPMENT

1 ———— 8½ x 4½ x 2½–inch/21.6 x 11.4 x 6.4–cm rectangular baking dish (or one that will accommodate the roast without being too large)

Small presoaked clay roasting pot or small rectangular roasting pan with deep sides

FOR THE ROAST

1 ———— 3-pound/1362-g boneless center-cut pork fillet or loin roast

1 ———— tablespoon/18 g coarse kosher salt

½ ———— teaspoon ground white pepper

2 ———— garlic cloves, smashed

2 ———— tablespoons/28 g butter

1 ———— bay leaf

3 ———— cups/705 ml whole milk as needed

FOR THE ONION SAUCE

2 ———— tablespoons/28 g butter

1 ———— medium onion, sliced

2 ———— tablespoons/16 g cornstarch

2 ———— tablespoons/30 ml water

½ ———— teaspoon ground nutmeg

MAKE THE ROAST

1. Preheat the oven to 350°F/180°C, or gas mark 4.

2. Season the roast all over with the salt and pepper. Put the meat in a small rectangular roasting pan with the garlic, butter and bay leaf. Pour in enough milk to almost cover the meat, about three-fourths of the way up the sides of the roast.

3. Place the pan in the preheated oven. Periodically, as the top of the roast browns, turn the meat, so that the browned part becomes submerged in the milk. Continue doing this, and eventually the whole roast will be caramelized and the flavor will infuse the milk. Continue to cook until the internal temperature reaches 150°F/65°C, about 1½ to 2 hours. Discard the bay leaf.

4. Transfer the roast to a cutting board, cover and let rest while you make the onion sauce.

MAKE THE ONION SAUCE

1. Melt the butter in a small skillet over medium-high heat. Add the onion and sauté until richly golden, about 5 to 7 minutes. Reduce the heat to medium.

2. Measure out and pour the milk from the roasting pan into the onions, adding more milk if needed to make 2 cups/470 ml. Make a cornstarch slurry by mixing the cornstarch, water and nutmeg together, then stir it into the milk. Bring the milk to a high simmer and continue stirring until the milk becomes the consistency of heavy cream, about 5 minutes.

3. Slice the pork into serving pieces, transferring to a serving platter. Ladle some of the onion sauce over and serve with extra sauce on the side.

Clam and Chouriço Stuffed Pork

Lombo de Porco Recheado com Amêijoas

SERVES 6 TO 8

The pairing of clams and pork is not unusual for the
Alentejo region. Go easy on salt because the sausage and clams contain salt. Use bottled clam broth if
there isn't sufficient juice from the raw clams.

---

4 ———	tablespoons/56 g butter, divided
2 ———	tablespoons/30 ml olive oil
½ ———	cup/50 g finely chopped scallion
4 ———	ounces/112 g chouriço sausage, casings removed and coarsely chopped (optional)
3 ———	garlic cloves, finely chopped, divided
⅔ ———	cup/65 g firmly packed cubed fresh bread
¼ ———	cup/60 ml milk
2 ———	eggs, lightly beaten
1 ———	cup/150 g chopped raw clams, juices reserved
4 ———	tablespoons/16 g finely chopped cilantro, divided
1 ———	teaspoon/6 g coarse kosher salt or to taste, divided
½ ———	teaspoon ground white or black pepper, divided
1 ———	3-pound/1362-g boneless center-cut pork roast, butterflied (the butcher can do this for you)
¼ ———	teaspoon ground nutmeg
1 ———	cup/235 ml reserved clam juices or 8-ounce/235-ml bottle clam broth
1 ———	cup/235 ml white wine

1. Preheat the oven to 350°F/180°C, or gas mark 4.

2. Place a medium skillet over medium-high heat. Heat 2 tablespoons/28 g of the butter and the olive oil. Toss in the scallion and sauté until soft, about 3 minutes. Mix in the chopped sausage and half of the garlic. Cook for 1 minute. Transfer to a bowl.

3. In another bowl, moisten the bread with the milk, then add to the scallions and sausage. Stir in the lightly beaten eggs, clams and 2 tablespoons/2 g of the cilantro. Sprinkle in ½ teaspoon of the salt and ¼ teaspoon of the ground pepper. Mix well and set aside.

4. Open up the pork loin and lay it on your workspace. Spread the filling lengthwise over half the roast to within 1 inch/2.5 cm around the edges. Fold the other half over or roll it up starting from the filling side. Using kitchen or butcher's string, tie the roast together so that the long edges meet.

5. Mash the remaining half of the garlic, remaining ½ teaspoon salt, remaining ¼ teaspoon pepper and nutmeg into a paste and rub it over the roast. Place the seasoned meat in a roasting pan. Melt the remaining 2 tablespoons/28 g butter and drizzle over the roast.

6. Combine the clam juice and wine and pour around the roast. Basting occasionally with the pan juices, roast for about 1 hour to 1 hour 15 minutes, until the meat is fork-tender and the internal temperature reaches 150°F/65°C on an instant-read thermometer. Cover and let rest for 10 minutes. Place slices of the pork on a serving platter and ladle any pan juices over.

Mushroom-Stuffed Pork with Pomegranate Sauce

Lombo de Porco com Molho de Romã

SERVES 6

The influence of Northern Africans in Portugal inspired me to use pomegranates to complement pork. Here I have paired pomegranates with a mushroom-stuffed pork loin, fusing the pomegranate and pork drippings to create a flavorful sauce. This stuffing is enough for 4 pork chops, or 2 pork tenderloins tied together or one 3-pound/1362-g center-cut pork roast. Depending on what cut you use, you may have some filling left over, which can be used to stuff mushrooms or roll in puff pastry or filo dough. Just bake until golden and use as appetizers.

FOR THE STUFFING

2	———	tablespoons/28 g butter
1	———	tablespoon/15 ml olive oil
1	———	large shallot or 2 tablespoons/20 g finely chopped onion
6	———	ounces/168 g mushrooms, cleaned, finely chopped (about 2 cups/140 g)
1	———	garlic clove, finely chopped
¾	———	cup/75 g plain fresh bread crumbs
¼	———	cup/15 g finely chopped parsley
1	———	teaspoon/6 g coarse kosher salt or to taste
¼	———	teaspoon ground white pepper
½ to 1	—	cup/60 to 120 g shredded St. Jorge or other semisoft cheese like Havarti

FOR THE MEAT

1	———	3-pound/1362-g center-cut pork roast

Coarse kosher salt as needed

Ground white or black pepper as needed

2	———	tablespoons/28 g butter

FOR THE STUFFING

1. In a large skillet, heat the butter with the olive oil. Add the shallot and sauté over medium-high heat until tender, about 2 to 3 minutes. Stir in the mushrooms and garlic and sauté until they give up their juices and the pan is almost dry.

2. Mix in the bread crumbs and parsley. Season the stuffing with salt and pepper. Stir well. Mix in the shredded cheese until it comes together, pulling away from the sides of the pan. Remove the pan from the heat and set aside to cool. It should yield approximately 1¾ cups/175 g of stuffing.

FOR THE MEAT

1. Preheat the oven to 350°F/180°C, or gas mark 4.

2. Place the meat on your cutting board. Using a long enough knife to reach half the length, insert the blade into the center of the short end of the roast, wiggling the blade to cut a 2-inch/5-cm wide pocket half the length of the roast. Turn the roast around and repeat from the other end, connecting the holes. (It is a bit larger than a tenderloin and that makes stuffing it easier, so butterflying and tying together is not really necessary, unless it is your preference.) Fill the opening of the roast with the stuffing, pushing the stuffing in the hole. Tie up the roast with kitchen string. Season the outside of the roast with salt and pepper.

3. Use the same skillet as for the stuffing, unwashed. Melt the butter and brown the stuffed roast on all sides, about 5 minutes. Transfer the browned roast to an oven-proof pan, and roast the meat for about 1 hour, checking the temperature at 45 minutes. Roast until the thermometer inserted into the thickest part of the meat reaches the internal temperature of 150°F/65°C, about 30 to 45 minutes more. Use the same unwashed pan for the sauce.

(continued)

FOR THE SAUCE

1 ——— cup/235 ml white wine

Juice of 3 to 4 pomegranates (about 2 cups/470 ml), or 3 tablespoons/60 g pomegranate molasses dissolved in 1½ cups/355 ml hot water

1½ ——— tablespoons/18 g sugar

1 ——— tablespoon/8 g cornstarch mixed with 2 tablespoons/30 ml cold water

Coarse kosher salt to taste

Ground white or black pepper to taste

FOR THE SAUCE

1. Pour the wine into the same skillet and deglaze the pan using the flat edge of a wooden spoon. Scrap up the caramelized bits on the bottom. Simmer over medium heat and reduce by half.

2. Pour the pomegranate juice into the wine. (If using pomegranate molasses, blend the molasses with the hot water first, then pour into the wine base.) Sprinkle in the sugar, stir and reduce the sauce again by half.

3. Turn off the heat. When the meat is done, transfer the meat to a cutting board or serving platter to rest for 3 minutes. Meanwhile, pour the pan juices into the pan of sauce and bring to a low boil. Whisk in the cornstarch slurry. Simmer over medium-low heat for 2 to 3 minutes, stirring frequently, reducing slightly and developing a light body. Adjust the seasoning with salt and pepper.

4. Serve the sliced meat on a platter or individual plates, spooning some of the sauce over or under or around the meat. Serve with your choice of vegetables. Extra sauce can be served on the side.

Variations

For pork chops: Make and stuff pockets in 1- to 1½-inch/2.5- to 3.8-cm thick boneless pork chops and close with toothpicks.

For pork tenderloins: Butterfly the tenderloins. Spread the stuffing lengthwise over the center of one tenderloin to within 1 inch/2.5 cm of the edges and cover it with another butterflied tenderloin; tie them together with kitchen string. Most often these are in the 1½-pound/680-g range and tying two together works. Follow the directions above, roasting for 30 to 35 minutes.

Roast Pork with Fennel

Lombo de Porco Assado com Funcho

SERVES 6 TO 8

The fennel used by the Portuguese is the wild form that doesn't contain a bulb. The fine fronds
are removed from the stems and finely chopped. The obvious anise flavor complements the flavors of cumin
and cinnamon but not overwhelmingly. The readily available variety in your supermarket can be substituted,
and even the bulb can be coarsely chopped used if desired.

¼ —— cup/60 ml olive oil

⅓ —— cup/40 g shredded carrot

½ —— cup/40 g chopped fennel fronds, plus more for garnish

2 —— garlic cloves, finely chopped

2 —— scallions, trimmed and finely chopped

¼ —— teaspoon ground cumin

¼ —— teaspoon ground cinnamon

1 —— cup/235 ml orange juice, divided

2 —— cups/200 g shredded fresh bread, heavy crusts removed

3 —— teaspoons/18 g coarse kosher salt, divided

1 —— 3-pound/1362-g boneless center-cut pork roast, butterflied

Ground pepper to taste

Orange wedges, for garnish

1. Preheat the oven to 350°F/180°C, or gas mark 4.

2. Heat the olive oil in a large skillet and lightly sauté the carrot, fennel, garlic and scallions until the garlic is lightly colored and aromatic, about 3 to 4 minutes. Transfer to a bowl and mix in the cumin, cinnamon and ¾ cup/180 ml of the orange juice. Add just enough of the torn bread to absorb the moisture. Add 2 teaspoons/12 g of the salt and mix with your hands until it comes together.

3. Lay the roast out on your workspace. Place the stuffing along the long side of the roast, leaving a 1-inch/2.5-cm margin on the sides. Roll up like a jelly roll or fold over and tie the roast with kitchen or butcher's string at 1-inch/2.5-cm intervals. Brush the roast with the remaining ¼ cup/60 ml orange juice, season with the remaining 1 teaspoon/6 g salt and the pepper to taste. Roast for about 1 hour to 1 hour 15 minutes, until the internal temperature reaches 150°F/65°C on an instant-read thermometer. Cover and let rest for 10 minutes, then slice. Garnish with finely chopped fennel fronds sprinkled over the top and serve with orange wedges.

Boneless Leg of Lamb with Sweet Pepper Paste
Perna de Borrego Assado

SERVES 6

Sweet pepper paste (*massa de pimentão*), along with fresh cilantro, can be used for more than seasoning pork. In fact, like my father before me, I love smearing it on lamb. You can either roast the leg of lamb whole or cut it into 2-inch/5-cm pieces and thread onto skewers to grill. You can make the paste yourself or purchase it at a Portuguese market or online.

5	garlic cloves, coarsely chopped
2	tablespoons/30 g Sweet Pepper Paste (page 367)
1	tablespoon/8 g sweet paprika
1	bay leaf, crumbled
2	tablespoons/8 g finely chopped cilantro
½	teaspoon ground black pepper
4	tablespoons/60 ml olive oil, divided
4	pounds/1818 g boneless leg of lamb
3	large onions, chopped into medium pieces
1	cup/235 ml white wine or red wine (red will darken the meat)
1¼	cups/295 ml water, divided
2	tablespoons/16 g cornstarch

Variation: Instead of roasting, cut the meat into 2- to 3-inch/5- to 7.5-cm pieces and toss with the seasoning paste and ½ cup/120 ml of white wine. Let stand for 1 hour, then thread onto skewers and grill. Serve with sautéed onions on the side.

1. Preheat the oven to 350°F/180°C, or gas mark 4.

2. Using a mortar and pestle, pound and crush the garlic into a paste. Incorporate the Sweet Pepper Paste, paprika, crumbled bay leaf, cilantro and black pepper. Drizzle in 2 tablespoons/30 ml of the olive oil, forming a loose paste. Rub the paste all over the leg of lamb and in the crevices. Tie with kitchen string to hold its shape.

3. Place the lamb in a roasting pan and cover. Reduce the oven setting to 300°F/150°C, or gas mark 2. Roast slowly for about 1½ to 1¾ hours, until the internal temperature reads 135°F/57°C, for medium-rare, when the thermometer is stuck in the thickest part of the meat. If you like your lamb done beyond medium-rare, continue to roast to the desire doneness. The meat should be fork-tender.

4. Transfer the meat to a platter and cover, resting for 10 minutes. Drain the fat from the roasting pan and place the roasting pan on a burner. Heat the remaining 2 tablespoons/30 ml olive oil in the roasting pan over medium heat. Add the onions and sauté until richly golden, about 5 to 7 minutes. Pour the wine and 1 cup/235 ml of the water into the pan to deglaze it and with a flat side of a wooden spoon or spatula, scrape up any caramelized bits (the fond) on the bottom of the pan.

5. Mix the cornstarch and the remaining ¼ cup/60 ml water in a cup, then stir into the pan. Bring to a boil, stirring, until slightly thickened, about 2 minutes. Ladle the sauce over the lamb and serve any extra on the side. Serve the lamb accompanied with rice and a vegetable.

Alentejo-Style Meatballs with White Beans

Almôndegas à Alentejana com Feijão Branco

SERVES 4 TO 6

One thing you don't see very often in Portuguese cooking is meatballs. Whether it is Greek or Roman influence or the other way around, these Alentejana meatballs are made of ground lamb. If you are not fond of lamb, feel free to substitute beef, pork or turkey, individually or in combination. This is as quick as it is easy and delicious. As a shortcut, I simmer my lemon-infused tender meatballs in a white wine, garlic and cilantro tomato sauce with precooked white kidney beans and cubed potatoes. Feel free to cook dried beans from scratch. Other beans can be substituted according to preference.

FOR THE SAUCE

¼ ——— cup/60 ml olive oil

1 ——— onion, coarsely chopped (about 1 cup/160 g)

2 or 3 — garlic cloves, finely chopped

1 ——— teaspoon/3 g sweet paprika

½ ——— cup/30 g finely chopped cilantro, divided

1 ——— bay leaf

¼ ——— cup/60 ml white wine

1½ ——— cups/270 g peeled, seeded, chopped tomatoes or 1 (14-ounce/392-g) can peeled tomatoes, drained and chopped

2 ——— cups/240 g peeled, medium rough cut (1½-inch/3.8-cm) Yukon gold potatoes

1 ——— cup/235 ml water, or as needed

FOR THE SAUCE

1. In a 4- or 5-quart/3.6- or 4.5-L pot over medium-high heat, warm the olive oil. Toss in the onion and sauté until lightly golden, about 5 minutes. Add the garlic, paprika, ¼ cup/4 g of the cilantro and the bay leaf. When the garlic is aromatic, about 1 minute, pour in the wine and bring to a boil. Reduce the heat to medium-low and simmer for 1 minute.

2. Mix in the tomatoes, stir, cover and simmer over low for 10 minutes. Add the potatoes. Pour in enough cold water to barely cover the potatoes. Recover and let simmer over medium-low heat until the potatoes are nearly fork-tender, about 15 minutes. Discard the bay leaf. Reserve.

(continued)

FOR THE MEATBALLS

1 ——— pound/454 g ground lamb

Juice of ½ lemon (about 2 tablespoons/30 ml)

2 ——— tablespoons/30 ml white wine

3 ——— eggs, lightly beaten

2 ——— garlic cloves, finely chopped

1 ——— teaspoon/6 g coarse kosher salt

½ ——— teaspoon ground black pepper

4 ——— thick slices stale bread, heavy crusts
       removed (about 4 cups/400 g packed)

½ ——— cup/120 ml milk

1 ——— cup/120 g all-purpose flour as needed

Olive oil as needed

TO ASSEMBLE

2 ——— cups/500 g precooked or canned
       white kidney beans, undrained

Coarse kosher salt to taste as needed

FOR THE MEATBALLS

1. In a large bowl, combine the lamb, lemon juice, white wine, eggs, garlic, salt and pepper. Moisten the bread with the milk, squeezing out any excess milk. Shred the bread into the ground lamb. Mix all the ingredients thoroughly.

2. Shape into meatballs the size of a golf ball, about 1½ inches/3.8 cm in diameter. Roll them in the flour and fry them in the olive oil until brown on all sides. Drain on paper towels or brown paper.

TO ASSEMBLE

1. Add the meatballs to the reserved sauce along with the beans and remaining ¼ cup/4 g cilantro. Taste for salt and add if needed. Gently stir, cover and simmer for about 25 minutes over medium-low heat, until the meatballs are thoroughly cooked. Serve in soup plates with olives, bread and a salad on the side.

Braised Lamb Shanks with Red Bliss Potatoes

Borrego com Batatas Vermelhas

SERVES 4 TO 6

Of all my grandson's favorite dishes, this one is by far his favorite. Succulent, falling-off-the-bone lamb, infused with spices, onions, tomato, wine and garlic, this is a savory delight, which is adapted from *Portuguese Homestyle Cooking*. This recipe is a repeat on our table, especially when he comes to visit. Whether you make it in a presoaked clay pot or a braising pan, you will have wonderful results.

---

4 ——— tablespoons/60 ml olive oil or 2 ounces/56 g salt pork

4 ——— pounds/1818 g lamb or goat forequarter shanks, cut into 4-inch/10-cm pieces (ask your butcher to do this for you)

3 ——— large onions, thinly sliced (about 2 cups/320 g)

1 ——— stalk celery, trimmed, coarsely chopped

2 ——— teaspoons/12 g coarse kosher salt

4 ——— garlic cloves, crushed

1 ——— bay leaf, crumbled

½ ——— teaspoon Jamaican whole allspice (9 or 10 berries)

½ ——— teaspoon marjoram or oregano

½ ——— teaspoon paprika

½ ——— teaspoon tumeric

½ ——— teaspoon black or white fresh ground pepper

Generous pinch (about ⅛ teaspoon) crushed, dried red chile pepper

1 ——— tablespoon/15 g tomato paste

1½ ——— cups/355 ml white wine

1½ ——— cups/355 ml water, divided

2 ——— tablespoons/16 g cornstarch

½ ——— cup/30 g finely chopped parsley (you can use mint if you prefer)

8 ——— medium red bliss or waxy potatoes, peeled

2 ——— carrots, peeled, cut into large chunks

1. Preheat the oven to 350°F/180°C, or gas mark 4.

2. Using a large, cast-iron frying pan, heat the olive oil or fry the salt pork, rendering the fat, until crispy pieces remain, about 3 minutes. Brown the pieces of lamb on all sides, 5 to 10 minutes, depending on how big and how many pieces you have. Transfer the browned lamb to a roasting pan. Scatter the onion slices and chopped celery over the meat.

3. Make a paste, using a mortar and pestle, by mashing the salt with the garlic. One by one, grind in the bay leaf, whole allspice, marjoram, paprika, tumeric, pepper and crushed red pepper, blending well. Set aside.

4. In a bowl, blend the tomato paste with the wine and 1¼ cup/295 ml water, stirring to dissolve the paste. Mix in the garlic and spice paste. Pour the seasoning solution over the lamb and cover.

5. Roast for 1 hour. Mix the cornstarch with ¼ cup/60 ml of the water to form a slurry. Stir the slurry into the pan, then add the parsley. Add the potatoes and carrots, spooning the braising sauce over them. Recover the pan. Cook until the meat is nearly falling off the bone, about 1 more hour. Serve the meat with the potatoes, ladled with some sauce. Serve extra sauce on the side.

Braised Goat of Poiares
Chanfana

SERVES 6

Those in the know say the best *chanfana* can be found in the town of Poiares on the Portuguese mainland. Adapted from Lucy Neves, this was traditionally served on weddings and feast days. The braised goat, done right, is highly praised. Although a 30-pound/13.6-kg goat is a lot for a small family, you can have a butcher cut it up and package it in desired portions or invite a few friends over. This is typically cooked in a low oven with red wine in a mineral-laden black clay oven-proof pot called a *caçoilo*, which has been prepared the day before. If you don't have a black clay pot you can use a red one (from kitchen stores) or a metal roasting pan; however, the amount of pan juices will be more and the flavor will be different. Do not use baby goat (*cabrito*) or a lamb weighing less than 15 pounds/6.8 kg for this recipe. The older goat requires longer slow cooking to break down the meat to fork-tenderness.

EQUIPMENT

1 ——— 4- or 5-quart/3.6- or 4.5-L unglazed clay pot (see headnote), presoaked for several hours in water (see Note)

5 ——— pounds/2270 g goat or lamb leg meat, or shoulder and ribs, cut into 2½- to 3-inch/6.4- to 7.5-cm chunks

3 to 5 — garlic cloves, whole

1 ——— large bay leaf, broken in half

½ ——— cup/30 g coarsely chopped fresh parsley

2 ——— teaspoons/6 g sweet paprika

½ ——— teaspoon crushed dried chile pepper

1 ——— tablespoon/18 g coarse kosher salt

3 ——— cups/705 ml red wine

¼ ——— cup/60 ml olive oil

1 ——— large onion, finely chopped, divided

2 ——— fresh mint leaves (optional)

4 ——— ounces/112 g salt pork, coarsely chopped, or 3 slices bacon

THE DAY BEFORE

1. Place the meat in a nonreactive bowl. Season the meat all over with the garlic, bay leaf, parsley, paprika, chile pepper and salt. Turn the meat to coat evenly with the seasoning. Pour the wine over the meat, enough to come level with the top of the meat. Drizzle the olive oil over the top. Marinate, turning occasionally, for a couple of hours to overnight. The longer the marinating time, the more winey the flavor will be.

THE NEXT DAY

1. If you are using a clay pot, *do not* preheat the oven. Clay pots go in a cold oven or they may crack. Otherwise, with a regular roasting pan, preheat the oven to 350°F/180°C, or gas mark 4.

2. Make a bed of half the onion in the bottom of the pot or pan. Transfer the meat and marinade on top, scattering the remaining onions and mint leaves over, followed lastly by the salt pork or bacon. Cover tightly with foil and place in the oven.

3. After 2½ hours, remove the cover or foil, and continue cooking, uncovered, for another 20 to 30 minutes, until the meat is falling-off-the-bone fork-tender. Occasionally, spoon some of the broth over the meat. The top of the meat will darken after the cover is removed. Serve with boiled potatoes and crusty bread to sop up the juice.

Note: To prep a new clay pot, fill it with water and add several cabbage or collard leaves with some onion peelings. Place the pot on a flame-proof diffuser over medium heat. Bring to a boil and reduce to a simmer. Simmer for about 2 hours and then drain. Before cooking, immerse the pot in water and soak for 24 hours.

Roast Kid
Cabrito Assado

SERVES 4 TO 6

If you never had goat before, this is a good introduction to the lamb alternative. The meat of a kid goat is succulent, more delicate in texture and flavor. You don't need to buy a whole goat unless you want to. Young goats, weighing no more than 12 pounds/5.4 kg, are typically used for this preparation. Unlike the previous recipe of *chanfana*, in which an older goat or lamb is slowly braised, the younger goat is first browned and then fully seasoned before finishing in the oven. This recipe calls for 5 pounds/2.3 kg of young goat. It sounds like a lot for 6 servings, but there is more bone than meat. You can double the seasonings for a whole goat. A butcher or specialty meat market can order, prep and cut the meat to your needs.

---

3 —— ounces/84 g salt pork, cut into strips

5 —— pounds/2.3 kg young goat, cut into 3-inch/7.5-cm serving pieces

Coarse kosher salt as needed

Ground pepper as needed

½ —— cup/120 ml olive oil, as needed

1 —— cup/235 ml white wine

1 —— large onion, sliced

½ —— cup/30 g chopped parsley

½ —— tablespoon/4 g paprika

4 —— garlic cloves, smashed

1 —— bay leaf

Medium pinch crushed dried chile pepper

1. Preheat the oven to 400°F/200°C, or gas mark 6.

2. Fry the salt pork in a large cast-iron skillet until the fat is rendered and crispy pieces remain, about 3 minutes. Season the meat with salt and ground pepper. Working in batches, brown the pieces of meat in the rendered fat, and olive oil, about 5 minutes. Transfer the browned pieces to a roasting pan. Pour the drippings over the meat.

3. Reduce the oven temperature to 350°F/180°C, or gas mark 4. Add the remaining ingredients over the pieces of meat, turning to coat. Cover, place the pan in the oven and cook for 1¼ to 1½ hours, until falling-off-the-bone tender. Discard the bay leaf. Serve with rice.

Note: You can also season the meat and toss in a bowl with the olive oil and rendered fat. Place the pieces on a sheet pan to brown in the oven, then transfer to a roasting pan and continue with step 3.

Baked Chicken with Béchamel Sauce

Galinha com Molho Branco no Forno

SERVES 8

For those of you who do not like salted codfish, this popular dish from Lisbon makes a great substitute
and is less expensive made with chicken. The creaminess of the sauce makes this deliciously rich and non-spicy on
the palate. Read the recipe through completely before beginning. You can omit the cream if you prefer. If you wish
to use chicken breasts, cut them into 2-inch/5-cm pieces and do not overcook. If you decide to cut
the recipe in half, make sure you cut the sauce recipe in half as well.

FOR THE BÉCHAMEL SAUCE

8	tablespoons/112 g butter
⅔	cup/80 g all-purpose flour
3	cups/705 ml cold milk
1	bay leaf
1	small onion, peeled, whole
2	whole cloves
¼	teaspoon nutmeg
½	teaspoon coarse kosher salt

Generous pinch ground white pepper or to taste

FOR THE CHICKEN

3	boneless, skinless, chicken thighs
¼	cup/60 ml olive oil
2	large onions, thinly sliced
2	carrots, peeled, cut into small cubes or thickly grated
1	tablespoon/4 g finely chopped fresh parsley
3	garlic cloves, finely chopped
1	bay leaf
¼	cup/60 ml white wine
2	teaspoons/12 g coarse kosher salt or to taste
¼	teaspoon ground white pepper or to taste

FOR THE BÉCHAMEL SAUCE

1. Melt the butter in a saucepan. Whisk in the flour, making a roux. When it starts to foam and is pale yellow, it should fall from the whisk like wet sand, about 2 minutes.

2. Gradually, while whisking, add the cold milk in a slow stream. (Adding the milk slowly will avoid a lumpy sauce. The butter-flour paste should be hot and the milk cold.) Pin the bay leaf to the onion with the stems of the cloves. Add to the pan along with the nutmeg, salt and pepper. While constantly stirring, cook over medium-low heat, simmering for about 20 minutes, until it thickens like heavy cream. Do not boil. Remove from the heat and reserve.

FOR THE CHICKEN

1. Cut the chicken into 2-inch/5-cm cubes and set aside.

2. Heat the olive oil in a 10-inch/25.4-cm skillet over medium-high heat. Add the onions and sauté until translucent, about 2 to 3 minutes. Mix in the chicken and continue to sauté until the chicken is lightly golden on each side, about 4 minutes. Reduce the heat to medium. Toss in the carrots, parsley, garlic and bay leaf. Stir, continuing to sauté, until the garlic is aromatic and the onions are golden, about 2 more minutes.

3. Pour in the wine and simmer for 1 minute. Season the chicken carefully with just a touch of salt and pepper or to taste—not too much because you will have salt in the béchamel sauce. Remove from the heat. Discard the bay leaf. Set aside.

FOR THE POTATOES

3 ——— cups/705 ml corn oil or as needed

3 ——— large potatoes, peeled, cut into fine julienne

TO FINISH

½ ——— cup/120 ml heavy cream

Coarse kosher salt as needed

Ground pepper to taste

FOR THE POTATOES

1. Heat the oil in a deep pot until it reaches 350°F/177°C but is not smoking. Working in small batches, fry the potatoes until golden. Drain well on paper toweling. Mix the drained fried potatoes with the sautéed chicken, onions and carrots.

TO FINISH

1. Preheat the oven to 350°F/180°C, or gas mark 4.

2. In a large bowl, combine the chicken mixture with half of the béchamel sauce and the cream, gently turning to blend everything. Taste for salt and pepper, and if you need to adjust, do so now. Transfer to a 9 x 13–inch/23 x 33–cm baking dish. Pour the remaining béchamel sauce evenly over the top. Bake until bubbly and slightly golden on top, about 30 minutes. Garnish with black Portuguese olives. Serve with a salad or sautéed green vegetable.

Note: For a shortcut on prep, frozen fried potato strings, cubes or rounds could be used in place of fresh fried ones.

Curried Chicken with Coconut Milk

Galinha com Caril e Leite de Coco

SERVES 4

Curry and coconut milk are not typical Portuguese ingredients. However, it works not only with the popular curried shrimp dish but also with chicken. Here is an economical and satisfying combination that goes well with rice. The coconut milk adds richness to the wonderful sauce infused with curry, cumin and tomato. Make sure you shake the can well before opening. If you prefer not to use coconut milk, you can substitute heavy cream instead.

4	tablespoons/56 g butter
¼	cup/60 ml olive oil
3	pounds/1362 g boneless, skinless chicken thighs, cut into 2-inch/5-cm pieces
1	large onion, chopped
1	large tomato, peeled, seeded and chopped
1	teaspoon/3 g paprika
1	garlic clove, finely chopped
¼	cup/15 g finely chopped parsley, divided
¼	cup/60 ml white wine
1	teaspoon/5 g tomato paste
1⅓	cups/313 ml coconut milk or heavy cream
1	tablespoon/6 g curry
1	teaspoon/5 ml hot sauce
¼	teaspoon ground cumin
1	teaspoon/6 g coarse kosher salt or to taste
¼	teaspoon ground white pepper
2	tablespoons/16 g cornstarch
1	tablespoon/15 ml water

Fluffy cooked rice

1. In a heavy-bottomed skillet, heat the butter with the olive oil until hot but not smoking. Working in small batches, sauté the chicken until lightly golden on all sides, about 5 to 10 minutes. Do not crowd the pieces of chicken or they will steam and not brown. Remove the browned chicken to a dish and cover.

2. Using the same pan, add the onion and sauté until golden, about 5 to 7 minutes. Mix in the chopped tomato, paprika, garlic and 2 tablespoons/ 8 g of the parsley. Stir, cover and simmer over medium-low heat for about 10 minutes, until the tomato breaks down a bit and becomes married to the onions.

3. Combine the wine with the tomato paste and stir into the tomato and onions.

4. In a small bowl, mix together the coconut milk, curry, hot sauce, cumin, salt and pepper and then stir into the pan. Mix the cornstarch with the water and stir into the sauce. Return the chicken to the pan, cover and simmer over medium-low heat until the chicken is tender and cooked through and the sauce is well blended, about 5 to 10 minutes. Taste for seasoning and adjust if necessary. Serve over cooked rice and garnish with the remaining 2 tablespoons/8 g parsley.

Piri-piri Chicken
Frango Piri-piri

Whatever the spelling, *frango piri-piri* (Portuguese) or *frango peri-peri* (African), this recipe has an interesting history. Little did Portuguese explorers know that they would later adopt a Portuguese-African dish that they helped create. This dish evolved in Angola and Mozambique (once Portuguese colonies) after Portuguese explorers and settlers brought tiny chile peppers (chiltepins, see page 364) from the Americas to Africa. The chiles were often referred to as *pimentos Africanos*. An African original, *frango piri-piri*, piri-piri chicken and peri-peri chicken all refer to basically the same dish where chicken is marinated in a hot chile pepper–infused concoction, then grilled. Other cooks simply season, grill and then baste the chicken with their chile concoction. Spicy-hot *frango piri-piri* is now so popular in Portugal that it is regarded as a Portuguese dish as well.

Usually, butterflied chicken and Cornish hens are laid flat to grill, but serving pieces can be used instead. I also like to use wings. The chicken pieces are coated with the seasoning, marinated for a couple of hours or overnight, chilled, and then brought to room temperature before grilling. If you choose to use the chile preparation as a condiment to serve on the side instead of basting or marinating with it, cut down the amount of chiles. Thai chiles are a perfect substitute for the chiltepin ones.

Keep in mind that whatever form of chiles you use for this recipe, whether it is liquid, dried (the hottest form) or bottled, too much will kill all the other flavors of the dish. You will only taste heat. Prolonged cooking will extract more heat from the chiles and make your dish spicier. So, for less heat, use a hot sauce or chile paste and add toward the end of cooking the chicken. Handle chiles very carefully. Food-safe gloves are recommended or wash your hands immediately after handling. If you should ingest or rub your eye, drink milk or bathe your eye with milk. Speaking from experience, it works wonders.

Chicken Rissoles
Rissois de Galinha

Although this dish is most often made with shrimp, the chicken filling is tasty as well, and is almost like chicken pot pie. These can even be made with shredded rabbit, poached salt cod, pulled pork or beef. I use olive oil to fry the onions, but corn oil is the oil I like to fry the assembled rissoles in. These are great to make and freeze, uncooked, for times when unexpected guests appear. Small or large, they are worth the work.

FOR THE FILLING

2	tablespoons/28 g butter
¼	cup/40 g finely chopped onion
¼	cup/30 g finely chopped celery
1	cup/235 ml milk
½	tablespoon/2 g finely chopped cilantro or parsley
1 to 2	teaspoons/5 to 10 ml hot pepper sauce or to taste
½	teaspoon coarse kosher salt or to taste
½	teaspoon freshly ground white pepper
¼	teaspoon nutmeg
2	tablespoons/16 g cornstarch
2	tablespoons/30 ml water
½	pound/227 g boiled skinless, boneless chicken thighs, trimmed of any fat and membranes, coarsely chopped (1½ cups/210 g)

FOR THE PASTRY

2	cups/470 ml milk
4	tablespoons/56 g butter
1	teaspoon/6 g kosher salt
2	cups/240 g flour

FOR THE FILLING

1. Melt the butter in a 1-quart/1-L saucepan. Add the onion and celery and sauté over medium-high heat until lightly golden, about 4 to 5 minutes.

2. Reduce the heat to medium-low, pour in the milk, and heat to really hot but not boiling. Add the cilantro, hot pepper sauce, salt, pepper and nutmeg and stir to combine.

3. Make a slurry by combining the cornstarch with the water. Stir into the milk and simmer over medium-low heat, stirring continuously, until it thickens, about 1 to 2 minutes. Stir in the chopped chicken, heat through for 1 minute, and remove from the heat. Set aside to cool completely. Makes about 2 cups/475 ml filling.

FOR THE PASTRY

1. Combine the milk, butter and salt in a 2-quart/2-L saucepan. Warm over medium heat until the milk is scalded, about 2 minutes.

2. Add the flour and as fast as you can, using a wooden spoon, incorporate the flour into the hot milk. Keep stirring fast until it forms a dough, about 1 minute. When the dough pulls away from the sides of the pan and forms a ball, remove the pan from the stove.

3. Turn the dough out onto a lightly buttered workspace (not stone). With a light touch, use a wooden spatula and your fingers to turn the warm dough onto itself and knead briefly until smooth. Don't overwork the dough. Divide the dough in half, forming two balls, and cover and keep warm.

(continued)

FOR FRYING

Egg wash of 3 beaten eggs mixed with 3 tablespoons/45 ml of water

Fine plain bread crumbs

Olive oil or corn oil, for frying

Variation:
Try making these with 1½ cups/210 g finely chopped shrimp, rabbit or shredded poached salt cod.

Note: For freezing, I find it easier to place each pastry, without overlapping, onto the tray after coating it with bread crumbs, covering them tightly with plastic wrap; they are then ready to freeze. Fry from frozen or let stand at room temperature for 15 minutes before frying.

FOR THE ASSEMBLY

1. It is important that the dough and work surface are warm for this method. Use a wooden board or other non-stone surface. Wipe it with a warm, barely damp cloth.

2. Use a warm wooden or nylon cutting board. Take half of the dough and shape it into a 4- to 6-inch/10-to 15-cm diameter log. Turn it so the short end is facing you. With your rolling pin, without separating the dough from the cylinder, roll out toward you some of the short end, about 5 inches/ 12.5 cm, to about ⅛ inch/3 mm thick. Place 1 scant tablespoon/15 g of filling in the middle.

3. Fold the rolled dough away from you and over the filling, pressing the edges of the far side together to seal, forming a half circle. The fold should be facing you. Using a 3-inch/7.5-cm diameter cutter, place it over the pressed side but not catching the folded edge and cut out the half-moon shape. Set aside on a plastic wrap–lined sheet pan or tray.

4. Repeat with the remaining dough until all the filling is used. The amount you get will depend on the size you make them and how thick you roll the dough.

FOR FRYING

1. Dip the rissoles in the beaten egg wash, then quickly into the plain bread crumbs, making sure to shake off any excess bread crumbs, and set back on the tray. Repeat with all the rissoles. At this point, you can cover and freeze the rissoles.

2. Fry the rissoles, two or three at a time, in hot oil until golden. Serve hot or at room temperature.

Dough is rolled out from a cylinder shape. Filling is added, covered over and sealed within. Rissoles are cut, eggwashed, breaded and fried.

Chile Chicken Wings

Asas de Frango Piri-piri

SERVES 4 AS AN APPETIZER

In Portugal, Cornish hen–size chickens are very popular. Bird's eye chiles are hard to get here, but you can use the hottest chile peppers or hot sauce available. I like to include paprika, cilantro and bay leaf in my robust, garlicky seasoning paste and sometimes even *massa de pimentão* (Sweet Pepper Paste, page 367), but feel free to be creative. You can adjust the spiciness by adding or reducing the amount of hot sauce. If you prefer a more vinegar flavor, you can add an extra 2 tablespoons/30 ml cider or white wine vinegar to the marinade. For a gathering, use this seasoning to make finger-licking chicken wings, as I have done, and serve as an appetizer.

---

8 —— garlic cloves, coarsely chopped

1 —— tablespoon/18 g coarse kosher salt or to taste

1 —— tablespoon/8 g paprika

1 —— bay leaf, crumbled

2 —— tablespoons/8 g finely chopped cilantro or parsley

1 —— teaspoon/5 g turmeric

½ —— teaspoon ground black pepper

¼ —— teaspoon ground cumin

½ —— cup/120 ml olive oil or melted butter

2 to 4 —— tablespoons/30 to 60 ml hot sauce or Chile Pepper Paste (page 365)

½ —— cup/120 ml cider vinegar

¼ —— cup/60 ml brandy

2 —— pounds/908 g chicken wings (6 to 8 per pound/454 g), or whole small chicken or parts

1. Using a mortar and pestle, mash the garlic with the salt, forming a paste. Mix in the paprika, bay leaf, cilantro, turmeric, black pepper and cumin.

2. In a cup, combine the olive oil, hot sauce, vinegar and brandy and then pour into the seasoning paste. Stir to blend.

3. Coat the chicken wings with the mixture.

4. Place the chicken wings in a single layer in a nonreactive dish. Cover and refrigerate, marinating for 1 to 2 hours or even overnight.

5. About ½ hour before cooking, reserving any residual marinade, transfer the chicken to another bowl. Let the chicken come to room temperature.

6. Grill the chicken wings over medium-hot coals, in a gas grill or under the broiler, basting periodically with any reserved marinade and turning frequently to avoid burning, until the juices run clear and the skin is crispy and richly colored. If using whole chicken or leg quarters, the juices of the meat should run clear and a meat thermometer should register 165°F/74°C when inserted into the thickest part of the thigh. Pile the wings on a platter and serve.

Chicken with St. Jorge Cheese
Galinha São Jorge

SERVES 2

This is a very tasty but simple way to liven up chicken breasts. The buttery wine sauce accented with the flavor of the garlicky chouriço sausage gives a subtly intense flavor to the chicken, which has creamy melted St. Jorge cheese on top. Keep in mind the sausage has salt when seasoning the chicken.

---

2 ——— tablespoons/28 g butter

2 ——— tablespoons/30 ml olive oil

1 ——— whole chicken breast, center bone removed, cut in half

½ ——— teaspoon coarse kosher salt, or as needed

¼ ——— teaspoon ground black or white pepper, or as needed

4 ——— ounces/112 g chouriço sausage, cut into ½-inch/1.3-cm pieces

½ ——— cup/120 ml white wine

1 ——— cup/120 g shredded St. Jorge cheese

1. In a large skillet set over medium-heat, melt the butter with the olive oil.

2. Season the chicken breast halves with salt and pepper.

3. Add the chicken halves to the pan and sauté for about 5 minutes on each side, until the juices run clear. Transfer to an oven-proof pan.

4. Add the sausage pieces to the same skillet and fry them just until they take on some color, about 2 minutes. Pour in the wine, deglazing the pan, and cook for 1 minute. Pour the pan juices over the chicken. Top the chicken breasts with the shredded cheese. Place in the oven, under the broiler, to melt the cheese and brown the top, about 3 to 4 minutes.

5. Served the chicken with the pan juices, accompanied with rice and a green vegetable.

Portuguese Home Remedies

Old-time Portuguese always have a home remedy for whatever ails you. When I was a kid, I was anemic, so my father would mix raw egg yolk and a touch of red wine with a teaspoon/5 g of sugar to build up my blood.

Whenever he had a cold, my grandfather José had his own concoction for getting rid of it.

He would scald milk with a garlic clove until it got very hot and then add 2 teaspoons/10 g of sugar.

Then he added, in a ratio of 3 to 1, with milk being the 3, a shot of homemade Portuguese *aguardente* (containing 100 percent alcohol, it is often referred to as "bang bang," Portuguese "fire water" or "moonshine," and is made from the stems, seeds and skins that remained from pressing grapes during winemaking). "Drink this immediately," he once told me as he gave me the recipe. "If you make it to bed without passing out, cover yourself well. Any perspiring that follows will chase away the cold bug." After hearing this, I thought the remedy would either kill me or cure me. Warning: Don't mix with aspirin or give to children. My grandfather lived to 97 years of age, so I guess that says it all.

Uncle Leo's Cough Syrup

Uncle Leo, as we called him, my husband's uncle, had this home remedy for sore throats and coughs.
He usually used homemade whiskey which we refer to as "bang bang."

---

1 ——— 8-ounce/227-g jar of honey

Juice of 1 lemon

1 ——— ounce/30 ml whiskey or substitute brandy

1. Heat the honey until hot, 10 to 15 minutes. Stir in the lemon juice and whiskey. Cool and take a teaspoon/5 ml as needed.

Chicken Giblets with Onions, Garlic and White Wine
Moelas Guisadas

SERVES 4

Chicken livers, stomachs and hearts sautéed with spices and onions is an old favorite. We usually eat this with rice on the side, or mix it with the rice. As an appetizer, use 1 pound/454 g of just the livers and purée everything after it has been cooked. Serve on toast points or crackers. Play with the vinegar, adjusting the amount to your taste.

1 —— pound/454 g chicken livers, hearts and stomachs, trimmed of fat and attachments

¼ —— cup/60 ml olive oil

1 —— large onion, finely chopped (scant 1 cup/160 g)

2 —— large garlic cloves, finely chopped

2 —— teaspoons/6 g sweet paprika

1 —— large bay leaf

3 —— tablespoons/45 ml white wine as needed

3 —— tablespoons/45 ml cider vinegar or wine vinegar as needed

Pinch of crushed dried chile pepper or dash of hot sauce to taste

1 —— tablespoon/4 g finely chopped cilantro or parsley

1 —— teaspoon/6 g coarse kosher salt or to taste

¼ —— teaspoon ground pepper or to taste

Chopped parsley, for garnish

1. Rinse the livers. Trim any extra fat that is visible.

2. Heat the olive oil in a medium skillet. Toss in the onion and sauté for about 7 minutes, until lightly golden.

3. Add the livers to the pan. Lightly fry to brown. Toss in the garlic, paprika and bay leaf. While stirring slowly, pour in the wine and vinegar. There should be just enough liquid to barely cover the livers. Add more wine and vinegar in equal amounts as needed.

4. Cover and simmer for 5 minutes. Add the dried chile, cilantro, salt and pepper. Continue to slowly simmer, covered, over medium-low heat until the stomachs are tender. If the liquid starts to evaporate before they are completely cooked, add just a little bit of water and stir. It is important that the pan stays tightly covered and the heat is not too high. Make sure you don't overcook the livers or they will be tough. They should be pale pink in the center and tender. Discard the bay leaf. Serve over rice. Garnish with parsley.

Roasted Brined Turkey

Peru Salmoura

SERVES 10-12

There was a time when turkeys would be force-fed with brandy before being slaughtered. Some say it was to give the meat flavor, but since most folks are not raising turkeys in their backyards, this recipe works nicely just the same. Brining draws out the impurity of any blood still in the meat, giving you a cleaner, more flavorful taste. Perhaps it is a method that was learned from the Jewish culture. It also helps it retain moisture. If you purchase a kosher processed turkey, check to see if it was pre-brined. It will save you the step. Bear in mind that brands of coarse salt vary in saltiness, so use the recipe as a guide. Just don't use regular table salt. For example: If I use 5 gallons/18 L of water and Morton Crystal coarse kosher salt, I would use 7 cups/2016 g. If I use Diamond Crystal coarse kosher salt for the same amount of water, I would use closer to 7½ cups/2160 g. The ½ cup/120 g more of salt is because Diamond Crystal salt has larger crystals and takes up more space in the measuring cup. Some cooks add bay leaves, wine, onions and other seasons to the brining solution. This recipe is simple. Recipes for stuffing are on pages 203 and 207.

This is the formula I use no matter what size bucket the turkey is in. Typically, I use a turkey that will fit in a 9-gallon/32-L food-safe bucket, maxing out at a 24-pounder/10.1 kg.

FOR THE BRINE

1 ——— dressed turkey, rinsed inside and out

For every gallon/3.6 L of water needed to cover the turkey completely use:

1½ ——— cups/432 g kosher coarse salt*

1 or 2 — whole lemons, juice and rinds

1 or 2 — whole oranges, juice and rinds

A large, clean 9-gallon/32-L bucket with lid to accommodate the bird

CAUTION: Trash bags are not a food-safe material and should not be used for brining. You can find food-safe brining bags at restaurant supply stores.

Diamond Crystal Salt measure, see headnote.

BRINE THE TURKEY THE DAY BEFORE COOKING

1. Place the rinsed, dressed turkey in the brining container (see note above). For every gallon/3.6 L of water you use to cover the turkey, dissolve in 1½ cups/432 g of coarse salt in a separate container before pouring it over the turkey. Add the juice of the lemons and oranges and the rinds to the salted water. Make sure the turkey is covered by 2 inches/5 cm of water. Give the turkey a spin and cover.

2. After you have covered the bird in the salted and flavored water with the citrus peels, cover and store below 40°F/4°C. During the cold seasons of the year, it is usually cold enough to store it in an unheated garage or back porch, or place it in a cooler with ice around the brining container. Leave the turkey to soak in the salted water overnight.

> *Note:* If outside temperatures are over 40°F/4°C, the bird needs to be refrigerated. I usually reserve a food-safe bucket that I have purchased new at a restaurant or kitchen supply store for brining turkeys and piglets.

FOR THE SEASONING PASTE

4 ——— garlic cloves, finely chopped

1½ —— tablespoons/12 g sweet paprika

1 ——— bay leaf, crumbled

½ ——— cup/30 g finely chopped parsley

½ ——— teaspoon freshly ground black pepper

2 ——— tablespoons/30 ml white wine or lemon juice

½ ——— cup/120 ml olive oil

Sliced bacon (optional)

1 ——— instant read thermometer

MAKE THE SEASONING PASTE

1. Preheat the oven to 350°F/180°C, or gas mark 4.

2. Remove the bird from the salted water, drain well, rinse with clean water and drain well again. Pat dry with paper towels.

3. Using a mortar and pestle, pound the garlic and mix in the seasoning ingredients, drizzling the oil in last, to form a paste. Rub the paste over and under the skin, completely coating the bird. At this point, my grandmother would drape bacon over the top of the bird before roasting. I don't.

4. Roast for 20 minutes per pound/454 g until the internal thigh temperature reaches 165°F/74°C. Make sure the thermometer is inserted in the thickest part of the thigh and is not touching the bone. The juices should run clear. Let the bird rest for 10 to 15 minutes before carving.

Note: Salt is not necessary in the seasoning paste when the bird has been brined. The amount of seasoning can be adjusted to your taste and the size of the bird.

Slow-Cooked Chicken in a Clay Pot

Frango na Púcara

SERVES 4 TO 6

Slowly cooking chicken in a clay pot with onions, tomatoes, wine and smoked bacon and chouriço, accented with the flavor of brandy, is an age-old dish of the Estremadura region of the Portuguese mainland. Traditionally, it is simple enough to combine all the ingredients in the pot and then set it to stew slowly until the chicken is tender and the juices condense into a flavorful sauce. Obviously, you may not have the clay pot, but you can make this dish in a heavy-bottomed Dutch oven with great results, or even in a slow cooker. I like to briefly sauté the bacon and onions with the garlic just long enough to release their flavors.

4	ounces/112 g smoked bacon, chopped
5	tablespoons/70 g butter
1	tablespoon/8 g paprika
1	pound/454 g small onions, peeled, halved
4	garlic cloves, smashed
1	bay leaf
¼	cup/15 g chopped cilantro
½	cup/30 g coarsely chopped parsley, divided
1	tablespoon/18 g coarse kosher salt or to taste
¼	teaspoon ground black pepper or to taste
1	4 pound/1.8 kg chicken, left whole or cut into serving pieces
½	pound/227 g chouriço sausage, cut into 6 pieces
2	cups/470 ml white wine
2	tablespoons/30 ml tawny port wine

1. Heat the bacon in a heavy-bottomed, 5-quart/4.5-L pot (such as a Dutch oven) set over medium heat. As it starts to sweat and release its fat, mix in the butter, paprika and halved onions, and sauté the onions until lightly golden, about 5 minutes. Toss in the garlic, bay leaf, cilantro, ¼ cup/15 g of the parsley, salt and pepper.

2. Add the chicken and sausage pieces, give everything a turn to coat, and let the chicken brown a bit to give it some color, about 5 to 10 minutes. Pour the white wine over, stir and cover tightly. Bring to a boil, reduce the heat to low and simmer slowly with an occasional stir. After 30 minutes, place the cover slightly ajar and continue to slowly simmer until the meat is just about falling off the bone. Add the port wine, stir to blend and simmer for 1 minute. Discard the bay leaf. Serve with the remaining ¼ cup/15 g parsley over the top and roasted potatoes and green beans on the side.

Duck with Rice
Arroz de Pato

SERVES 4 TO 6

Rice simmered in duck stock and then finished in the oven is so flavorful. The golden rice, combine with chouriço sausage and duck meat, is one not to miss. Don't be thrown by the length of this recipe. Read it through completely. It is my attempt to give detailed steps to the novice, even though the more experienced will have no problem.

Traditionally, a whole duck, minus the feathers and webbed feet, was boiled in salted water with perhaps a spice or two, if the cook desired. The meat was mixed with partially cooked rice and then baked off, which resulted in overcooked duck, especially the breast meat, which in my opinion ruined the dish. Cooking duck is not like cooking chicken. Since duck breast is delicate, you really want a little pink in it so that it remains tender. It requires less cooking time than the rest of the carcass and the legs require the most time. To manage the different cooking times, I updated this recipe to still include duck meat in the rice but the breast meat is cooked separately. The breast meat is served sliced, on top or to the side of the rice. The breast meat should be springy but not mushy.

There isn't much meat on the carcass without the breast, but the small amount is good to add to the rice as well. However, if the duck is not cooked enough, removing the meat from the skin and bones will require some effort. The point of this dish is to give distinctive duck flavor from the carcass to the stock, and ultimately the rice, which I would not be able to do if I used just duck breasts. For purists, chicken broth is not an alternative for this dish. In this updated version, to give additional flavor to the stock, I use celery and carrot along with parsley. For those who haven't cooked duck before, see the notes following this recipe. Before you begin, organize your ingredients in groups and in order of use.

FOR THE STOCK

1	4- to 5-pound/1818- to 2270-g duckling, fresh or thawed from frozen
½	pound/227 g chouriço sausage, link intact
1	carrot, peeled
1	celery stalk, trimmed
3	scallions, trimmed, heavy outer green removed
1	tablespoon/15 ml olive oil
2	teaspoons/12 g coarse kosher salt
3	garlic cloves, peeled, smashed
2 or 3	whole cloves
1	bay leaf
½	cup/120 ml white wine
1½ to 2	quarts/1.5 to 2 L water, or as needed

FOR THE STOCK

1. Carefully, starting at the center breast bone, make a cut, keeping as close as you can to the bone as you cut down close to the ribs (a boning knife makes this easier). At the same time with the other hand, peel back the breast meat. As you cut down, you should be able to lift out one of the breast halves, with the skin intact, from the body of the duck, leaving the carcass. Repeat on the other side. Set aside the breast meat with the skin intact.

2. Separate the legs from the carcass. Place the remaining duck carcass with the separated legs, chouriço, carrot, celery, scallions, olive oil, salt, garlic, whole cloves and bay leaf in an 8-quart/7.2-L pot with the wine and enough water to cover the ingredients completely by 2 inches/5 cm. Cover and bring to a boil over medium-high heat. Reduce the heat to medium-low and simmer for 20 minutes. Remove the sausage link to a dish and continue to simmer the stock, covered, for about 1 hour, until the duck meat is cooked and easily pulled from the carcass bones with a fork. Remove just the carcass from the pot and set aside to cool. Continue to cook the legs until the meat easily falls off the bones, or it will be difficult to remove.

(continued)

FOR THE BREAST MEAT

Reserved duck breasts, plus any extra duck breasts you are using (see Note)

Coarse salt as needed

¼ ——— teaspoon ground white or black pepper, or as needed

3. Reserve the broth and set the legs aside with the carcass. When cool enough to handle, remove all the meat from the carcass, the legs and the wings. Cut the meat into bite-size pieces and transfer to a dish and reserve. Cut the sausage into ¼-inch/6-mm round slices and set aside. Strain the stock and let stand to cool so the fat rises to the top. Spoon the fat off into a small bowl or use a defatting cup and reserve. Do not discard the fat. (See Note.)

FOR THE BREAST MEAT

1. While the stock is cooling, take the breasts and, with a sharp knife, score the skin by carefully making shallow crosshatch cuts in the skin but do not go completely through to the meat. Season both sides of the breasts with coarse salt and ground black pepper to taste. Cover and place in the refrigerator for 30 minutes.

After removing any giblets from the duck cavity, the breast meat is removed from the duck.

Note: For 4 larger portions of breast meat or for 6 servings, ask your butcher for 2 additional individual duck breast halves. I often find them vacuum-packed in the supermarket freezer. Just prepare them the same as the two halves that come with the whole duck.

To defat the broth, it is helpful if you have one of those defatting cups where the broth is let out the bottom of the cup while the fat is at the top. In any event, you need to let the broth settle a little for the fat to rise. If you make the stock a day ahead, chill it and then just scoop off the solid fat. Save the fat and use it for sautéing. It is flavorful and, unlike chicken fat, it is a healthier form of fat. Use the fat to coat seasoned potatoes, then pan roast them for a unique flavor.

FOR THE RICE

3 ——— tablespoons/45 ml olive oil

2 ——— tablespoons/28 g butter

½ ——— cup/80 g finely chopped onion

1 ——— teaspoon/3 g paprika

1 ——— garlic clove, finely chopped

Grated peel of a whole orange

¼ ——— cup/15 g finely chopped parsley, divided

1 ——— bay leaf

1 ——— teaspoon/6 g coarse kosher salt

Pinch of crushed dried chile pepper (optional)

½ ——— cup/120 ml white wine

1½ ——— cups/278 g long-grain rice (not instant)

3 ——— cups/705 ml duck stock, defatted, divided (see Note)

1 ——— orange, cut into slices, for garnish

FOR THE RICE

1. Preheat the oven to 375°F/190°C, or gas mark 5.

2. While the breasts are chilling, start the rice. In a 2½-quart/2.3-L pot, warm the olive oil with the butter over medium heat until hot but not smoking. Toss in the onion, paprika, garlic, grated orange peel, 1 tablespoon/4 g of the parsley, bay leaf, salt and crushed dried chile. Let the ingredients sweat for 1 minute to bring the flavors together.

3. Pour in the wine and bring to a simmer over medium heat, slightly reducing, about 1 minute. Give all a stir and then mix in the rice. Let the rice sizzle for a minute in the base to absorb the flavors.

4. Pour in 2 cups/470 ml of the defatted duck stock. Cover and bring to a boil. Reduce the heat, stir, recover and simmer until half done, about 10 minutes.

5. Mix the reserved chopped duck meat and sausage slices into the half-cooked rice. Transfer all of the rice and meat with its broth to a 9 x 13–inch/23 x 33 cm–baking dish. Pour the remaining 1 cup/235 ml hot stock over the rice. Place in the oven and bake until the broth is completely absorbed and the rice is golden and crispy on top, about 35 to 40 minutes.

6. When the rice has been cooking in the oven for 20 minutes, prepare the duck breasts. In a preheated hot skillet (I like to use a cast-iron one) without any fat, brown the breasts, skin side down, for 5 to 8 minutes, until the skin is golden and crispy and the fat has been rendered. Holding back the breasts, tilt the excess fat from the skillet. Turn the breasts over and cook for 2 to 3 minutes. The breast meat should be pink inside but not raw; again, springy but not mushy. The internal temperature should be 165°F/74°C. Set aside for 4 minutes and keep warm.

7. Remove the rice from the oven and discard the bay leaf. Slice the breast meat and serve on top or on the side of the rice. Garnish with the remaining 3 tablespoons/12 g parsley and orange slices. Serve hot with green beans, beets or leafy greens on the side.

Valencia-Style Rice

Arroz à Valenciana

SERVES 6 TO 8

Portuguese cooks adapted this savory rice dish from Valencia, Spain. Although it has a mix of meat and shellfish, it is the wonderful, flavorful rice that makes this dish. In any case, we have our own adaption, which involves marinating the meat prior to combining it with the shellfish and rice. This version I have adapted from my friend John Borges, retired owner of the former Boulevard Ocean View Restaurant, a Portuguese restaurant in Gloucester, Massachusetts. Since time was a factor, John used a restaurant method of separately prepping the meats, sauce and rice, then assembling it as orders were placed. Although lengthy, the recipe is easy to make. The recipe here is more traditional in method and perfect for home cooks and entertaining. *Read it through first, and be sure to read the notes at the end, and have all the ingredients ready in order of use before you start.* The recipe may be cut in half.

EQUIPMENT

16-inch/40.5-cm paella pan with cover (12-inch/30.5-cm for half the recipe) or a wide skillet with shallow, sloped sides

MARINATE THE MEAT THE DAY BEFORE

3 ——	boneless, skinless chicken thighs, trimmed of any visible fat, cut into 1-inch/2.5-cm pieces
1 ——	pound/454 g pork tenderloin, cut into 2-inch/5-cm cubes
1 ——	cup/235 ml white wine, or as needed, divided
2 ——	garlic cloves, finely chopped, divided
2 ——	tablespoons/30 ml wine vinegar, divided
2 ——	bay leaves, divided
2 ——	teaspoons/10 ml hot pepper sauce, divided
2 ——	teaspoons/6 g paprika, divided
2 ——	teaspoons/12 g coarse kosher salt or to taste, divided

MARINATE THE MEAT THE DAY BEFORE

1. Place the cubes of chicken and pork in separate nonreactive bowls (glass, ceramic or stainless steel).

2. Combine half of the remaining ingredients in a small bowl, mixing well to blend, forming a marinade. Pour the marinade over the pork. Make sure enough wine has been added so the meat is completely covered. Turn the meat to coat evenly with the marinade. Cover and set in the refrigerator to chill overnight. Repeat the procedure with the remaining half of the ingredients and the chicken thighs.

(continued)

½ ——— cup/120 ml olive oil

4 ——— ounces/112 g linguiça or chouriço sausage, sliced into ½-inch/1.3-cm rounds

8 ——— ounces/227 g medium shrimp (size 26/30), shelled and deveined, shells reserved

1 ——— large onion, finely chopped (about 1 cup/160 g)

2 ——— cups/360 g peeled, seeded and coarsely chopped very ripe tomatoes

5 ——— garlic cloves, finely chopped

1 ——— teaspoon/3 g sweet paprika

½ ——— teaspoon ground turmeric (optional)

½ ——— teaspoon toasted saffron, crumbled and steeped in 2 tablespoons/30 ml hot water (see Note)

¼ ——— teaspoon ground cumin

1 ——— bay leaf

1 ——— teaspoon/5 g Chile Pepper Paste (page 365) or hot sauce to taste

1. About ½ hour before you are ready to start cooking, drain the marinade from the pork and the chicken and discard. If needed, gently blot the excess moisture from the pork with paper towels.

2. In a paella pan or large, deep skillet, heat the olive oil over medium-high heat until hot but not smoking. Sauté the sausage slices until they pick up some color, about 2 minutes, then transfer to a platter. Add the shrimp and sauté for about 2 minutes. Remove to the platter as well and cover. Without thoroughly cooking through, working in small batches and without crowding, brown the cubes of pork and chicken on all sides. Transfer to the platter, cover and keep warm. Repeat until all the pork and chicken are browned.

3. To the same pan, add the onion and sauté until just translucent, about 2 to 3 minutes. Add the tomatoes, garlic, paprika, turmeric, saffron, cumin, bay leaf and Chile Pepper Paste. Stir well to meld the flavors. Cover tightly. Simmer over low heat until the flavors are married to the onions, about 10 minutes.

4. Add the rice, stirring it into the base and letting it sizzle, about 1 to 2 minutes, until it is translucent. Spread it out evenly across the bottom of the pan. From this point on, no matter how tempted, do not stir.

Note: While it is typical to use safflower powder in some Portuguese dishes, I suggest saffron, since those with severe allergies to ragweed could have severe problems with the safflower.

A simple shrimp broth can be made by using the shells of uncooked shrimp and boiling them in 3 cups/705 ml water, then straining.

If you get carried away and wish to use lobster, make sure your pan is large enough. Although it is not really traditional in this dish, you can add it in one of two ways. Either steam or boil it separately, cut it into serving pieces, then, unshelled, place it on top, garnishing the rice, or cut into uncooked serving pieces and pan-fry for 5 minutes, at the same time you brown the meats. Remove it from the pan. Then, return the lobster pieces (shells left intact) to the pan at the same time the little neck clams are added. Make sure you provide picks to remove the meat from the shells.

2 ——	cups/360 g medium-grain starchy rice, such as Bomba or Arborio
1 ——	cup/235 ml white wine, such as vinho verde or medium-bodied white table wine
4 ——	cups/940 ml hot shrimp broth as needed (see Note)
½ ——	cup/120 ml tawny port (optional)
4 ——	tablespoons/16 g finely chopped cilantro or parsley, divided
1 ——	teaspoon/6 g coarse kosher salt or to taste
8 ——	littleneck clams, scrubbed (counts or manila clams)
10——	mussels, scrubbed, beards removed
4 ——	ounces/112 g bay scallops (optional)
4 ——	ounces/112 g baby squid with tentacles, cleaned, cut crosswise into 1-inch/2.5-cm rings (optional)
1 ——	cup/140 g frozen peas, thawed, or peas and carrots mixed

5. Slowly pour in the white wine over the rice and simmer for a minute or two. Add the shrimp broth, port wine, 2 tablespoons/2 g of the cilantro and the salt. Cover. Bring to a boil over medium-high heat, then reduce the heat to medium. Without stirring, simmer the rice for 10 minutes.

6. When the rice has absorbed most of the liquid, arrange the clams and mussels evenly over the top of the rice. Recover and continue to simmer for 10 minutes.

7. Arrange the scallops, squid, browned meats, sausage and peas over the rice and continue to simmer, without stirring, with the cover removed, for 10 more minutes.

8. The rice should be done, the broth evaporated and shellfish open. Continue cooking, uncovered, without stirring, so that the rice develops a crusty caramelized bottom. Arrange the sautéed shrimp over the top of the rice to heat through, and cover. Remove from the heat and let stand for about 10 minutes to absorb any extra broth. Discard the bay leaf. Garnish with the remaining 2 tablespoons/2 g cilantro. Serve from the pan.

Seafood

Peixe e Marisco

Fish Tales

When you ask a Portuguese person what is his or her favorite fish or shellfish, the first most likely response is *bacalhau* (dried salted codfish), *sardinhas* (sardines), *chicharros* (a variety of horse mackerel, about the size of smelts), *amêijoas* (clams), *camarão* (shrimp) and, of course, *lapis* (a variety of sea urchin). Fish a little deeper and you will find the Portuguese also enjoy octopus, monkfish, red fish, sea bream, scup, sea bass and more. Many who grew up along Portugal's coastline made a living from the sea. Many, as well, who migrated to the United States especially, to the East Coast in cities like Gloucester, New Bedford and Fall River, Massachusetts, continued to make a living as fishermen for many years. More than a form of livelihood, fish and shellfish are an integral part of the Portuguese Mediterranean-style diet.

Now that there is so much emphasis placed on eating a diet of more fish, it's important to know whether you are getting your money's and your health's worth. First, you want to make sure you are getting the freshest fish. Don't purchase any fish with dull, sunken eyeballs that smells foul, though I have yet to find a fish market that will let me get really up close to a prospective purchase to take a whiff. Chances are that when you walk into a fish market, if it smells foul, the seafood is not too fresh. Every fish market has its particular day when the fish come in, and it is a good idea to get to know your fishmonger.

Fish Tales (continued)

Second, unless a person is a huge fish lover, and because there is little waste with fish, I would allow 4 to 6 ounces/112 to 168 g per person when purchasing fillets. Fillets are best for pan searing, baking and frying. If you are purchasing a whole fish, allow a little more. Unless you are cooking a whole fish, the fish can be cut up and used in various dishes. If the recipe you are working on doesn't call for a seafood or shrimp stock, don't throw the fish frames or shrimp shells out. The frames and the head (don't use the gills or innards) can be used to make a flavorful fish stock that can be used in soups, fish stews and seafood sauces. Even the shrimp shells can be used to make a quick and simple stock. Simple is best when you are in a hurry because you can add fresh seasoning as needed. Stocks can be frozen in 1- and 2-cup/235-and 460-ml containers, but be sure to write the date on a label. Uncooked shrimp shells as well as cut-up frames can be placed in a container, covered completely with water and frozen for when you have time to make a stock. If you need extra frames but don't want a whole fish, ask your fish market if they have any frames available for purchase.

Finally, when is it done? It depends on the fish and the cut. Some cooks say it is ready when the flesh flakes easily with a fork. I suggest removing it from cooking when the flesh is opaque and almost flaking because residual heat will finish the job. You can always tell when, for example, whole large sardines cooking on the grill are done. Even if they are golden, wait until you see the "whites of their eyes," meaning their eyeballs will turn white when they are done and the skin will be nicely bronzed. There are those who do like their fish really done, but seriously, don't overcook your fish. You want the fish to be moist, not dry, especially if it isn't in its skin.

With so many varieties of fish and shellfish to pick from, we Portuguese could eat a different fish every day without boredom. If one favorite is unavailable, we will surely find another fish to enjoy.

Shrimp Mozambique

Camarão à Moda de Moçambique

SERVES 2 TO 4

This recipe, shared by Anne Marie Viviers of South Africa, has made its way throughout the Portuguese network. Briny shrimp, simmered in a garlicky, tomato and wine-based sauce with just the right amount of kick and spice is perfect as a starter or ladled over rice as a meal. The present use of a popular brand-name seasoning powder with saffron is typical in this dish, but since it contains monosodium glutamate, I have adapted the recipe so that just the spices are used.

---

4 ——— tablespoons/56 g butter, divided

¼ ——— cup/40 g finely chopped onion

8 ——— garlic cloves, finely chopped

⅓ ——— cup/23 g finely chopped fresh cilantro or flat leaf parsley, divided

1 ——— teaspoon/3 g ground turmeric

½ ——— teaspoon saffron, crushed

½ ——— cup/120 ml warm water

1 ——— tablespoon/15 g tomato paste

½ ——— cup/120 ml white wine or light beer

1 ——— tablespoon/15 ml fresh lemon juice

2 ——— teaspoons/10 ml hot chile sauce or generous pinch of crushed red pepper (optional)

1 ——— teaspoon/6 g coarse kosher salt or to taste

½ ——— teaspoon ground white pepper

1 ——— pound/454 g medium shrimp (26/30 count) peeled and deveined

Hot cooked rice (optional)

1. Melt 2 tablespoons/28 g of the butter in a 3-quart/2.7-L saucepan over medium heat. Toss in the chopped onion and sauté just until translucent, about 2 to 3 minutes. Mix in the garlic, half of the cilantro, turmeric, saffron, water and tomato paste. Cover and simmer the ingredients for 2 to 3 minutes to allow the flavors to mingle.

2. Stir in the wine, lemon juice and chile sauce. Cover and raise the heat to medium-high to bring the ingredients to a boil. Reduce the heat to medium-low and simmer for 2 minutes.

3. Taste, and then season with salt and pepper. Add the shrimp and give them a turn in the sauce. Cook for 3 minutes over medium-low heat until the shrimp are just curled and have turned opaque pink. Stir in the remaining 2 tablespoons/28 g butter. Spoon the shrimp into bowls. Serve with boiled rice on the side and plenty of crusty bread to dip in the flavorful broth. Garnish with remaining cilantro.

Grilled Shrimp with Spicy Garlic Sauce

Gambas Grelhadas com Molho d'Alho

SERVES 4 TO 6

Vinegar, onion, tomato and spices together create the complex flavors of this shrimp's garlic sauce. Though ketchup is not a traditional Portuguese ingredient, it has been adapted for some time now from the global market as a shortcut to using tomatoes in some dishes. You can use strained concentrated ground tomatoes to make your own homemade tomato ketchup (recipe below). Alternatively, there is a wonderful substitute and shortcut by using some hot and spicy ketchup now available on grocery shelves. If you make the mistake of purchasing shrimp that are already shelled, substitute fish or clam broth. Adjust the cooking time if using smaller shrimp. The sauce can be made a day or several hours ahead.

FOR THE HOMEMADE "KETCHUP-STYLE" SAUCE

2 ——— cups/360 g canned ground tomatoes, finely strained to remove seeds

1 ——— tablespoon/15 ml white vinegar

1 ——— tablespoon/12 g sugar

2 ——— teaspoons/5 g onion powder

2 to 3 — teaspoons/10 to 15 ml hot sauce or to taste

1 ——— teaspoon/6 g coarse kosher salt

FOR THE RICE

2 ——— pounds/908 g jumbo deveined shrimp with shells (or desired size)

3¾ —— cups/881 ml water

1 ——— teaspoon/6 g coarse kosher salt

¼ ——— teaspoon ground white pepper

1 ——— cup/185 g long-grain rice (not instant)

FOR THE HOMEMADE "KETCHUP-STYLE" SAUCE

1. Combine all the ingredients in a small saucepan. Bring the ingredients to a boil over medium-high heat. Reduce the heat and simmer over medium heat for 2 minutes. Allow to cool. Makes about 1¼ cups/360 g.

FOR THE RICE

1. As you peel and devein the shrimp, do not discard the shells. Set the shrimp aside. Place the shells in a small pot with the water. Cover and bring to a boil over medium-high heat. Reduce the heat and simmer for 15 minutes. Remove the shells with a slotted spoon and discard.

2. Reserving 1 cup/235 ml of the strained stock, return 2½ cups/588 ml of the stock to a boil. Stir in the salt, ground pepper and rice. Recover, reduce the heat to medium-low and simmer the rice until tender, about 15 to 20 minutes (depending of the type of rice you use). Turn off the heat and keep hot.

FOR THE SAUCE AND SHRIMP

1 ——— tablespoon/14 g unsalted butter

5 ——— garlic cloves, finely chopped

1 ——— cup/235 ml reserved shrimp stock

1 ——— cup/240 g ketchup sauce
(see above)

Chopped cilantro or parsley as needed

Salt and pepper to taste

Black olives

FOR THE SAUCE AND SHRIMP

1. Melt the butter in a skillet and add the garlic, cooking just until the garlic becomes aromatic, about 30 seconds. Do not brown. Stir in the reserved stock, ketchup sauce and cilantro to taste. Bring to a boil over medium-high heat, then reduce the heat to medium-low and simmer until the sauce is reduced by half and has the consistency of light ketchup or cream, about 5 to 7 minutes. Set aside.

2. Season the shrimp with the salt and pepper. Grill over a hot fire, about 2 to 3 minutes on each side, adjusting the time to the size of the shrimp. Transfer the shrimp to a serving platter. Drizzle the sauce over the grilled shrimp and garnish with chopped cilantro and olives. Serve with the rice and additional hot sauce on the side. Don't forget some crusty bread to dip into the zippy sauce. This dish can be used as an appetizer as well.

Shrimp Baked on a Tile with Onions and Cream

Gambas Assadas na Telha

SERVES 2 TO 4

On the island of Terceira, in the Azores, there is a little restaurant in the town of Angra de Heroísmo that serves shrimp baked on a clay tile—a typical European roof tile. At one time, new unglazed tiles were used. These tiles, shaped by smoothing clay over a person's thigh, have one end narrower than the other. It looks like a hollowed-out log split in half lengthwise but without end caps. A plop of bread dough would be placed at each end, then the ingredients for the dish would be placed in the middle, and the whole thing was baked; the bread would expand as it baked, preventing any spillage. Today, though hard to find outside Portugal, these clay tiles are made specifically for cooking. They have a food-safe glaze and end caps so the juices that normally would have been absorbed by the dough and unglazed tile will not spill out. If the end caps are still a bit shallow, adding a fist-size piece of bread dough to each end will help prevent leakage. A shallow ceramic baking dish also works well. Colossal size shrimp are dramatically perfect to serve on a tile but can be pricey. I suggest using a minimum size of 16/20 shrimp per pound. Here is my interpretation of that dish, to which I have added a touch of cream.

1	pound/454 g colossal/jumbo shrimp ($^{16}/_{20}$) or preferred size, shell on
2	tablespoons/30 ml olive oil, or as needed
1	large onion, peeled and thinly sliced
2	medium very ripe tomatoes, seeded, coarsely chopped, well drained of any juice
4	garlic cloves, coarsely chopped
½	cup/30 g finely chopped fresh cilantro or parsley
1	teaspoon/6 g coarse kosher salt or to taste
¼	teaspoon ground white pepper or to taste
¼	teaspoon crushed dried chile pepper or to taste
⅓	cup/80 ml heavy cream, or as needed

1. Preheat the oven to 350°F/180°C, or gas mark 4.

2. Devein the shrimp and, reserving the shells, peel the shrimp, leaving just the tail shell intact. Rinse and pat dry.

3. In a bowl, mix the olive oil with the onion, tomatoes, garlic, cilantro, salt, pepper and chile pepper. If using the tile, add a fistful of dough to each end, pressing it into the clay.

4. Scatter half of the tomatoes, onions and seasoning over the bottom of the tile or baking dish and arrange the shrimp, tails up, on top. Add the rest of the tomato, onions and seasoning on top of the shrimp.

5. Drizzle the cream over, coating the shrimp. If using the tile, set the filled tile on a sheet pan so that it is level and steady in the oven and to catch any juices that may leak out. Bake for about 35 to 45 minutes depending on size, until the shrimp are opaque pink, curled and cooked through. Adjust the cooking time if you use a different size shrimp.

Variation

Optional rice as a side: While the shrimp are baking, make a quick stock by placing the shrimp shells in a medium pot and covering with enough water for 1½ cups/270 g of rice. Bring the water and shells to a boil, then strain out the shells. Return the water to a boil, add 1 teaspoon/6 g of coarse salt and cook the rice until tender, about 20 minutes. Serve the shrimp with the rice and sautéed greens.

Shrimp Cataplana
Camarão na Cataplana

SERVES 6

Most often you hear of Clams Cataplana (recipe in *Portuguese Homestyle Cooking*), but if you are allergic to bivalves, here is a variation using shrimp. Garlic and heady spices mingle and infuse shrimp as they simmer with cherry tomatoes, white wine and a bit of heat. Although this dish is named for the hinged tin-lined copper pot that resembles a clam shell, you can use a deep 4-quart/3.6-L pot with a tight-fitting lid.

¼ — cup/60 ml extra virgin olive oil

4 — ounces/112 g linguiça or chouriço sausage, sliced into ¼-inch/6-mm rounds

4 to 6 — large scallions, trimmed of heavy darker green stems and cut crosswise into thin rounds (about ½ cup/50 g)

2 — teaspoons/6 g paprika

2 — garlic cloves, finely chopped

1 — bay leaf

¼ — teaspoon crushed dried chile pepper, hot sauce or Chile Pepper Paste (page 365)

½ — cup/120 ml white wine

12 — cherry or grape tomatoes, halved

2 — pounds/908 g extra-large shrimp, shelled and deveined

½ — cup/30 g finely chopped cilantro or parsley or to taste, divided

1 — teaspoon/6 g coarse kosher salt as needed

¼ — teaspoon ground white pepper

2 to 3 — tablespoons/28 to 42 g softened butter

Black olives, for garnish

1. Heat the oil in the bottom of a cataplana pan or 4-quart/3.6-L pot with a tight-fitting lid. Toss in the sliced sausages and cook just to give them some color, about 2 minutes.

2. Mix in the scallions and cook just until they are translucent, about 2 minutes. Stir in the paprika, garlic, bay leaf and crushed chile pepper. When the garlic is very lightly golden and aromatic, about 1 minute, pour in the wine and tomatoes and stir. Simmer for just a minute, then add the shrimp, turning them in the base to coat.

3. Mix in ¼ cup/15 g of the cilantro. Sprinkle the salt and pepper over all as needed. Recover and cook for 3 minutes, until the shrimp are opaque pink and the tail is curled over but not too tightly. Be careful not to overcook the shrimp. Remove from the heat. Discard the bay leaf. Add the softened butter, give a toss with the shrimp, and serve immediately with the olives and remaining ¼ cup/15 g cilantro to garnish.

Mussels, Clams and Shrimp with White Beans
Feijoada de Marisco

SERVES 6 TO 8

Shrimp, clams and mussels comingle with flavorful white kidney beans that give body to the heady, spicy sauce accented with sautéed slices of chouriço sausage. You can adjust the shellfish types and amounts to your preference, making it your own. Adjust the cooking times to the size and type of clams and shrimp you use so that the shellfish are not overcooked.

¼ —— cup/60 ml olive oil

½ —— cup/80 g chopped onion

½ —— pound/227 g chouriço sausage, cut crosswise into ½-inch/1.3-cm round slices

1 —— very ripe tomato, peeled, seeded and coarsely chopped

½ —— cup/30 g finely chopped fresh parsley or cilantro, divided

2 —— garlic cloves, chopped

2 —— teaspoons/10 ml hot sauce or crushed dried chiles or to taste

1 —— teaspoon/5 g Sweet Pepper Paste (page 367)

1 —— bay leaf

1 —— cup/235 ml white wine, beer or clam stock

1 —— pound/454 g mussels, scrubbed and rinsed

1 —— pound/454 g small clams, scrubbed and rinsed

1 —— pound/454 g large shrimp, shelled and deveined

3 —— cups/750 g cooked white butter beans or white kidney beans

1 —— teaspoon/6 g coarse kosher salt or to taste

½ —— teaspoon ground white pepper or to taste

1. Heat the olive oil in a 5-quart/4.5-L heavy-bottomed pot or one large enough to accommodate all the ingredients. When the olive oil is hot but not smoking, add the onion and sausage slices. Sauté until the onions are translucent and the sausage has picked up some color, about 2 minutes.

2. Stir in the tomato, ¼ cup/15 g of the parsley, garlic, hot sauce, Sweet Pepper Paste and bay leaf and cover. Cook over medium-low heat until the tomato has broken down and married well with the onions, about 10 minutes.

3. Mix in the wine and simmer for 1 minute, reducing by half. Add the mussels and clams and give them a stir in the base. Cover tightly and simmer over medium-low heat for 10 minutes, then add the shrimp and cooked beans. Taste for salt as needed, and add along with ground pepper, adjusting to taste. Continue to simmer for about 3 minutes more until the shellfish are open, the shrimp are opaque pink and slightly curled and the beans are heated through. Remove the bay leaf and serve, sprinkled with the remaining ¼ cup/15 g parsley.

Dried Salt Codfish

If asked, the Portuguese will recommend the fillets of the dried fish that still have the bones and skin intact, because the skin and bones infuse more flavor into the resulting dish. However, you can get boneless and skinless fillets, which are especially perfect for making codfish cakes. Gaining popularity lately, the non-dried salted cod eliminates the need for reconstituting, and has a more buttery mouthfeel with a softer flavor. Some soaking, however, is still required to remove some of the salt. Although dried salted cod is available from various sources, the Norwegian cod is highly sought because it is thought to taste better.

To use dried salted codfish, you must rehydrate and desalinate the fish at least one to two days before cooking. Cut the fish into serving pieces, rinse them and put them in a good-size bowl, covering them with plenty of cold water. Rinse the fish and change the water about every 3 hours, about 7 times in the course of just 24 hours. A pound/454 g of boneless fillet may take as little as 24 hours. On the other end, if the pieces are really thick, have skin and are encrusted with salt, it could take 48 hours. Do not soak more than 2 pounds/908 g in the same bowl; give them plenty of room and water. Taste a small piece for saltiness and soak for another 3 hours if needed. Times are approximate since one fillet may have more salt than another.

I suggest water for the primary soaking medium because it is less expensive. You can do the final soak with milk if you are planning to bake or grill the fish so that it keeps some moisture. Milk also lessens the saltiness of the fish.

Precooking Dried Salt Cod

When recipes call for soaked dried salt cod to be poached in water before it is used in a recipe, there are occasions when sometimes we poach the fish in milk or even olive oil. The following less expensive method is the one I suggest most often.

---

1. Bring a large pot of water to a full boil over high heat. Turn off the heat.

2. Rinse the presoaked fish and add to the pot. Cover and allow to sit for 15 to 30 minutes (depending on the thickness of the fish), until the cod is opaque. Remove the pieces as they become opaque.

3. Drain the cod. Depending on the recipe, use whole pieces or discard bones and skin, if present, and place the fish in a bowl. Use as needed.

Note: To poach reconstituted salt cod in milk, use scalded milk instead of water, a trick I learned in Portugal. This helps the fish retain its moisture, sweetness and tenderness while tempering the salt. It also tames the fishiness of the flavor. Not all Portuguese cooks poach the cod this way. Our family did not use milk to make codfish cakes, but I find it improves other salt cod dishes to which little or no extra moisture is added. If you are using the cod in a casserole, you can poach the fish completely in simmering milk, which can be pricey, or cut your cost a little by first poaching in water. After draining, remove the bones and skin. Transfer the flaked fish to a bowl and pour scalded, not boiled, milk over, just to cover. Let stand, covered, at room temperature for 20 to 30 minutes. Drain well, taste again for salt, and use the fish as needed.

Poaching fish in olive oil instead of water or milk is a bit more expensive but also helps the fish retain moisture while giving it a silky mouthfeel. This technique is not to fry the cod, so the oil must not be hotter than 175°F/80°C.

Baked Salt Cod with Shrimp and Scallops

Bacalhau com Camarão e Vieiras no Forno

SERVES 4 TO 6

The Arabic influence on casseroles did not get wasted on the Portuguese. Mashed potatoes simply seasoned and dressed with butter or olive oil are layered with salt cod, shrimp, sweet bay scallops and a light but aromatic *refogado*, the Portuguese onion- and tomato-infused sauce. Just one bite of the potatoes, seafood and the sauce is scrumptiously comforting. Adapted from João B, the potatoes are delicious with olive oil as well as with butter. It is a matter of personal preference. For this dish, I like the butter. If you use olive oil, use a flavorful one.

FOR THE FISH

1 ——— pound/454 g salt cod, soaked for 24 to 36 hours in several changes of cold water

Scalded milk as needed

FOR THE POTATOES

6 ——— large potatoes, peeled and cut into 2-inch/5-cm cubes

½ ——— cup/112 g softened butter or light olive oil

1 ——— teaspoon/6 g coarse kosher salt

½ ——— teaspoon ground white pepper

FOR THE SAUCE

¼ ——— cup/60 ml olive oil

1 ——— large onion, coarsely chopped

2 ——— garlic cloves, finely chopped

1½ ——— cups/270 g seeded and coarsely chopped fresh tomato

1 ——— teaspoon/3 g paprika

½ ——— cup/30 g chopped fresh parsley, divided

FOR THE FISH

1. Drain and rinse the fish, then poach it (see page 103) in boiled water with the heat off for 15 minutes. Transfer fish to a bowl and pour in just enough scalded milk to cover the fish. Let it stand for 15 minutes. Drain and cool slightly. Remove and discard any bones and skin. Hand flake the fish into medium pieces. Set aside.

FOR THE POTATOES

1. In a pot, cook the potatoes in water to cover until very tender, about 20 to 25 minutes. Drain, then mash them until smooth, blending in the butter or olive oil. Season with salt and pepper. Keep warm and reserve.

FOR THE SAUCE

1. While the potatoes are cooking, heat the olive oil in a saucepan and sauté the onion until lightly golden, about 5 minutes. Add the garlic. When the garlic is aromatic, about 1 minute, stir in the chopped tomatoes, paprika and ¼ cup/15 g of the parsley. Cover and cook over medium-low heat for 10 minutes. Mix the pieces of salt cod into the onion and tomato base, then simmer for 2 minutes to heat through.

TO ASSEMBLE

1 —————— pound/454 g large shrimp, shelled and deveined, patted dry

½ —————— pound/227 g small bay scallops

1 —————— egg, beaten

TO ASSEMBLE

1. Preheat the oven to 350°F/180°C, or gas mark 4.

2. Transfer half of the mashed potatoes to a lightly oiled casserole dish, about 9 x 13 inches/23 x 33 cm, and spread fairly evenly on the bottom. Ladle the fish, onion and tomato mixture over the potatoes. Scatter the shrimp and scallops on top. Spread the remaining warm mashed potatoes over everything, sealing the edges. Brush the top of the potatoes with a light coating of beaten egg. Bake in the oven until lightly golden on top and heated through, about 25 minutes. Sprinkle with the remaining ¼ cup/ 15 g parsley and serve.

Grilled Salt Cod with Onions

Bacalhau Grelhado João do Porto

SERVES 4

Grilled salt cod steaks drizzled with fruity olive oil glisten atop a bed of sliced potatoes, hard-boiled eggs and caramelized onions. You might instead consider poaching this fish in olive oil, but with the price of olive oil, for the home cook, we will take a different route. This is adapted from a wonderful dish I enjoyed at the historical Majestic Café in the city of Porto in northern Portugal. It elevated the popular dish of *Bacalhau Gomes de Sá* (in *Portuguese Homestyle Cooking*) out of the casserole dish, where it shined, grilled and plated in an elegant way. Here, salt cod with the skin and bones is cooked on the grill. In addition to adding flavor, the skin holds the fish steaks intact.

ONE OR TWO DAYS AHEAD

4 ———— 4-ounce/112-g crosswise-cut salt cod steaks, 1 inch/2.5 cm thick, with skin and bones (see prep on page 102)

Whole milk as needed

TO COOK

4 ———— red bliss potatoes, scrubbed, unpeeled

¾ ———— cup/180 ml extra virgin olive oil, divided, plus more for brushing

2 ———— large onions, thinly sliced

Coarse kosher salt to taste, if needed

Ground white pepper to taste

4 ———— hard-boiled eggs, peeled

4 ———— garlic cloves, smashed

Pinch of crushed dried chile pepper (optional)

¼ ———— cup/15 g finely chopped parsley

ONE OR TWO DAYS AHEAD

1. Start soaking the salt cod (see page 102). Rinse well, then place in a large bowl with enough cold water to cover. Change the water about six times over the next 24 to 36 hours. Drain, rinse, return the fish to the bowl and pour in just enough milk to cover the fish. Let stand for 3 more hours. Drain and pat dry.

TO COOK

1. Cook the unpeeled potatoes in boiling salted water until fork-tender, about 20 minutes. Reserve and keep warm.

2. In a medium skillet set over medium heat, warm ¼ cup/60 ml of the olive oil until hot but not smoking. Toss in the onions and sauté until golden, about 5 minutes. Remove from the heat, cover and set aside but keep hot.

3. Remove the fish from the soaking water and rinse. Blot excess moisture from the fish with a paper towel. Brush the fish with olive oil and season with salt if needed and ground pepper. Grill the fish for 10 minutes per inch/2.5 cm of thickness, about 5 minutes on each side. If thicker, grill 5 to 8 minutes on each side. Test the thickest part of the fish to see if it is opaque and just starting to flake. Transfer the fish to a dish and cover.

4. Assembly is easy. Seasoning as you go with salt and pepper, remove the potato peels if desired, slice and arrange the potatoes in two side-by-side rows (about 4 slices each row) on individual dinner plates, setting the slices end to end in straight rows the length of the fish steak. Slice the eggs and arrange the slices end to end, on top of the potato slices, and season again as needed. Set one cod steak, skin side down, on top of the eggs on each plate. Spoon some of the hot onions on top of the fish. Warm the garlic in the remaining ½ cup/120 ml olive oil with the crushed chile pepper. Drizzle all with the heated olive oil, giving each plate a smashed garlic clove, then garnish with the chopped parsley and serve.

Heavenly Salt Cod with Tomatoes, Onions and Peppers

Bacalhau do Céu

SERVES 4

Well-worn pages of Cousin Evelina's personal cookbook hold many recipes that she frequently made. This one, adapted from faded script and some letters obliterated by age, was one of her favorites. "Heavenly" perfectly describes this casserole of salt cod with sautéed peppers, boiled potatoes and lightly caramelized onions.

A DAY OR TWO AHEAD

1	pound/454 g salt cod

THE NEXT DAY

2 to 3	cups/470 to 705 ml scalded milk as needed
4	large potatoes, unpeeled
½	cup/120 ml olive oil, divided
4	large onions, thinly sliced
1	bay leaf
4	medium very ripe tomatoes, peeled, seeded and chopped, or 1½ cups/ 270 g canned, drained
2	garlic cloves, chopped
4	red or green bell peppers, stemmed, seeded and thinly sliced lengthwise
1	tablespoon/8 g flour
1	teaspoon/6 g coarse kosher salt, or as needed
¼	teaspoon ground white pepper, or as needed

A DAY OR TWO AHEAD

1. Soak the salt cod for 24 to 48 hours in several changes of cold water, about every 3 hours. After soaking, drain and rinse the fish. The length of soaking time depends on whether or not the cod is boneless and skinless (takes less time) and the thickness of the pieces.

THE NEXT DAY

1. Place the soaked cod in a pot of boiled water and shut off the heat. Poach for 15 minutes. Remove the fish, set in a medium bowl and cover with scalded milk. Let stand for 15 minutes. Reserve ½ cup/120 ml of the milk and discard the rest. Blot the fish with a paper towel and hand-shred the fish into another bowl, discarding any bones and skin.

2. In a pot, boil the potatoes until fork-tender, about 20 to 25 minutes. Drain and set the potatoes aside to cool.

3. Heat ¼ cup/60 ml of the olive oil in a large skillet over medium-high heat. Sauté the onions with the bay leaf until the onions are soft and richly golden, about 7 minutes.

4. Mix in the tomatoes and garlic. Cover and continue cooking until the tomatoes are married to the onions and the garlic is aromatic, about 10 minutes. Add the peppers and simmer in the sauce for 1 minute.

5. Separately, mix the flour with the ½ cup/120 ml of reserved cool milk, just enough to form a slurry. Stir into the tomato base and continue to cook for 3 minutes. Remove the bay leaf. Taste for salt and adjust to taste. Season with pepper to taste.

TO ASSEMBLE

1 ——— cup/100 g plain bread crumbs

3 ——— tablespoons/42 g softened butter

TO ASSEMBLE

1. Preheat the oven to 350°F/180°C, or gas mark 4. Drizzle a 9 x 13–inch/ 23 x 33–cm baking dish with some olive oil, spreading it to coat the bottom. Peel the boiled potatoes and slice them into ½-inch/1.3-cm rounds. Lay the potatoes on the bottom of the baking dish. Next, make a layer of the fish followed by the peppers, onion and tomato base. Mix the bread crumbs with the softened butter and then scatter the crumbs fairly evenly over the top. Bake for 30 to 45 minutes, until the bread crumbs are golden on top and everything is heated through.

Charcoal Grilled Salt Cod with Punched Potatoes

Bacalhau à Lagareiro com Batatas à Murro

SERVES 2

This is such an easy and popular dish, especially in the summer when backyard grills are always heating up. Grilled salt cod is served up with sautéed onions and peppers with red bliss waxy potatoes roasted with a salt and olive oil coating. If you don't have a grill, use a stove top cast-iron grill pan or broil the fish. Everything is topped with a drizzle of extra virgin olive oil and a scattering of chopped garlic. Follow the directions on page 102 to prepare the fish.

EQUIPMENT
Fish spatula

4 to 6 — waxy red bliss potatoes, whole, unpeeled

1 — cup/240 ml olive oil, divided

Coarse kosher salt to taste

1 — large onion, peeled and quartered

1 or 2 — red or green bell peppers, cored, seeded and cut into large pieces

¼ — teaspoon ground black pepper, or as needed

Pinch of crushed dried chile pepper (optional)

6 — garlic cloves, coarsely chopped

2 — 4-ounce/112-g steaks of presoaked dried salt cod, skin on (see page 102)

Olives, for garnish

1. Preheat the oven to 400°F/200°C, or gas mark 6.

2. Rinse the potatoes and pat dry. Put the potatoes in a bowl and drizzle with 2 tablespoons/30 ml of the olive oil, turning to coat. Roll the potatoes lightly in the coarse salt and transfer to a small sheet pan. Roast for 50 minutes, or until tender with crispy skins.

3. Meanwhile, heat ¼ cup/60 ml of the olive oil in a small skillet over medium heat. Add the onion and bell peppers. Sauté until the onions are lightly golden and the peppers are tender, but with a little bite, about 5 minutes. Season with salt, pepper and pinch of crushed dried red chiles. Remove from the heat. Keep hot and set aside.

4. Warm the remaining olive oil. Some folks prefer to add the garlic at the end, uncooked. Others add the chopped garlic to the olive oil, infusing it as it warms. I will leave that decision to you. Set aside.

5. Preheat the grill or broiler.

6. While the potatoes are roasting, drain the fish from the soaking water, rinse and pat dry. About 15 minutes before the potatoes are done, brush the salt cod with the warm olive oil, infused or not with garlic. Place on the grill, skin side up. Grill for 5 minutes on each side per 1 inch/2.5 cm of thickness. If the fish steaks are thicker than 1 inch/2.5 cm, grill for 8 minutes on each side. Use a fish spatula to turn the fish over onto the skin side and grill for another 5 to 8 minutes.

7. Remove the potatoes from the oven. With a closed fist, give them a little punch, hard enough to just break open the skin on top. Transfer to serving plates with the fish and onions and peppers on the side. Drizzle the remaining warm olive oil over all. If the garlic was kept separate, scatter it over all and serve. Garnished with olives.

Saint Martin
São Martinho

Now and then you hear of a dish with the added title of *São Martinho*. According to Roger Texeira, owner of Adega Restaurant in Woburn, Massachusetts, every year on November 11 there would be a celebration in St. Martin's honor, especially in the Azorean island of Terceira. The basic oral history is that shortly after having joined the military as a young man, St. Martin's generous heart and numerous acts of kindness made him realize a dislike for the path he had taken as a soldier. He then entered the monastery. He became so loved, especially by the poor, that after many years he became the bishop of Turones.

In his honor, it is tradition to celebrate with roasted or boiled chestnuts, corn and especially *Áqua Pé,* the fresh pressed wine from the new harvest that has been blended with brandy. On the island of Madeira, which lies south of the Azore islands, comes a dish in his honor as well, *Bacalhau São Martinho.*

Saint Martin's Grilled Salt Cod with Potatoes
Bacalhau à São Martinho com Batatas

SERVES 4

This particular dish is usually served when tasting new wine on the Portuguese island of Madeira. A heady seasoning paste infuses prepped salt cod before it is tossed on a grill to cook. It is then dressed with a tangy vinaigrette and accompanied by boiled potatoes and a green vegetable. In this dish, it is important to have pieces of cod with similar thickness for even cooking. The intact skin holds the flesh together while grilling. Since the fish and the pepper paste have salt, use any additional salt only as needed.

A DAY OR TWO AHEAD

2 ——— pounds/908 g salted codfish fillets, bones and skin intact, presoaked in several change of cold water for at least 24 hours, refrigerated (see page 102)

A DAY OR TWO AHEAD

1. Drain the fish from the soaking water, rinse and pat dry. Taste a middle piece of the fish for salt. If too salty, soak a little longer in fresh water. Drain and rinse the fish and pat dry. With a sharp knife, cut the fish lengthwise, starting along the backbone, into 2-inch/5-cm wide strips, then cut crosswise in half. Transfer to a bowl and reserve.

FOR THE SEASONING PASTE

8	———	garlic cloves, peeled
½ to 1	—	teaspoon coarse kosher salt to taste
2	———	teaspoons/10 g Chile Pepper Paste (page 365) or dried crushed red hot pepper or to taste
¼	———	teaspoon black pepper
¼	———	teaspoon white pepper
4	———	tablespoons/60 ml olive oil

FOR THE DRESSING

½	———	cup/120 ml apple cider vinegar
½	———	cup/30 g plus 2 tablespoons/8 g finely chopped fresh parsley
½	———	cup/80 g finely chopped red onion
1	———	teaspoon/6 g coarse kosher salt or to taste
¼	———	teaspoon ground black pepper
1	———	cup/235 ml Portuguese or extra virgin olive oil

TO ASSEMBLE

| 4 | ——— | medium potatoes, peeled and quartered |

FOR THE SEASONING PASTE

1. Go easy with salt in this seasoning paste. There is already salt in the fish and the chile pepper paste. Using a mortar and pestle, crush and pound the garlic with the salt. Mix in the chile pepper paste and ground black and white peppers. Drizzle in the oil, mixing it well with the garlic to form the seasoning paste.

2. Add the seasoning paste to the bowl of fish, gently turning the fish to coat, making sure both sides of each piece are all coated. Cover the bowl and let the fish stand in the seasoning paste for 30 to 60 minutes at room temperature. (You can season the fish overnight if you want a stronger flavor, then continue with the recipe the next day.)

FOR THE DRESSING

1. In a medium bowl, mix the vinegar, ½ cup/30 g of the parsley, onion, salt and pepper together. Gradually drizzle in the olive oil while whisking briskly to emulsify it. If the vinaigrette dressing is too thick, whisk in additional oil and vinegar in the same ratio as listed above. Let stand for at least ½ hour for the flavors to meld.

TO ASSEMBLE

1. Place the potatoes in a pot, cover with water and bring to a boil over high heat. Cook for about 20 minutes, until tender, and reserve.

2. Grill or broil the fish for 5 minutes on each side for 1-inch/2.5-cm thick pieces. Adjust the cooking time to a little more or less per side depending on the thickness of the fish fillets. The fish should be opaque but not flaking.

3. Once the fish is done, set the fish aside until it is cool enough to handle. Use your hands or two forks to remove any bones and skin, and flake the fish into medium pieces. Place the fish in the middle of a platter and surround with the boiled potatoes. Drizzle some of the dressing over the fish and potatoes and sprinkle with the remaining 2 tablespoons/8 g finely chopped parsley. Accompany with extra dressing and hot pepper sauce on the side if desired. Make sure the wine is flowing to quench the fire.

Braised Monkfish with Tomatoes and Onions

Tamboril com Tomates e Cebolas

SERVES 6 TO 8

Living near the ocean gives me great opportunities to enjoy seafood. My friend Tony dos Santos, who is originally from Ponte de Muçela, in northern Portugal, taught me this easy recipe. I have used monkfish in the past with great results and I like it because it doesn't have a lot of bones. Flavors of peppers, onion, white wine, tomatoes and herbs infuse this wonderful fish in a way that brings you to the Mediterranean without actually going there. You also can substitute sea bass, halibut, grouper or your favorite non-endangered firm-fleshed white fish.

¾ —— cup/180 ml olive oil, divided

1 —— large onion, sliced into ¼-inch/6-mm rounds, divided

1 —— red or green bell pepper, cut into slices, divided

1½ —— cups/270 g finely chopped fresh tomatoes, divided

1 —— cup/235 ml white wine

¼ —— cup/60 ml water or fish stock

2 —— tablespoons/30 g tomato paste

¼ —— cup/15 g finely chopped parsley, divided

1 —— tablespoon/8 g paprika

3 —— garlic cloves, finely chopped

1 —— tablespoon/18 g coarse kosher salt

¼ —— teaspoon white pepper

4- to 5- —— pound/1.8- to 2.2-kg whole fish (headless optional), scaled, innards removed

12—— baby new potatoes, peeled, halved, parboiled and drained

Olives, for garnish

1. Preheat the oven to 350°F/180°C, or gas mark 4.

2. Coat the bottom of a baking dish large enough to accommodate the fish with ½ cup/120 ml of the olive oil. Scatter half of the onion across the bottom of the dish followed by half of the pepper.

3. In a medium saucepan, combine the remaining ¼ cup/60 ml olive oil, 1 cup/180 g of the tomatoes, the wine, water, tomato paste, 2 tablespoons/ 7 g of the parsley, paprika, garlic, salt and ground pepper. Cover and bring to a low simmer over medium heat. Simmer for just 3 minutes. Drizzle one-third of the sauce over the onions and peppers.

4. Rinse the fish and pat dry. Place the fish in front of you on a cutting board. With a sharp knife, make three or four 1-inch/2.5-cm wide and deep slits into both sides of the fish, evenly spaced, about 1 to 2 inches/2.5 to 5 cm apart from one another. Place the fish on the onions, peppers and sauce in the baking dish.

5. Drizzle some of the sauce into the belly and top slits. Sprinkle 1 tablespoon/ 4 g of the parsley over the top of the fish followed by the remaining ½ cup/ 90 g chopped tomatoes and the remaining slices of bell pepper and onion. Spoon the remaining sauce over the fish. Nestle the parboiled potatoes into the sauce, around the fish.

6. Cover the dish loosely with foil and bake for 20 minutes. Remove the foil and continue to bake, uncovered, for about another 10 to 15 minutes, basting occasionally with the juices, until the potatoes are tender and the fish is cooked to opaque or desired doneness. Serve right from the pan, garnished with the olives and remaining 1 tablespoon/4 g parsley. Sautéed greens make a great side to this dish.

Grilled Mackerel with Villain Sauce

Cavalas Grelhadas com Molho Vilão

SERVES 4

It is said, according to oral history, that Villain Sauce comes from an enclave of unsavory people who once lived on the outskirts of the city of Funchal, the capital of Madeira. True or not, this well-seasoned vinaigrette is the perfect complement to an oily fish like mackerel as well as for drizzling over freshly grilled sardines. Cooking fish over an open fire was something my father really enjoyed. Like him, Portuguese cooks pride themselves on their ability to make vinegar sauces that have just the right amount of tang that brightens without hiding the flavor of the fish. Grilling mackerel over an open flame gives the best flavor and allows the excess oil of the fish to drip away. If you have allergies to ragweed and the like, do not use the safflower.

FOR THE VILLAIN SAUCE

1	medium onion, finely chopped
½	cup/120 ml red wine vinegar
½	cup/30 g finely chopped parsley, divided
3	garlic cloves, smashed, then coarsely chopped
½	teaspoon ground safflower, saffron or paprika
1	teaspoon/6 g coarse kosher salt or to taste
1	cup/235 ml Portuguese or extra virgin olive oil

FOR THE FISH

4	garlic cloves
1	teaspoon/6 g coarse kosher salt
1	large bay leaf, crumbled
½	teaspoon ground white pepper or to taste
Four	1-pound/454-g fresh whole mackerel, dressed (if the fish has not been prepared by a fishmonger, see Prepping Whole Fish [page 119])
12	small boiling potatoes

FOR THE VILLAIN SAUCE

1. Combine the onion, vinegar, ¼ cup/15 g of the parsley, garlic, safflower and salt in a medium bowl. Gradually whisk in the olive oil, whisking until it is completely married to the vinegar. Set aside. If you like more tang, increase the vinegar, 1 tablespoon/15 ml at a time to your preference.

FOR THE FISH

1. Using a mortar and pestle, make a paste by pounding the garlic with the salt, crumbled bay leaf and pepper, grinding the ingredients to blend. Divide the paste fairly evenly, about 1 teaspoon/5 g per fish, lightly coating the inside of the fish bellies. Let stand for 1 hour.

2. Put the potatoes in a pot and cover with water. Bring to a boil over medium heat and cook until they are fork-tender, about 15 to 20 minutes. Cover and keep hot.

3. While the potatoes are cooking, grill the fish over a wood fire, white hot coals or a gas grill, about 5 to 10 minutes on each side (depending on the thickness of the fish). The skin should be crispy, the eyes opaque white and the flesh almost flaking. Arrange the fish and potatoes on a platter, then drizzle the Villain Sauce over all. Garnish with the remaining ¼ cup/15 g parsley and serve.

Garlic and Wine–Infused Fish Kabobs
Espetada de Peixe em Vinho d'Alhos

SERVES 4

Born on the Portuguese island of Madeira, Roger Texeira, who now lives in the States, shares a few of his recipes in this book. Once you get him started on the subject of fish, there is no stopping until you have his recipes. Traditionally in Madeira, Roger would use black scabbard for this dish, but it can be hard to get. Bay laurel branches are typically used as skewers, imparting flavor to the fish. I have substituted firm white fish, like halibut. Especially for those of you who love to grill, this recipe is so simple and flavorful.

EQUIPMENT
Wooden skewers

2 ——— garlic cloves, finely chopped

2 ——— teaspoons/12 g coarse kosher salt or to taste

½ ——— teaspoon ground white or black pepper or to taste

¼ ——— cup/15 g finely chopped parsley

Several bay leaves as needed

4 ——— tablespoons/60 ml olive oil

½ ——— cup/120 ml white wine

1 ——— small onion, finely chopped

1 ——— teaspoon/5 g Chile Pepper Paste (page 365) or hot sauce

4 ——— firm white fish steaks, cut into 2-inch/5-cm cubes

1. Place the wooden skewers in a shallow dish and cover with water. Soak for at least 30 minutes.

2. Using a mortar and pestle, mash the garlic with the salt, making a paste. Incorporate the pepper and parsley and crumble in 1 bay leaf. Drizzle in the olive oil to combine the ingredients, mixing well to marry the flavors. Stir in the wine, onion and chile pepper paste.

3. Put the fish in a bowl and pour the marinade over, giving the fish a turn to coat evenly. Cover with plastic wrap and marinate for about an hour, refrigerated. Occasionally give the fish a turn in the marinade.

4. Preheat the grill.

5. Thread the fish onto the soaked wooden skewers, alternating pieces of fish with a bay leaf. Grill for 8 minutes, then turn. Basting with the marinade, grill for 5 to 8 more minutes depending on the thickness. It should be opaque but not quite flaking. Stop basting 1 minute before the fish is done. Be careful not to dry out the fish by overcooking. The fish can also be broiled. Serve with rice, a salad or steamed vegetables.

Sardine Fillets with Garlic and Lemon

Filetes de Sardinhas com Alho e Limão

SERVES 4

Lourdes Silva, a former fado singer, frequently fries her sardines after a simple preparation. Any which way sardines are prepared, there will not be a lack of happy campers. Adapted from *Portuguese Homestyle Cooking*, this makes a great light meal.

---

1 ——— dozen fresh (preferably) or thawed frozen large sardines, scales removed, well chilled

Coarse kosher salt as needed

½ ——— teaspoon ground pepper or to taste

1 ——— tablespoon/4 g finely chopped parsley

½ ——— teaspoon paprika

1 to 2 — garlic cloves, finely chopped

Juice of 1 lemon

2 ——— eggs, lightly beaten

Plain panko bread crumbs, finely crushed as needed

Olive oil as needed

1. Trim the body and tail fins from the sardines. Slice the bellies lengthwise from just under the head to the tail. Place the sardine belly side up on your workspace and remove the innards with your finger. Grab the fish by the head or tail bone with your dominant hand, and with two fingers of the other hand, one on each side of the backbone, lightly press the flesh down in the opposite direction as you carefully lift the main bone up and out along with some rib bones. The backbone may come out in pieces. The smaller rib bones should come out with it. Rinse and pat dry.

2. Transfer the fish fillets to a shallow dish. Season it with salt and pepper. Sprinkle the parsley, paprika and garlic over and drizzle with the lemon juice. Cover and let it stand for ½ hour.

3. Heat ¼ cup/60 ml of olive oil, to start, in a medium skillet. One by one, dip in beaten egg and dust the fillets on both sides with the bread crumbs, shaking off the excess, then sauté until lightly golden, about 1 minute on each side. Add more oil to the pan as needed. Drain on paper towels. Serve with a salad of seasoned sliced boiled potatoes, roasted peppers and sautéed onions, drizzled with rich olive oil.

(continued)

Sardines are scaled and gutted. The head and backbone are removed. The fillets are marinated, then coated with egg and bread crumbs and pan fried.

Prepping Whole Fish

Use the back edge of a knife blade, the blade of scissors or a scaling tool to run over the back of the fish to remove the scales. These scales can fly all over the place, so get a large plastic bag, such as one from the grocery store, and perform this task with your hands, fish and tool inside the open bag. It will help contain the mess. Using scissors, cut off the fins and tail end fin. Then, with the sharp point of a paring or boning knife, slit the belly of the fish from just under the gill to the midpoint of the tail. Reach in with your finger and remove the innards, then rinse.

Baked Fish Fillets with Shellfish and Cilantro Stuffing

Filetes Recheados com Marisco e Coentros

SERVES 6

The stuffed fish fillet of Atasca Restaurant in Cambridge, Massachusetts, promises not to disappoint. I have adapted it here, as it is one of my favorite recipes for stuffed fish fillets. The briny flavors of shellfish are rounded and softened with the inclusion of St. Jorge cheese and lemony fresh cilantro. You can use just shrimp or just the clams if you prefer.

FOR THE TOPPING

1	garlic clove, peeled, finely chopped
1	teaspoon/6 g coarse kosher salt or to taste
1	teaspoon/3 g paprika
2	tablespoons/8 g finely chopped cilantro or parsley

Freshly ground white pepper

Portuguese or extra virgin olive oil as needed

1	cup/150 g finely chopped almonds or pine nuts (optional)

FOR THE STUFFING AND FISH

1	cup/100 g firmly packed finely hand-shredded fresh bread crumbs
½	cup/120 ml milk
¼	cup/40 g coarsely chopped, peeled and deveined shrimp
¼	cup/40 g coarsely chopped clams
¼	cup/30 g shredded St. Jorge or Havarti cheese
2	tablespoons/8 g finely chopped cilantro, divided
1	garlic clove, finely chopped
1	teaspoon/6 g coarse kosher salt or to taste
½	teaspoon ground white pepper or to taste
6	large sole or flounder fillets

Olive oil as needed

FOR THE TOPPING

1. Using a mortar and pestle, mash the garlic with the salt to form a paste. Mix in the paprika, cilantro and white pepper.

2. Drizzle in just enough olive oil to bring it to a spreading consistency. Mix with the chopped almonds. Set aside until ready to use.

FOR THE STUFFING AND FISH

1. Preheat the oven to 350°F/180°C, or gas mark 4.

2. In a bowl, combine the fresh bread crumbs and just enough milk to moisten them. Squeeze out any excess milk and drain off. Mix in the shrimp, clams, cheese, 1 tablespoon/1 g of the cilantro, garlic, salt and pepper.

3. Lay out the fillets of fish. Divide the filling into 6 parts (about ¼ cup/ 30 g each). Roll up the fillets around the stuffing and fasten with a toothpick. Place the fish, seam side down, on a lightly oiled baking dish or pan. Lightly press a generous spoonful of the topping onto the top of the fish. Any extra topping can be scattered around the rolled fish. Bake for 30 minutes. Serve with potatoes or rice and sautéed greens.

Squid Stuffed with Scallops and Shrimp

Lulas Recheadas com Vieiras e Camarão

SERVES 4 TO 6

Put fried squid aside for a day and try soft, tender squid with a stuffing of sausage and shellfish bathed in a sea of tomato and wine garlic sauce. The key to this dish is not to overcook the squid into a rubbery mess. Fresh, cleaned squid bodies can be obtained from the fish market or supermarket frozen fish section. Make sure they are of decent size (4 to 6 inches/10 to 15 cm in length) because it is harder to insert the stuffing into smaller squid bodies. You can also use the tentacles; just chop them up and mix into the stuffing. I prefer to use shellfish in this, my contemporary version. Squid doesn't require as much cooking as octopus.

FOR THE SAUCE

½ ——— cup/120 ml olive oil

1 ——— small onion, thinly sliced

1 ——— pint/300 g cherry or grape tomatoes, rinsed, coarsely chopped

½ ——— cup/120 ml white wine or fish stock

1 ——— tablespoon/15 g tomato paste

1 ——— garlic clove, finely chopped

¼ ——— cup/15 g finely chopped cilantro or parsley

1 ——— bay leaf

1 ——— teaspoon/6 g coarse kosher salt or to taste

½ ——— cup/120 ml water

FOR THE SAUCE

1. Heat the oil in a large skillet. Add the onion and sauté until they are lightly golden, about 4 to 5 minutes. Toss in the tomatoes, white wine, tomato paste, garlic, cilantro, bay leaf and salt. Bring to a boil over medium-high heat. Reduce the heat to medium-low and simmer for 1 minute. Pour in the water, stir, taste for salt, adjust the seasoning and simmer for 5 minutes more. Turn off the heat and reserve.

(continued)

FOR THE SQUID

10 —— large or 20 medium squid bodies (about 3 pounds/1362 g), fresh or thawed, without tentacles, cleaned (see page 242)

3 to 4 —— cups/300 to 400 g packed, shredded fresh bread, heavy crusts removed

½ —— cup/120 ml milk, or as needed

½ —— cup/80 g coarsely chopped raw scallops

½ —— cup/80 g coarsely chopped raw shrimp

¼ —— cup/40 g finely chopped prosciutto or chouriço or linguiça sausage

¼ —— cup/40 g finely chopped onion

¼ —— cup/15 g finely chopped fresh cilantro or parsley

2 —— garlic cloves, finely chopped

¼ —— teaspoon coarse kosher salt or to taste

¼ —— teaspoon ground white pepper

4 —— tablespoons/56 g butter, melted

1 to 2 —— teaspoons/5 to 10 ml hot sauce or to taste

Toothpicks as needed

FOR THE SQUID

1. Rinse the squid bodies and pat dry.

2. In a medium bowl, combine the shredded bread with the milk, letting it stand for 5 to 10 minutes until absorbed. Add a little more if needed. After standing, squeeze the excess milk from the bread and drain off. Break up and crumble the bread back into the bowl. Mix in the scallops, shrimp, prosciutto, onion, cilantro, garlic, salt and pepper. Pour in the melted butter and hot sauce and mix thoroughly.

3. Stuff each squid body, leaving about 1 inch/2.5 cm of space at the top. Hold the opening closed and fasten it horizontally by threading a toothpick through both edges. Set aside. Do not stuff to full capacity as the bodies will shrink somewhat when they cook.

4. Arranging in a single layer, place the stuffed squid in the sauce. Cover and bring to a simmer over medium-low heat, cooking for 10 to 15 minutes, depending on their size, until fork-tender. Serve this as an appetizer, or with a salad as a light meal. As a full meal, serve with boiled potatoes, spooning some of the sauce over the potatoes.

"Purple Stew"

Someone contacted me looking for Portuguese "purple stew." I had never heard it put quite that way, but the only purple-looking stew I could think of was stewed octopus, which we call *Polvo Guisado*. What, you may wonder, gives it the red-purple color? Some folks have dubbed it purple stew because of the color extracted from the red wine, but if you use white wine, you will see more clearly that some of the red-purple color comes from the octopus itself as it becomes tender.

It might seem logical that octopus would cook as quickly as squid, but it actually needs to cook for almost an hour and there is a fine line that crosses it from perfectly tender to overcooked rubber toughness. Cooking octopus is a little tricky, and you must watch the pot constantly, checking for doneness. When perfectly cooked, the octopus will be tender to the bite and have taken on a red-purple hue. If the pieces start to shrink too much, it is a sign that they are getting overcooked. Each octopus will need a slightly different amount of cooking time because the amount of water they hold varies with their size and age.

I usually use thawed, frozen octopus for a few reasons. One is that fresh is not always available, and another is that the frozen one has already had the ink sac removed. Finally, aside from watching the cooking time, there isn't any need for extra tenderizing methods with the frozen octopus. The freezing seems to have already tenderized the meat, so you will obtain perfectly tender octopus by first sweating the octopus with an onion for at least 5 to 10 minutes in a covered pot with very little olive oil at the start of most recipes. Expect the octopus to give up water as it sweats. Of course, you can opt to use fresh octopus. The typical old method of tenderizing octopus is to beat it with a dowel or stick. Some cooks use what we call *aguardiente*, or "bang bang," which is Portuguese whiskey, to tenderize by marinating overnight, while others even add a cork or two to the cooking pot.

Of the following octopus recipes, the first has the simplest of seasonings: a vinaigrette drizzled over the cooked octopus to make a tantalizing salad that can be scooped onto a bed of lettuce. In cousins Tony and Noelia's recipe of stewed octopus, the influence from the island of Graciosa is evident, and a Madeiran friend shared his mother's marinated then stewed version. As with all the recipes, make sure you read the recipes through as well as any notes at the end of the recipes.

Prepping Octopus

It is said the best octopus comes from the waters around Portugal and Spain. In fish markets you may find the frozen ones that are labeled imported from Spain. That is what I recommend whenever possible. The average size for the recipes in this book is about 3 to 4 pounds/1350 to 1800 g. Take the thawed or fresh octopus and lay it on your workspace. With a sharp knife, separate the legs from the head by cutting between the top of the legs and below the eyes. If you are planning to use the head, make a second crosswise cut above the eyes and discard the sections with the eyes. Make a slit in the head, turn it inside out and remove the ink sac, innards and tags that attach them to the inside of the head. Sometimes the frozen ones have already had the ink sac and innards removed. Rinse the head well. Peel the skin off the head by simply grabbing the edge of the skin and pulling it from the meat. It comes off fairly easily. Set aside.

Now remove the mouth beak. In the center of the top of the legs (mantel), you will see and feel a hard, dark cartilage. Using your finger, push it through from one side or the other and you should have a hole, the diameter of your finger, in the middle. Rinse the octopus and it is ready to cook.

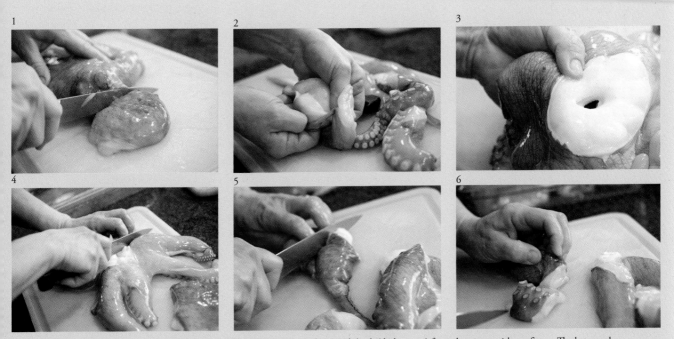

First I remove the head and peel off its skin by tugging firmly. Then I push the mouth beak (dark center) from the center with my finger. The legs are then separated and cut as needed before cooking.

Octopus Salad

Salada de Polvo

SERVES 2 TO 4

While visiting the town of Óbidos in central Portugal, just a bit north of Ericeira, we enjoyed lunch at a sidewalk café inside the walls of the town. Tender bites of octopus dressed with a simple vinaigrette make a great starter or lunch. This salad is a great way to introduce someone to octopus.

1	2½- to 3-pound/1135- to 1362-g octopus, fresh or thawed, cleaned (see page 125)
½	cup/120 ml olive oil, divided
1	large onion, peeled, quartered
1	bay leaf
1	cup/235 ml water
1	red bell pepper, stemmed, seeded and cut into medium pieces
1	small red or sweet onion, roughly chopped
2 or 3	garlic cloves, chopped
2	tablespoons/8 g finely chopped fresh cilantro or parsley
2	tablespoons/30 ml wine vinegar

Scant teaspoon of Dijon mustard

Coarse kosher salt to taste

Ground black pepper to taste

Fresh lettuce greens, rinsed

Black olives, for garnish

1. Prep the octopus following directions on page 125. Separate the legs of the octopus at the mantel so that you have eight. Cut each of the legs into 2- to 3-inch/5- to 7.5-cm lengths and set aside.

2. In a heavy pot with a tight-fitting lid, heat ¼ cup/60 ml of the olive oil over medium-high heat. Throw in the onion quarters and bay leaf and sweat the onion for about 5 minutes.

3. Add the pieces of octopus. Give them a stir and cover tightly. Reduce the heat to medium-low and let the octopus sweat for about 10 minutes. If it is about 2½ pounds/1135 g, let it sweat for just 5 minutes.

4. Add the water, then give it a stir. Recover tightly, bring to a boil, then reduce the heat to medium-low and cook, simmering slowly, for 40 to 45 minutes, depending on the thickness of the legs. After 30 minutes, keep checking for tenderness using the tines of a fork. Cut a small piece from the thickest part of the leg and taste for tenderness. If it is a little chewy, cook a few minutes more, but not too long. It will take on a reddish purple color when it is just about done. It should be tender, not rubbery. Drain and discard onion and bay leaf. Allow the octopus to cool slightly. Transfer the pieces of octopus to a bowl and mix with the chopped red pepper, chopped red onion and garlic.

5. Make the dressing in a cup or small bowl, whisking together the cilantro, vinegar, mustard, salt and black pepper. Drizzle in the remaining ¼ cup/60 ml olive oil. Mix well and drizzle over the salad, turning the pieces to coat. If serving shortly, let stand at room temperature for at least 30 minutes to absorb the flavors, or chill in the refrigerator for serving later. Serve this on a bed of lettuce or simply on a plate with some olives and bread. This is a great lunch for two but can also be served as a starter.

Note: If the octopus is closer to 2½ pounds/1135 g and the legs do not look too thick at the top, it may take only 40 minutes total, but you need to keep checking it to make sure it doesn't overcook.

Variation: If you wish to grill the octopus, prep it but *do not* cut up the legs. Cook as directed above, then throw the legs on the grill and cook, turning, for 2 or 3 minutes just to give it a light char.

Octopus Stew of Graciosa Island

Polvo Guisado à Moda da Graciosa

SERVES 4

While I was visiting family in the Azores, cousin Tony Ortins shared his recipe for octopus stew. Some versions are less spicy, but Tony loves to add his personal touch to this dish. He, like many Portuguese cooks, tenderizes the octopus by beating it on his workspace with a stick. There in the town of Luz, on the island of Graciosa, a little woman named Terezinha was whacking a fresh octopus with a heavy stick, preparing her simple version in the shore-side café. She used part of the day's catch to cook for local fishermen and those in the neighboring boatyard.

1	3- to 4-pound/1350- to 1,800-g octopus, fresh or thawed, cleaned (see page 125)
¼	cup/60 ml olive oil
1	medium onion, coarsely chopped
4	garlic cloves
2	bay leaves
1	teaspoon/6 g coarse kosher salt or to taste
½	teaspoon paprika
½	teaspoon cumin
¼	teaspoon ground white pepper

Generous pinch of nutmeg

½ to 1	tablespoon/7.5 to 15 g Chile Pepper Paste (page 365)
4	tablespoons/16 g finely chopped parsley, divided
3	Jamaican allspice berries
12	very small (1½ to 2 inch/3.8 to 5 cm diameter) new potatoes, peeled
1	cup/235 ml water as needed
1	cup/235 ml white or rosé wine (red wine will make the stew dark but you can use it if you wish)
1	rounded tablespoon/15 g tomato paste
1	tablespoon/15 ml port wine

1. After you have prepped and rinsed the octopus, if it is not previously frozen, you need to pound it with a mallet or heavy dowel to tenderize it. Cut the legs into 2- to 3-inch/5- to 7.5-cm lengths.

2. In a heavy pot with a tight-fitting lid, heat the olive oil over medium-high heat. Throw in the onion and sauté until they are golden, about 5 to 7 minutes.

3. Give a quick stir and add the octopus. Cover tightly. Reduce the heat to medium-low and let the octopus sweat for about 10 minutes, especially if it is large. It will give up a lot of water. Toss in the garlic, bay leaves, salt, paprika, cumin, ground pepper and nutmeg. Mix in chile pepper paste, 1 tablespoon/4 g of the parsley, allspice berries and potatoes. If there is not enough liquid at this point to cover the potatoes, add the water.

4. Recover tightly and simmer over medium-low heat for about 30 minutes. Check it at this time, piercing a fat piece with a fork or tasting a fat piece to make sure it is not chewy. It should be almost done. Mix the wine, tomato paste and port wine together then stir into the broth along with 1 tablespoon/4 g of the parsley. Recover tightly and continue to simmer for 5 to 10 more minutes, making sure the liquid does not evaporate. If it looks like it is getting dry, add some water in small increments. You don't want too much liquid. Every octopus lets out different amounts of water.

5. Keep checking for tenderness. Be careful not to let it overcook or the octopus will be rubbery. The octopus will be reddish purple in color and easily pierced with a fork when it is just about tender. Total cooking time should be about 40 to 50 minutes, after a 10-minute sweating period, depending on the thickness of the legs. Sometimes I turn off the heat at 40 minutes and then let it sit covered, in its own heat, to finish. The trick is to keep testing for tenderness. Serve with extra hot sauce on the side and plenty of bread to sop up the broth. Garnish with the remaining 2 tablespoons/8 g parsley.

Madeiran Wine and
Garlic Marinated Octopus Stew
Polvo à Moda da Madeira

SERVES 4

Arcenia Texeira of Madeira, a chef in her own right, never beat the octopus to tenderize it. The wine does the work for you, she would say. Garlic, wine and a bit of chile infuse the octopus overnight before it is cooked.

A DAY BEFORE

1	3- to 4-pound/1350- to 1800-g octopus, thawed and cleaned (see page 125)
5	garlic cloves, crushed
1	tablespoon/15 g Chile Pepper Paste (page 125) or hot sauce
1	teaspoon/6 g coarse kosher salt or to taste
½	teaspoon ground white pepper or to taste
2	bay leaves
1	cup/235 ml white wine

A DAY BEFORE

1. Cut the octopus into 2-inch/5-cm pieces. Rinse and place in a bowl.

2. Season with the garlic, Chile Pepper Paste, salt, white pepper and bay leaves. Pour the wine over and turn the octopus to coat in the seasoning. Cover and chill overnight.

(continued)

Note: At any time during the cooking, if the liquid looks like it is evaporating, lower the heat and add the reserved marinade in small increments. If you don't have a tight-fitting lid for your pot, or if the heat is too high, the liquid can evaporate more quickly.

THE NEXT DAY

¼ ——— cup/60 ml olive oil

1 ——— cup/180 g coarsely chopped onion

1 ——— head garlic or 8 large cloves, peeled, thinly sliced

¾ ——— cup/45 g coarsely chopped flat Italian parsley, divided

12——— baby red bliss potatoes, peeled, halved, or 6 medium boiling potatoes, cut into 2-inch/5-cm pieces

1 ——— red bell pepper, stemmed, seeded and cut into 1-inch/2.5-cm pieces

1 ——— tablespoon/8 g cornstarch mixed with 2 tablespoons/30 ml water

THE NEXT DAY

1. Reserving the marinade, strain the octopus and set the pieces in a separate dish.

2. Heat the olive oil in a 4-quart/3.6-L pot set over medium-high heat until hot but not smoking. Add the onion and cook over medium-high heat until they are lightly golden, about 5 minutes. Toss in the garlic and half of the parsley.

3. When the garlic becomes slightly aromatic, about 1 minute, add the strained octopus and cover the pot. The octopus will release a lot of water from its meat as it sweats in the oil and onions, about 10 minutes. Stir, recover and continue to simmer over medium heat for 20 to 25 minutes more, then check the liquid level. If the level of the liquid is almost dry, add about ½ cup/120 ml of the reserved marinade.

4. Give the octopus a stir and add the potatoes and red pepper. Recover, reduce the heat to medium-low and simmer, cooking slowly, for about another 10 to 15 minutes, checking periodically for tenderness. Test a fat piece and if it is still chewy or tough, let it cook some more. Total cooking time should be about 40 to 50 minutes, tops. Reminder: Depending on the weight, the thickness of the legs and the size of the pieces, the cooking time can vary from one recipe to another. It can take almost 50 minutes if the legs are really thick, so taste test at 40 minutes to prevent overcooking. The thick part of the legs should be easily pierced with a fork.

5. When the octopus is almost tender, add the cornstarch slurry. Simmer for another minute or two and serve with the remaining parsley scattered over the top.

Octopus and White Kidney Beans

Feijoada de Polvo

SERVES 2 TO 4

Here the octopus is first cooked separately, then added to a second pot. This way, the stew is not watered down. The addition of the beans complements the octopus. You will find one octopus can release more water than another and shrink quite a bit during the cooking process, so the amount of water added to the pot is flexible.

FOR THE OCTOPUS

1	3- to 4-pound/1362- to 1818-g octopus, fresh or thawed, cleaned (see page 125)
¼	cup/60 ml olive oil
1	onion, peeled, quartered
1	bay leaf
1	cup/235 ml water, or as needed

FOR THE BEANS

¼	cup/60 ml olive oil
½	cup/80 g finely chopped onion
1	very ripe tomato, peeled, seeded and coarsely chopped
2	large garlic cloves, finely chopped
1½	tablespoons/23 g Chile Pepper Paste (page 365), hot sauce or crushed dried chiles or to taste
1	bay leaf
1	cup/235 ml white wine
1½	cups/375 g cooked white butter beans or kidney beans
½	cup/30 g finely chopped fresh parsley or cilantro, divided
1	teaspoon/6 g coarse kosher salt or to taste
½	teaspoon ground white pepper or to taste

FOR THE OCTOPUS

1. Cut the octopus legs into 2- to 3-inch/5- to 7.5-cm pieces.

2. In a heavy pot with a tight-fitting lid, heat the oil over medium-high heat. Throw in the onion and let it sweat for about 5 minutes.

3. Add the bay leaf. Give a quick stir and mix in the octopus. Cover tightly. Reduce the heat to medium and let the octopus sweat for about 10 minutes.

4. Depending on the amount of water the octopus releases, you may need ½ to 1 cup/120 to 235 ml of the water, just so the pot isn't dry. If there seems to be a lot of water, just use ½ cup/120 ml, then give it a stir. Cover tightly, bring to a boil over high heat, then reduce the heat to medium-low and cook, simmering slowly, for about 35 minutes more. Check for tenderness by eating a piece and making sure it isn't chewy and if needed, cook for about 5 minutes more, until fork tender. Remove the octopus with a slotted spoon to a dish and set aside.

FOR THE BEANS

1. Heat the olive oil in the bottom on a heavy-bottomed pot that is large enough to accommodate all the ingredients. Add the onions and sauté until golden, about 5 minutes.

2. Stir in the tomato, garlic, Chile Pepper Paste and bay leaf. Cover tightly and cook over medium-low heat until the tomatoes have broken down and married well with the onions and the sauce has taken on a slightly rusty color, about 10 minutes.

3. Mix in the wine and simmer over medium heat for about 1 minute and reduced by half. Add the cooked beans with ¼ cup/15 g of the parsley. Mix in the drained octopus pieces, turning them in the sauce. Taste for salt and add with ground pepper, adjusting to taste, and cook just until the beans are heated through, about 3 minutes more. Remove the bay leaf and serve, sprinkled with the remaining ¼ cup/15 g parsley.

Soups

Sopas

Soups are the heart of a Portuguese meal. We take pride in our soups, which are typically laden with vegetables, legumes and leafy greens. Many early immigrants, like my father, survived in the United States by eating soup. My grandmother would make a huge pot of soup, which would last them for a few days and provide them with much needed nutrients, especially on a cold winter's night. Then she would make some more. It was the most economically delicious thing to make.

Soups are one of the easiest things to prepare and, usually, you have most of the ingredients in your pantry. Fresh vegetables, a little rice or pasta, some seasoning, a piece of chicken or beef (or not) and legumes can all be whipped up into a delicious soup in no time. Plus, making soup from scratch ensures you know what's in it. With increased awareness of commercial processed food ingredients, it makes more sense than ever to prepare your own soups—or anything, for that matter. What could be easier and healthier? Don't be shy about making your own soup. Be creative!

A Few Words on Stock

More and more it seems chicken broth is added to soups and even stews to enhance their flavors. I don't know whether people think adding chicken broth makes everything taste good or whether it is a matter of "when in doubt, add chicken broth." I recently saw a seafood dish that incorporated chicken broth. Chicken-flavored shrimp and fish? Good grief, why not just eat chicken? Instead, use a light vegetable, shrimp or fish stock for a seafood dish.

Of course, I occasionally use chicken broth for a soup, but it isn't always necessary. In fact, I believe sometimes it may camouflage the flavor of the primary ingredient(s) in the soup. Using plain water as the medium in a distinctive soup or stew allows the main ingredient's flavor to come through as the recipe intends. However, I will say yes, there are some soups and stews that do need a little extra touch. So I offer my rule of thumb: think first if the dish really needs the lift. If it is a very traditional dish with specific ingredients that uses water and is delicious as it stands, perhaps it should be left alone. For example, *caldo verde* soup is made with water, potato, kale, onion, olive oil and sausage—very specific main ingredients. Could you use chicken broth in it? Well, yes, and it would taste good, but it would not be the true version. Remember to use stocks to enhance, not to camouflage. I also encourage you to use a simple homemade stock whenever possible or an organic commercial one with the least amount of additives. You can make a batch and freeze it in portions. Leave store-bought stocks for a last alternative or for when you have time constraints. After all, homemade soups are healthier and easy to make.

Giving Body to Soups

There is something to be said for a flavorful soup that has a broth with body, but you ask how does one give body or get a thickened soup broth? Typically, a form of starch is used.

An old method, still used today, especially by many Europeans, is the use of bread, particularly day-old or hardened bread. With heavy crusts removed, bread is torn and tossed into a steaming broth of vegetables, where it soaks up some broth. Today, depending on the desired results, one might use a stick immersion blender or food mill to purée ingredients. Then you may pass the puréed soup through a sieve, china cap or chinois to lighten the soup.

If you are allergic to wheat, legumes are not just an alternative. They have always been part of the Portuguese diet, especially in soups, where they are often cooked in the broth and mashed against the inside of the pot, or cooked separately and then processed through a food mill placed over the soup pot, passing the meat of the beans into the broth, thickening it.

Cornstarch or flour mixed with cold water to make a slurry and tempered with broth can be gradually added to boiling broth to give it body (although we don't often do that with Portuguese soups).

For a velvety texture, add a touch of cream by tempering about ¼ cup/60 ml when the soup is done. Do not allow the broth to boil once the cream is added or the broth will curdle. For a lighter texture, pass the puréed soup through a sieve and then a fine chinois. This will aerate it, giving it a lighter, smoother body and mouthfeel.

It is common to find rice and small pasta comingling in the same soup. The extra starch gives body to the soup, not to mention that in the old days it filled people up and kept hunger at bay. As you make and taste soups, you will experience the different mouthfeel that results from the various starches. Try the recipes that follow and see which texture you like best.

Aunt Ana's Pot Luck Soup

Sopa de Panela da Tia Ana

SERVES 6

My aunt Ana, it could be said, almost never served the same soup twice. With a little bit of this or that, combined with a handful of rice, a chicken leg or a lamb chop here, a carrot there, my *tia's sopas* were made with what she had on hand. Fortunately, I stopped by to visit on my way home from school just when she was cooking this version. In this particular soup of the pot, or "pot luck soup," she, like many Portuguese cooks (myself included), used the leftover vegetable broth from a Portuguese boiled dinner (see *Portuguese Homestyle Cooking*), making the need for salt almost unnecessary. If you haven't made a boiled dinner, good-quality low-sodium vegetable stock can also be used to make this soup, but the flavor will be less concentrated.

1	ounce/28 g lean salt pork or 2 tablespoons/30 ml olive oil
1	lamb chop, with bone, trimmed of visible excess fat
1	medium onion, finely chopped
1	medium tomato, peeled, seeded and coarsely chopped
2½	cups/625 g cooked red or white kidney beans
1	large potato, coarsely chopped
½	pound/227 g link of chouriço sausage
8	cups/1880 ml broth from a boiled dinner (you can add water or vegetable stock to the broth to yield 8 cups/1880 ml)
3	carrots, cooked and mashed
4	ounces/112 g fresh green beans, trimmed and cut into 1-inch/2.5-cm pieces
1	cup/70 g roughly chopped green cabbage
¼	cup/25 g elbow macaroni

Coarse kosher salt to taste (the broth may have sufficient salt if it is from a boiled dinner)

1. Fry the salt pork in an 8-quart/7.2-L pot set over medium heat, rendering the fat from it. Remove the crisp pieces. Alternatively, heat the olive oil until hot but not smoking. Add the lamb chop and fry until lightly golden on both sides, about 2 minutes on each side. Remove to a dish and reserve. Toss in the onion and sauté until translucent, about 2 to 3 minutes.

2. Stir in the peeled, chopped tomato and cover tightly. Cook over medium-low heat until it is broken down and married to the onion, about 10 minutes.

3. Mix in the beans, chopped potato, link of sausage and the browned lamb chop. Pour in the broth. Cover tightly and bring to a boil over medium-high heat. Reduce the heat to medium-low and simmer until the potatoes are almost done, about 20 minutes.

4. Add the mashed carrots, green beans, chopped cabbage and pasta. Simmer for 10 to 15 minutes more. Adjust the seasoning to taste.

5. To serve, remove meat from the lamb chop, discarding the bone, and cut into small pieces. Slice the sausage into ¼-inch/6-mm rounds and serve with the meat on the side or return all to the pot. Ladle into soup plates and serve with crusty bread slices.

Chicken with Rice Soup

Sopa de Galinha com Arroz

SERVES 4

Chicken soup is always popular in a Portuguese home. When I was growing up, it was most frequently served in our house as the first course to Sunday dinner. Continuing with tradition, it is the first soup my grandchildren were introduced to. This soup is more substantial than my grandmother's *canja*, which was basically the broth of chicken accented with minimal shredded chicken, giblets, a squirt of lemon juice and maybe a mint leaf. One of my granddaughters prefers my aunt's version while her sister loves my grandmother's. Here I have added celery and give the optional addition of chickpeas, which were my father-in-law's trademark.

---

3 —— chicken thighs, skin removed

6 —— cups/1410 ml water

1 —— medium onion, finely chopped (about 1 cup/160 g)

½ —— cup/65 g finely chopped celery

1 —— carrot, peeled and thinly sliced into scant ¼-inch/6-mm rounds

½ —— cup/82 g short-grain rice

½ —— tablespoon/9 g coarse kosher salt or to taste

¼ —— teaspoon ground white or black pepper or to taste

½ —— cup/120 g cooked chickpeas, well drained (optional)

Lemon wedges, for serving

1. Combine the chicken and water in a 3½- to 4-quart/3.2- to 3.6-L pot. Cover and bring to a boil over medium-high heat. Reduce the heat to medium-low and simmer until the meat is nearly falling off the bones, about 30 minutes. Using a slotted spoon, transfer the meat to a dish. Set aside until it is cool enough to handle.

2. Return the soup to a boil and add the onion, celery, carrot, rice, salt and pepper. Reduce the heat to medium-low and simmer until the rice is done, about 20 minutes. Meanwhile, remove and discard the bones from the meat and hand-shred the chicken into pieces.

3. When the rice is done, add the chickpeas, return the shredded meat to the pot and heat through. If the soup is too thick for your taste, you can thin it with a small amount of water or additional stock. Serve with lemon wedges on the side to squeeze over the soup if desired.

Cabbage and Kidney Bean Soup with Rice

Sopa de Repolho com Feijão Branco

SERVES 6 TO 8

Kidney beans pull the flavors of cabbage and vegetables together in this simple, light soup, which is perfect for an easy supper on a cold night—or any time, really. It is another soup that tastes even better the next day, after all the ingredients have come together to give you the indescribable, satisfying taste.

A DAY AHEAD

1 —— pound/454 g dry white kidney (cannellini) beans; soak overnight in a bowl with enough cold water to cover by 2 inches/5 cm, or two 1-pound/454-g cans white kidney beans (if using the latter, cut the water to 6 cups/1410 ml and skip step 1)

THE NEXT DAY

8 —— cups/1880 ml water, divided

1 —— medium onion, finely chopped (about 1 cup/160 g)

1 —— medium potato, peeled, coarsely chopped (about 1 cup/150 g)

2 —— carrots, peeled, finely chopped

1 —— garlic clove, finely chopped

½ —— cup/82 g short-grain rice

4 —— ounces/112 g fresh green beans, cut into ½-inch/1.3-cm pieces

1 —— teaspoon/6 g coarse kosher salt or to taste

½ —— teaspoon ground white pepper or to taste

2 —— cups/140 g finely shredded green cabbage

4 —— tablespoons/60 ml olive oil

THE NEXT DAY

1. Drain the beans from the soaking water and rinse. Place them in a 2½-quart/2.2-L pan and cover them with 3 cups/705 ml of the fresh water. Cover and bring to a boil over medium-high heat. Reduce the heat to medium-low and simmer for about 45 minutes, until very tender and easily mashed with a fork. Skip this step if using canned beans.

2. Place a food mill over a 4-quart/3.6-L pot. Empty the beans with their cooking liquid into it. Process the cooked beans through the food mill, alternating hand cranking and flushing them through the holes with the remaining water 5 cups/1175 ml. Only the skins of the beans should be remaining in the food mill when you are finished. You can also leave some beans whole for added texture to the soup.

3. Add the chopped onion, potato, carrots and garlic. Cover the pot and set it over medium-high heat. Bring the ingredients to a boil, then reduce the heat to medium-low. Simmer until the potato is very tender, about 20 minutes. Using a long-handled fork or the back of a large spoon, roughly mash the potato against the inside of the pot.

4. Toss in the rice, green beans, salt and pepper and stir. Cover and continue simmering for about 15 minutes. Stir in the cabbage. Continue simmering for another 10 to 15 minutes, until the cabbage is tender but not mushy. Drizzle in the olive oil and stir well. Ladle into bowls and serve.

Spinach with Rice Soup

Sopa de Espinafres com Arroz

SERVES 4

Simple and delicious, this spinach soup, another specialty of my aunt Ana, is light, utilizes fresh spinach and marries well with carrots, tomato and potato. It is another way of enjoying the flavor of spinach besides sautéing, steaming or making a salad out of it. Make sure you rinse the spinach well, especially the back of the leaves.

3	medium carrots, peeled, cut into chunks (about 1½ cups/195 g)
2	medium all-purpose boiling potatoes, peeled, quartered
1	small onion, coarsely chopped
½	cup/90 g coarsely chopped, peeled, seeded tomato
6	cups/1410 ml cold water
¼	cup/40 g short-grain rice or small pasta
1½	teaspoons/9 g coarse kosher salt or to taste
¼	teaspoon ground black or white pepper
10	ounces/280 g fresh savoy spinach, trimmed of heavy ribs, rinsed, roughly chopped
3	tablespoons/45 ml olive oil

1. Toss the carrots, potatoes, onion and tomato into a 3½- to 4-quart/3.2- to 3.6-L pot. Stir in the water. Cover and bring to a boil over medium-high heat. Reduce the heat to low and simmer until all the vegetables are very tender, about 20 minutes. Working in batches with a blender or food mill, or simply using a stick blender right in the pot, purée the broth. For a smoother texture, pour the soup through a fine sieve.

2. Return the broth to a boil and then stir in the rice, salt and pepper. Recover the pot and simmer over medium-low heat for about 10 minutes.

3. Add the spinach and the olive oil. Continue simmering for 10 more minutes, until the rice is done and the spinach is tender. Serve hot.

Kidney Bean with Pumpkin Soup

Sopa de Feijão com Abóbora

SERVES 4 TO 6

This is a nutritious fall soup, perfect for making use of pumpkins and squash. The sweetness of pumpkin comingling with the kidney beans, sweet potato and tomato, accented with cinnamon, gives it a comforting, homey taste. Not only is it perfect for vegetarians, but it is also easy to make. If you haven't any pumpkin or squash, use a yellow turnip, called rutabaga, which is sweeter than the white turnip.

2	tablespoons/30 ml olive oil
½	cup/80 g finely chopped onion
½	cup/90 g coarsely chopped, peeled, seeded tomatoes
1	garlic clove, finely chopped
1	teaspoon/3 g sweet paprika
½	teaspoon cinnamon or to taste
1	bay leaf
6	cups/1410 ml water, or as needed
3	cups/750 g cooked red kidney beans with cooking broth
1	cup/120 g 1-inch/2.5-cm diced, peeled, seeded pumpkin, Blue Hubbard or butternut squash
1	cup/120 g 1-inch/2.5-cm diced, peeled sweet potato (optional)
½	cup/50 g small pasta, like orzo or ditalini pasta (optional)
½	teaspoon coarse kosher salt or to taste
¼	teaspoon ground black or white pepper

1. In a 4-quart/3.6-L soup pot, heat the olive oil. Toss in the onion and sauté until soft and translucent, about 2 to 3 minutes. Stir in the tomatoes, garlic, paprika, cinnamon and bay leaf. Cover and simmer for about 10 minutes over medium-low heat.

2. Pour in the water. At this point, you can either purée the beans using a food mill to hold back the skins (resulting in a skinless bean broth) or leave the beans whole, and add them to the pot. If using whole beans, press some against the inside of the pot to give the soup some extra body.

3. Add the diced pumpkin and sweet potato. Cover and bring the contents of the pot to a boil over medium-high heat. Reduce the heat to medium-low and simmer until the vegetables are nearly fork-tender, about 20 minutes. Toss in the small uncooked pasta, stir in the salt and pepper, and continue cooking for 10 minutes more, until the pasta is cooked. Alternatively, cook the pasta in a separate pan until al dente, drain and then add to the soup.

Variation: The simplest version is without potato or pasta, and yet if you add them—plus some leafy greens like spinach, kale, cabbage, Swiss chard or beet greens—you have a heartier soup.

Velvet Shrimp Bisque
Veludo de Camarão

SERVES 6

This recipe is adapted from the restaurant at the Beira Mar Hotel on the island of Terceira, in the Azores. The chef was so gracious to share her recipe, in which she incorporates freshly made fish stock. I have adapted the recipe to include a simple shrimp stock. It is a bit more sophisticated than the traditional style. The modern use of cream to add a velvety finish to the soup is more common in restaurants than in traditional homes. For this recipe, make your stock ahead or use premade fish stock.

FOR THE SHELLFISH STOCK

2 —————— pounds/908 g medium shrimp, with shells

2 —————— stalks celery, trimmed, chopped

1 —————— carrot, peeled, chopped

1 —————— cup/235 ml white wine

3 —————— sprigs cilantro

6 —————— cups/1410 ml water

FOR THE SHELLFISH STOCK

1. Peel and devein the shrimp. Reserving the shrimp, place the shells, celery, carrot, wine, cilantro and water in a 3-quart/2.7-L pot. Cover, bring to a boil, reduce the heat to a simmer and cook for 20 minutes.

Note: It is not uncommon for Portuguese cooks to boil the shrimp unpeeled, but this can overcook the shrimp, which will be cooked separately at a different time in the recipe. I suggest cooking the shells separately in water, and to prevent overcooking, cook the shelled shrimp when the recipe states. This method extracts the essence of the shrimp and ensures a flavorful shrimp broth that you can use in a soup, for cooking rice or for the recipe itself, enhancing the flavor of the dish.

The texture of this soup is up to you. After puréeing, you will have a rustic puréed soup. If you want a lighter texture, then pass it through a china cap. For a finer and lighter texture, pass again through a double-mesh sieve or a finer mesh chinois. The china cap looks like a conical-shaped colander and the chinois is conical shaped but with a mesh sieve. They involve a little more work to pass the soup through. The result, however, is a lighter, contemporary, smooth mouthfeel. Yum, in any case! I use this method in the next two recipes for the chestnut and the garlic soups.

FOR THE SOUP

3 ——— tablespoons/45 ml olive oil

½ ——— cup/80 g finely chopped onion

3 ——— tablespoons/45 g tomato paste

2 ——— garlic cloves, finely chopped

1 ——— bay leaf

6 ——— cups/600 g shredded day-old bread, heavy crusts removed (use Portuguese bread or another crusty peasant or artisan bread like Italian, Greek or French)

1 ——— teaspoon/6 g coarse kosher salt or to taste

¼ ——— teaspoon white pepper

Dash of hot sauce or ¼ teaspoon cayenne pepper (optional)

½ ——— cup/120 ml heavy cream (optional)

2 ——— tablespoons/30 ml tawny port wine

¼ ——— cup/15 g finely chopped cilantro, for garnish

Toasted bread, cut into triangles

FOR THE SOUP

1. In a 5-quart/4.5-L pot, heat the olive oil over medium-high heat until hot but not smoking. Add the onion and sauté until translucent, about 2 to 3 minutes. Reduce the heat to medium-low and mix in the tomato paste, garlic and bay leaf, stirring until well blended and the garlic becomes aromatic, about 1 minute. Cook over medium-low heat, covered, until the onions are married with the ingredients, about 7 minutes.

2. Strain the shrimp stock with a mesh strainer. Pour the strained shrimp stock into the onion and tomato base, cover and bring to a boil. Add all of the reserved peeled shrimp, reduce the heat to medium-low and simmer for just 3 minutes. With a slotted spoon, remove 6 of the shrimp and reserve.

3. Add the shredded day-old bread to the hot soup and stir. Remove the bay leaf and turn off the heat.

4. When the bread has softened in the broth, use a stick immersion blender, food mill or food processor to purée the soup. For a smoother texture, pass the soup through a sieve into another pot, pressing on the solids to squeeze out the soup. Discard the solids. Return the strained soup to the pot. Taste for salt and add if needed. Stir in the white pepper and hot sauce.

5. Just before serving, temper the cream in a cup or bowl with some of the soup, warming it up so that it doesn't curdle. Then, briskly whisk the warmed cream into the pot of soup until it is well dispersed throughout and heat without boiling for 1 minute. Drizzle in the port wine and stir. Ladle the soup into individual serving bowls and garnish each with a reserved shrimp and a smattering of chopped cilantro. Serve with the toast points.

Purée of Chestnut Soup

Sopa de Castanhas

SERVES 4 TO 6

Have extra chestnuts left over from roasting or boiling? Great! If you have about 3 cups/435 g, then you are in luck! When chestnut season is here, I sometimes purchase extra chestnuts so that I can make this soup. I even cook some chestnuts ahead and freeze them short term for future use. Some specialty stores carry chestnuts already cooked, but that can get more expensive. Instead of leaving the chestnuts whole, serving them puréed is perfect around the holidays, especially Christmas. Since chestnuts can be heavy, I do pass the soup through a sieve or chinois to lighten it up. For an extra creamy texture, I sometimes add light cream.

A DAY OR TWO AHEAD

1 ——— pound/454 g chestnuts

FOR THE SOUP

¼ ——— cup/60 ml olive oil or butter

1 ——— small onion, coarsely chopped (about ½ cup/80 g)

½ ——— cup/90 g peeled, seeded, chopped tomato

2 ——— garlic cloves, peeled, any green sprouts removed

1 ——— teaspoon/3 g paprika

2 ——— tablespoons/8 g finely chopped cilantro or parsley

6 ——— cups/1410 ml cold water or vegetable stock

1½ ——— cups/355 ml water

¼ ——— cup/40 g short-grain rice

1 ——— teaspoon/6 g coarse kosher salt, or as needed

½ ——— teaspoon ground white pepper

¼ ——— cup/60 ml light cream (optional)

Variation: Skip the rice, reduce the water or broth to 4 cups/ 940 ml and pass the soup through an extra-fine sieve; serve as a light and elegant first course.

A DAY OR TWO AHEAD

1. Preheat the oven to 400°F/200°C, or gas mark 6.

2. With a sharp paring knife, cut a deep crosshatch on the point of each chestnut or cut a deep horizontal slit all around the middle through just the skin of each chestnut. Spread on a baking sheet and roast for 25 minutes, or boil for 20 minutes in salted water. Whichever method you use, quickly peel the shell and inner skin as soon as they have cooled enough to handle, or use a kitchen cloth to prevent burning your fingers. It hurts, trust me. But, if they get too cool, chestnuts are more difficult to peel, so keep them warm, either in the oven or in the hot water, removing them gradually, and peel. You should have about 3 cups/435 g cooked and peeled.

FOR THE SOUP

1. Heat the oil in a 3½- to 4-quart/3.2- to 3.6-L pot over medium heat. Sauté the onion until it becomes translucent, about 2 to 3 minutes. Toss in the tomato, garlic, paprika and cilantro. When the garlic becomes aromatic, about 1 minute, pour in the cold water and add all but 5 of the chestnuts. Cover and bring to a boil. Reduce the heat to medium-low and simmer for 5 minutes, or until the chestnuts are falling-apart tender. Using a stick immersion blender, or working in batches using a food mill, purée the soup. Chop the reserved chestnuts and set aside for garnish.

2. Meanwhile, boil 1½ cups/355 ml water in a separate pot. Add the rice and salt. Cook for about 20 minutes, until tender, then drain.

3. Add the drained, cooked rice to the soup pot and heat through. Add salt if needed and ground pepper. Warm the cream with a small amount of the soup. Just before serving, stir into the soup. It should have the consistency of heavy cream. Garnish the soup in the middle of each bowl with the chopped chestnuts. Use extra stock or water to thin if it is too thick.

Garlic Soup
Açorda de Alho

SERVES 4 TO 6

How one can be of Portuguese roots and not like garlic, I couldn't tell you. But I can tell you how to make this flavorful "garlic fix." This is a contemporary version of an *açorda* (the Alentejo's rustic bread soup with garlic) that I was raised on, which is basically a broth with bread, garlic, cilantro and hard-boiled egg (the recipe is in my book, *Portuguese Homestyle Cooking*). Inspired by my father's *açorda*, I have increased the garlic and added a few vegetables to the broth followed by the bread. I then puréed this country dish and finished with a touch of cream to bring it up a level, then garnished it with chopped hard-boiled egg.

⅓	cup/80 ml olive oil
1	tablespoon/14 g butter
1	head garlic, peeled, green stems removed, coarsely chopped
¼	cup/40 g coarsely chopped, peeled, seeded tomato
½	cup/60 g finely chopped cilantro, divided
1	stalk celery, trimmed and coarsely chopped
¼	cup/30 g chopped carrot
3	scallions, trimmed of dark green stems, chopped
1	teaspoon/3 g paprika
1	bay leaf
6	cups/1410 ml water or vegetable stock
3	cups/300 g shredded day-old Portuguese, Italian or French bread, heavy crusts removed
1	teaspoon/6 g coarse kosher salt or to taste
¼	teaspoon white ground pepper or to taste
½	cup/120 ml light cream (optional)
3	hard-boiled eggs, shelled, chopped

1. Heat the olive oil and butter in a 4-quart/3.6-L soup pot over medium heat. Add the garlic, tomato, ¼ cup/4 g of the cilantro, celery, carrot, scallions, paprika and bay leaf. Cover and let them sweat over medium-low heat for 4 minutes to release their essence.

2. As the garlic becomes more aromatic but not burning, pour the water into the pot. Cover and bring to a boil over medium-high heat, then lower the heat and simmer for about 20 minutes. Remove the pot from the heat. Add the bread, allowing it to absorb some of the broth.

3. Remove the bay leaf and, using a stick blender, regular blender or food mill, purée the soup to the desired texture. Taste for salt and adjust to your taste. If you want a finer, smooth texture, pour through a mesh strainer or china cap set atop another pot and press the soup through, then discard the solids. Season with pepper.

4. Temper the cream with some warm stock so that it doesn't curdle, then whisk into the soup pot. Heat through. Ladle into bowls. Garnish servings with the remaining ¼ cup/4 g chopped cilantro and chopped egg.

Watercress, Chickpea and Green Bean Soup

Sopa de Agrião, Grão e Feijão Verde

SERVES 4 TO 6

Watercress is a delicate, peppery flavored, underused green that is best purchased shortly before using. The green gives a little lift to the soup, matching nicely with the nuttiness of the chickpeas and softer flavor of the green beans. You might see it in salads here and there, but we like to add it to soups. Loaded with fiber and antioxidants, and vitamins A and C, this soup is a quick, inexpensive first course or great lunch.

5	medium Yukon gold potatoes, peeled, quartered (about 4 cups/480 g)
1	medium onion, finely chopped (about ½ cup/80 g)
8	cups/1880 ml water
½	pound/227 g green beans, cut into ½-inch/1.3-cm pieces
2	bunches watercress, thick stems removed, rinsed
2	cups/490 g cooked chickpeas, drained (canned may be substituted)
1	carrot, peeled, finely chopped
4	tablespoons/60 ml olive oil
1	garlic clove, finely chopped
1	tablespoon/18 g coarse kosher salt or to taste
¼	teaspoon ground white pepper or to taste
½	cup/90 g orzo or other small pasta

1. Combine the potatoes, onion and water in a 4-quart/3.6-L pot. Cover the pot and bring to a boil over medium-high heat. Reduce the heat to medium-low and simmer for 20 to 25 minutes, or until the potatoes are nearly falling apart. Purée the soup with a stick blender.

2. Return the broth to a boil, toss in the remaining ingredients and cover. Simmer the soup over medium-low heat, stirring frequently to prevent the starch from sticking to the bottom of the pot and burning, for 10 to 12 minutes, or until the pasta is al dente. Alternatively, cook the pasta separately, then add to the soup. Serve with black olives and crusty bread on the side.

Sweet Potato Soup with Green Beans and Cilantro

Sopa de Batata Doce

SERVES 6

This is a nice fall soup that makes a wonderful starter for Thanksgiving. It is very simple to make. The sweetness of the potato and the cilantro make an unexpected but flavorful combination. Using water or vegetable stock instead of chicken broth, as some cooks do, allows the flavor of the sweet potatoes to come through.

¼	cup/60 ml olive oil
1	medium onion, peeled, chopped
½	cup/80 g chopped, peeled and seeded tomato
1	garlic clove, finely chopped
¼	teaspoon ground cumin
6	cups/1410 ml water or vegetable stock
4	medium sweet potatoes, peeled and cut into cubes (about 4 cups/480 g)
½	pound/227 g fresh green beans, rinsed and cut into 1-inch/2.5-cm pieces
1 to 2	tablespoons/4 to 8 g finely chopped cilantro or parsley, divided
1½	teaspoons/9 g coarse kosher salt or to taste
¼	teaspoon white pepper

1. Heat the oil in a 4-quart/3.6-L soup pot over medium heat. Toss in the onion and sauté until lightly golden, about 5 minutes.

2. Add the tomato, garlic and cumin, stir and cover. Simmer, covered, over medium-low heat for about 10 minutes, until the tomatoes are soft and are married to the onions.

3. Pour in the water and stir. Add the sweet potatoes and recover. Bring the soup to a boil. Reduce the heat to medium-low and simmer until the potatoes are very tender, about 15 to 20 minutes. Using a stick blender, you can purée the soup right in the pot.

4. Return the soup to a simmer and throw in the green beans with half of the cilantro. Season the soup to taste with salt and pepper. If you want, you can thin the soup with extra stock or water. When the green beans are just tender, about 10 minutes, turn off the heat. Serve the soup with the remaining cilantro as a garnish.

Madeiran Countryside Vegetable Soup
Sopa do Campo à Madeirense

SERVES 8 TO 10

This vegetarian-friendly soup from the island of Madeira comes from workers in the fields, and nothing could be easier. Calling for freshly harvested vegetables, this recipe is simple to make and gives sustenance to keep going. Although this makes a large pot, any extra soup tastes even better the next day.

3 —— quarts/2.7 L water or vegetable stock

2 —— cups/500 g dried kidney beans, soaked overnight in water to cover, drained, or 4 cups/1000 g canned beans, undrained

2 —— white or yellow sweet potatoes, peeled, quartered

2 —— medium carrots, peeled, cut into ½-inch/1.3-cm rough chunks

1 —— medium all-purpose white potato, peeled, roughly cut

1 —— cup/120 g peeled, cubed butternut or Blue Hubbard squash or sweet pumpkin

1 —— medium onion, coarsely chopped

2 —— garlic cloves, chopped

2 —— cups/200 g green beans cut into 1-inch/2.5-cm lengths

2 —— cups/140 g coarsely chopped kale or cabbage or combination

1 —— cup/100 g elbow macaroni or other small pasta (optional)

1 —— tablespoon/18 g coarse kosher salt or to taste

Freshly ground pepper to taste

⅓ —— cup/80 ml Portuguese or extra virgin olive oil

1. In a large 8-quart/7.2-L soup pot, combine the water, presoaked beans, sweet potatoes, carrots, white potato, squash, onion and garlic. Cover the pot and bring to a boil over high heat. Reduce the heat to medium-low and simmer for 30 minutes. Mash a few of the potatoes and squash with a fork against the inside of the pot.

2. Add the green beans, kale and pasta and simmer for 10 minutes. Season with salt and pepper and stir. When the pasta is al dente, drizzle in the olive oil, simmer 1 additional minute and serve.

Cream of Linguiça Soup

Sopa de Linguiça

SERVES 4

This is a contemporary soup I created when Caroline Pacheco emailed me in search of this soup. Based on her description, the use of linguiça sausage reached a new height. The garlicky, paprika- and wine-infused pork sausage is delightful as a soup. The addition of cream tames the flavor so it is not overpowering (at least for me). It is a great soup for a simple meal, accompanied by a salad, some bread and olives. Still, this soup is elegant enough when passed through a fine sieve to be served as a first course for a special dinner. Caroline enjoyed my version, garnished with a dollop of the Puréed White Kidney Beans with Chouriço (page 225) or a sprinkling of chopped herbs.

¼ ——— cup/60 ml olive oil

½ ——— cup/80 g finely chopped onion or shallot

12 ——— ounces/340 g linguiça, casing removed

1 or 2 — garlic cloves, finely chopped

¼ ——— cup/60 ml white wine

1 ——— tablespoon/15 g tomato paste

2 ——— cups/470 ml water

2½ ——— cups/625 g precooked red or white kidney beans, with broth, or 1-pound/454-g can kidney beans, undrained (see Note)

1 ——— teaspoon/6 g coarse kosher salt or to taste

¼ ——— cup/30 g thinly sliced linguiça, for garnish

¼ ——— cup/60 ml light cream

Puréed White Kidney Beans with Chouriço (page 225), for garnish (optional)

Finely chopped parsley or cilantro

1. Heat the oil in a 3-quart/2.7-L pot over medium-high heat until hot but not smoking. Add the onion and sauté until lightly golden, about 5 minutes.

2. Cut the linguiça into small pieces and toss into the onion. Cook until the sausage takes on some color, about 2 to 3 minutes. Reduce the heat to medium. Stir in the garlic. Mix the wine with the tomato paste and add to the pot. Simmer for 1 minute.

3. Add the water along with the beans and their broth. Stir well and bring to a boil. Reduce the heat to medium-low and simmer for 10 minutes. Add salt if needed. Remove from the heat.

4. Using a stick blender, regular blender or food mill, purée the soup.

5. Sauté the slices of linguiça for garnish. Just before serving, quickly whisk in the cream. Ladle the soup into soup plates and garnish with the slices of linguiça, chopped or whole, or the puréed kidney beans, and then scatter finely chopped parsley over to serve.

Note: To serve as a light, elegant first course for a special occasion, before adding the cream, pass the puréed soup through a fine strainer, china cap or sieve, working it through. Then return to the stove to keep warm. Add the cream just before serving and garnish as in step 5, or float small toast points topped with a bit of Puréed White Kidney Beans with Chouriço (page 225) in the center of the soup as a garnish. Red beans will give it a deeper color.

If you have the time, use the dried beans, soaked overnight and cooked separately in fresh, unsalted water for 45 minutes.

Black-Eyed Pea Soup with Beet Greens

Sopa de Feijão Frade com Folhas de Beterraba

SERVES 6

In recent years I have converted to loving beets. Not the bland canned or jarred ones, but fresh ones. So much so that I just love them roasted and drizzled with an orange-infused dressing. But moreover, I love their greens. I have taken to adding beets to my garden patch and snip the greens as they grow. Thinking of what to do with this leftover bean salad we had eaten for two days as a lunch and a side, I did what Portuguese mothers and grandmothers do . . . I made soup, and did it with what I had on hand. Using the leftover tangy, vinaigrette-dressed black-eyed pea salad and incorporating chopped beets greens, I felt my father's presence. These greens carry even more nutrition than the beets themselves. I did use chicken broth in my creation, but vegetable broth will make it vegetarian friendly. The secret to this soup is to make the salad first and let it stand in its seasoning for at least several hours or overnight to absorb the flavors. The cilantro in the seasoning really clenches the soup. The salad is even better if made a day or two ahead.

FOR THE BEAN SALAD

½	pound/227 g dried black-eyed peas
½	cup/80 g finely chopped red onion
3	tablespoons/45 ml olive oil
1	tablespoon/15 ml wine vinegar or cider vinegar
1	tablespoon/4 g finely chopped cilantro
1	garlic clove, finely chopped
1	teaspoon/6 g coarse kosher salt or to taste

FOR THE SOUP

6	cups/1410 ml vegetable or chicken stock
½	cup/90 g rice
4	cups/280 g trimmed, rinsed beets greens, heavy stems removed, about 1 pound/450 g

Salt to taste

FOR THE BEAN SALAD

1. Soak the black-eyed peas in enough cold water to cover by 2 inches/5 cm. Let stand for several hours.

2. Drain the peas, place in a soup pot and cover with fresh water. Bring to a boil, turn down the heat and simmer for about 45 minutes. Drain. Transfer the black-eyed peas to a bowl and add the onion, olive oil, vinegar, cilantro, garlic and salt. Mix well, cover and let stand in the refrigerator for 2 to 4 hours, occasionally giving them a stir.

FOR THE SOUP

1. In a 4-quart/3.6-L soup pot, combine the black-eyed pea salad and the stock, then cover. Bring to a boil over medium-high heat. Toss in the rice and stir. Reduce the heat to medium and cook until the rice is almost done, about 10 to 12 minutes.

2. While the rice is cooking, roughly chop the greens. It will look like a lot, but these greens shrink like spinach. Add the greens to the pot and continue to cook over medium-low heat until the rice and greens are tender, about 10 minutes more. I don't think it will need salt but adjust to your taste. Ladle into bowls and serve.

Tomato Soup with Potatoes and Poached Eggs

Sopa de Tomate

SERVES 4

Use the meatiest, ripest tomatoes you can find for this soup or any recipe that calls for fresh tomatoes. In the fall, when I have an abundance of very ripe tomatoes in the garden, I love to make this soup. The intensity of tomato flavor spiced with paprika and cumin gives this soup a unique taste. The potatoes are usually roughly sliced into ¼-inch/6-mm rounds, but I cut them into ½- to ¾-inch/1.3- to 2-cm cubes.

3	tablespoons/45 ml olive oil, preferably Portuguese, Spanish or Italian
1	cup/160 g finely chopped onion
4	cups/720 g firmly packed, very ripe, coarsely chopped, peeled, seeded tomatoes
1	tablespoon/4 g finely chopped parsley or cilantro
1	bay leaf
1	large garlic clove, peeled, finely chopped
½ to 1	teaspoon sweet paprika
½	teaspoon ground cumin
2	cups/470 ml water
1	large potato, peeled, cut into ½-inch/1.3-cm cubes
1	teaspoon/6 g coarse kosher salt or to taste
½	teaspoon ground white or black pepper or to taste
4 to 6	slices day-old bread
2	garlic cloves
4 to 6	eggs

1. In a 3-quart/2.7-L pot, heat the oil over medium heat until hot but not smoking. Toss in the onion and sauté until lightly golden, about 5 minutes. Add the tomatoes, parsley, bay leaf, chopped garlic, paprika and cumin. Cover and simmer over medium-low heat until the tomatoes are married to the onions, about 10 minutes. Add the water, stir and recover. Simmer for 10 more minutes. Remove bay leaf. Purée and strain to remove any seeds at this point if desired.

2. Add the potato. Recover and return the soup to a boil. Reduce the heat to medium-low. Season with the salt and pepper and continue to simmer, covered, until the potatoes are tender, about 10 to 15 minutes.

3. While the soup is simmering, toast the bread and rub one side of each slice with a garlic clove. Set aside.

4. Poach the eggs separately in simmering water to the desired firmness or, when the potatoes are tender, crack the eggs into a bowl and slowly slide them one by one into the simmering broth to poach to the desired firmness. Place a slice of toast in the bottom of each soup plate and ladle the soup over, including an egg set on each slice of toast for each plate. Serve immediately.

Variation: To serve as an elegant first course, purée the soup and replace the traditional poached eggs and toast with a touch of cream and a sprinkling of chopped hard-boiled egg.

Clams, Scallops and Shrimp Soup
Sopa de Marisco

SERVES 6

On a recent visit to the seaside town of Ericeira, I joined my cousins Lili and Abel at a popular seafood restaurant, Estrela do Mar in Ribamar, where I enjoyed the best seafood soup. The owner wasn't willing to share his recipe so, as we ate, I wrote down flavors we all tasted and what was in the soup. The briny shrimp and clams with scallops, swimming in a well-spiced garlicky broth of curry, saffron, turmeric and cumin, and the surprising taste of peas, grabbed my attention. His version was thick enough that one could almost consider it a stew. I am sure there was something I could not identify, but this is an adapted, somewhat lighter version.

FOR THE STOCK

1 —— pound/454 g medium shrimp, peeled, shells and shrimp reserved separately

6 —— cups/1410 ml water

1 —— cup/235 ml white wine

2 —— celery stalks, chopped medium

1 —— small carrot, peeled, chopped into small chunks

1 —— cup/100 g precooked split peas, with their broth (optional)

½ —— cup/30 g chopped parsley

1 —— bay leaf

Generous pinch of saffron, toasted in a dry skillet, crumbled

FOR THE STOCK

1. Combine the shrimp shells in a 3-quart/2.7-L pot with the water, wine, celery, carrot, cooked split peas, parsley and bay leaf. Bring to a boil and reduce to a simmer. Simmer for 30 minutes, until the vegetables are tender. Strain. Add the toasted saffron to the stock and reserve.

(continued)

Note: Nail brushes, available in your department store's toiletry section, are the perfect little brush for scrubbing clam and mussel shells of grit. Keep this brush for the sole purpose of scrubbing the shellfish and nothing else. Throw it in the dishwasher for cleaning and store it in a small plastic bag to prevent accidental use on other food items.

FOR THE SOUP

1	pound/454 g littleneck or small clams
2	tablespoons/28 g butter
2	tablespoons/30 ml olive oil
¾	cup/120 g finely chopped onion
¼	cup/45 g finely chopped, peeled, seeded tomato
3	garlic cloves, finely chopped
2	teaspoons/6 g sweet curry
2	teaspoons/6 g ground turmeric
½	teaspoon cumin seeds, toasted in a dry skillet, then ground
½	teaspoon coarse kosher salt or to taste
¼	teaspoon ground white pepper
4	tablespoons/16 g finely chopped cilantro, divided
½	teaspoon hot sauce or to taste
1	large Yukon gold or other boiling potato, peeled, cut into 1-inch/2.5-cm cubes
¼	cup/60 ml red wine vinegar
¼	cup/60 ml freshly squeezed lemon juice
1	pound/454 g small bay scallops
1	cup/235 ml heavy cream

FOR THE SOUP

1. Under a steady stream of running water, scrub the outside of the clam shells of any grit using a clean new nail brush (see Note). Rinse the clams well, drain and set aside.

2. Heat the butter and olive oil together in a 4-quart/3.6-L soup pot. Dump in the onion and sauté until translucent, about 2 to 3 minutes.

3. Stir in the chopped tomato, garlic, curry, turmeric, cumin, salt, pepper, 2 tablespoons/8 g of the cilantro and hot sauce. Let the ingredients sizzle for about 1 minute. Dump in the diced potato. Pour in 5 cups/1175 ml of the reserved shrimp stock, wine vinegar and lemon juice. Cover and bring to a boil, then reduce the heat to medium-low and simmer for about 15 minutes, until the potatoes are nearly done, then add the scrubbed clams. Cover the pot and cook for 6 minutes. Add the scallops and reserved shrimp, then simmer for 3 minutes. If the scallops are large, cook them for 2 minutes before adding the shrimp, then simmer for 3 minutes. Gently stir. Discard any clams that fail to open.

4. Warm the cream in a small bowl by stirring in some of the hot broth to temper it and prevent curdling. When the cream seems warm enough, transfer it back to the pot of shellfish and simmer over low heat for about 30 seconds, stirring to blend well. The potatoes should be done, and the shellfish just tender. Garnish with the remaining 2 tablespoons/8 g cilantro. Don't forget to serve with bread for dipping.

Legumes, Vegetables and More

Legumes e Hortaliças e Mais

From the land, the Portuguese harvested a variety of crops: wheat, corn, legumes, root vegetables, olives, greens, nuts, tomatoes and fruits. More traditionally, with some exceptions, you would see vegetables most often in soups. Today, there is a wider variety of cultivated and imported vegetables that are utilized in Portuguese kitchens and not just in a soup pot. My father would use rutabagas, also known as yellow turnips, in his *sopa de couves* (kale soup) and also in a boiled dinner. Beet, kale and spinach greens sautéed with onions and garlic, sweet potatoes baked in breads and carrots in sweet fried fritters are all wonderful ways of enjoying vegetables. Taro root, called *inhames*, similar to a potato, is a very popular vegetable served in stews in the Azores and Madeira. We even make jam and preserves from tomatoes, spaghetti squash and quince.

When I wasn't in my father's garden, I might have been in my grandfather's. Having lost his hands in an industrial accident during the 1930s, my grandfather José enlisted the help of family for his small vegetable garden. Hoeing the dirt around the tomato plants and watering, my brothers and I would work under my grandfather's watchful eye. Today, when I till the soil around my garden plants, I feel his presence, instructing me silently as though he were sitting on one of my shoulders, and my father on the other side. It was a learning experience, although at the time I didn't realize it. Teaching gardening to the young and the rewards of growing your own vegetables, even if it is just tomatoes, are invaluable.

Whenever possible, use the freshest vegetables you can find, whether you grow them in your garden or purchase them from a farmers' market or the produce section of the supermarket. They are such an important part of our diet. Even the simplest method of vegetable preparation does not have to be boring. Tomato jam and spaghetti squash preserves add life to toast, as well as desserts. Use a splash of one of the vinaigrette sauces (*molhos*) on page 368 to give life to boiled potatoes and even fresh cheeses. The recipes in this chapter can be made vegetarian by eliminating the use of sausage or prosciutto where they are included with the ingredients.

Eggs Poached in Tomato Sauce
Ovos Escalfados no Molho de Tomate

SERVES 6

This is an old but still especially flavorful use for an abundance of tomatoes in the garden. I happen to like my eggs poached, but my friend Marguerite's cousin Regina likes to scramble hers right with the tomato base. The sweetness of the onions counteracts the acidity of the tomatoes, leaving the base the perfect complement to the eggs. Either way, they are wonderful. You can poach the eggs whole as directed or stir to scramble them with the tomato base.

½ —— cup/120 ml olive oil

1 —— medium onion, finely chopped

6 —— very ripe tomatoes, peeled, seeded, coarsely chopped

8 —— garlic cloves, finely chopped

Pinch of kosher salt or to taste

Ground pepper to taste

6 —— eggs

1 to 2 — tablespoons/4 to 8 g finely chopped cilantro or parsley

1. Heat the oil in a skillet set over medium heat until hot but not smoking. Toss in the onion and sauté until lightly golden, about 5 minutes. Mix in the tomatoes and garlic. Cook, stirring, until the excess juices are evaporated, about 4 minutes. Season with salt and pepper.

2. Crack the eggs into a shallow bowl. With the tomato base evenly covering the bottom of the skillet, make evenly spaced wells for each egg, then carefully lower and nestle each egg into the sauce. Simmer the eggs, spooning some of the sauce over them, for about 4 to 5 minutes, or until desired firmness. Serve, ladled over slices of toast, garnished with the cilantro.

Portuguese Croque Madame–Style Sandwiches

Francesinhas

SERVES 2

Rumor has it that this sumptuous sandwich was started in the northern city of Porto on the mainland. It is similar to the French sandwich *croque madame*, but heartier. Whatever the true origin, it is a big hit in cafés in Portugal, especially in Porto; it is such a hit that spin-offs of the sandwich are happening everywhere. Having enjoyed it there at a few different places, I noticed some cooks place a poached or over-easy fried egg on top of the cheese, while others place it under the cheese. Some versions of the sauce vary slightly. A fork and knife are required for this he-man of a sandwich. I have adapted the recipe here, for the home cook. You can make the sandwich leaner by using only the ham and one other choice of meat ingredients.

FOR THE SAUCE

2 ——— tablespoons/30 ml olive oil as needed

¾ ——— cup/120 g finely chopped onion

2 ——— garlic cloves, finely chopped

½ ——— teaspoon paprika

1 ——— bay leaf

¼ ——— cup/60 g tomato paste

½ ——— cup/120 ml water

½ ——— cup/75 g chopped boiled ham or *presunto* (prosciutto)

½ ——— cup/120 ml beer or white wine

2 ——— tablespoons/30 ml brandy of choice

½ ——— teaspoon coarse kosher salt or to taste

Hot sauce to taste

FOR EACH SANDWICH

2 ——— slices artisan or Portuguese bread, ½ inch/1.3 cm thick, or crusty roll cut in half horizontally

½ ——— 4- or 5-inch/10- or 12.5-cm piece linguiça sausage, split, sautéed

1 ——— thin beef, pork or chicken medallion, grilled or sautéed, sliced lengthwise

1 ——— slice boiled ham

4 ——— very thin slices mild melting cheese, such as St. Jorge or Havarti

1 ——— fried or poached egg to your liking

Olives, for garnish

FOR THE SAUCE

1. Heat the oil in a large pot over medium-high heat. Toss in the onion and sauté until golden, about 5 minutes. Mix in the garlic, paprika and bay leaf.

2. Blend the tomato paste with the water and stir into the onion. Add the chopped ham. Pour in the beer, brandy, salt if needed and hot sauce. Stir well to mix thoroughly, cover and simmer for about 10 minutes. Remove the bay leaf. Remove the sauce from the heat.

3. Using a stick blender or other means, purée the sauce. Strain and reserve the hot sauce until needed. Make sure it is hot before ladling over sandwiches so that it will soften the cheese.

FOR EACH SANDWICH

1. Place a slice of bread on a plate. Layer each of the meats, one by one, on top of the other. Add a second slice of bread on top followed by a fried or poached egg on top of the bread. Arrange 2 slices of cheese, crisscross, over the egg, covering it completely. (This sandwich can also, with or without the egg, be placed in an oven-proof pan and set under a broiler just to melt the cheese, then transferred to a shallow serving bowl. The egg can be placed under the cheese before placing in the oven or on top of the cheese after melting.)

2. Spoon some of the hot sauce (about ¼ to ½ cup/60 to 120 ml) over the top, melting the cheese a bit. Add some olives on the side. Serve with fried potatoes.

Madeiran Potatoes with Egg and Cheese

Batatas à Madeirense

SERVES 2 TO 4

Adapted from a Madeiran friend's verbal recipe, this dish is simple and perfect for home or a potluck take-along. Baked with a cheese topping, the buttery onion–egg yolk sauce adds a richness that complements the potatoes.

---

1 pound/454 g boiling potatoes (that hold their shape), peeled, cut into medium cubes

2 hard-boiled eggs, shelled, yolks and whites separated

1 cup/235 ml milk, divided

Generous 1 tablespoon/14 g softened butter

¼ cup/40 g finely chopped onion

Coarse kosher salt as needed

Ground pepper as needed

Hot sauce to taste (optional)

½ cup/60 g coarsely grated soft Azorean or Havarti cheese

1 tablespoon/4 g finely chopped parsley

1. Preheat the oven to 350°F/180°C, or gas mark 4.

2. In a pot, boil the potatoes in salted water until fork-tender, about 25 minutes.

3. Meanwhile, in a small bowl, combine just the egg yolks with ½ cup/120 ml of the milk, mashing them into a sauce. Chop the egg whites and reserve.

4. Add the remaining ½ cup/120 ml milk, butter, onion, salt, pepper and hot sauce. Add the cooked potatoes to the egg yolk sauce and turn to coat. Transfer to an oven-proof baking dish. Sprinkle the top with the grated cheese. Place under the broiler just to melt the cheese and give it a little color, about 5 to 10 minutes. Garnish with the parsley and chopped egg white.

Potatoes Roasted with Sweet Pepper Paste

Batatas Assadas com Massa de Pimentão

SERVES 6

Here I let my Alentejo blood influence the seasoning of the beloved potato. Layering sweet paprika with the salt-brined sweet pepper paste (*massa de pimentão*) gives the flavor a dimension worth tasting.

---

2 —— garlic cloves, halved

1 —— teaspoon/3 g sweet paprika

1 —— scant tablespoon/15 g Sweet Pepper Paste (page 367)

1 —— bay leaf, crumbled

2 —— tablespoons/8 g finely chopped parsley

¼ —— teaspoon ground black pepper

2 —— tablespoons/30 ml white wine

2 —— tablespoons/30 ml olive oil

6 —— medium-large red bliss or other roasting potatoes, peeled, rinsed

1. Preheat the oven to 375°F/190°C, or gas mark 5.

2. Using a mortar and pestle, mash the garlic with the paprika, making a paste. Incorporate the pepper paste, crumbled bay leaf, parsley, black pepper and wine. Drizzle in the olive oil and mix to make a spreadable paste.

3. Pat the potatoes dry and cut them into quarters. Put the potatoes into a large bowl and add the seasoning paste. Turn to coat them in the paste. Transfer to a roasting or baking dish and cover with foil. Roast for 30 minutes. Remove the foil, turn the potatoes and continue to roast them for 30 minutes more, uncovered, until tender. Season with salt if needed.

Note: If you cannot get the Sweet Pepper Paste, add 1 more teaspoon/3 g of paprika and mash the garlic with 2 teaspoons/ 12 g of coarse salt. The flavor will not be the same, but the potatoes will still be tasty.

Potatoes with Green Herb Sauce

Batatas Cozidas com Molho Verde

SERVES 6

There is one vegetable the Portuguese have no question about, and that is the potato. Potatoes are so versatile and are a great source of potassium. Why mash them when we can drizzle them with a number of different sauces? Here, the aromatic herbs, garlic and seasoning liven up the potatoes. We punch salt-roasted ones, scatter garlic over them and add a little stream of great Portuguese extra virgin olive oil over these earthly delights. Roasted, boiled or added to braises, potatoes deserve great praise. Here, the simply boiled potato is far from boring. Drizzled with herb sauce, the potatoes spring to life.

---

1 —— large onion, finely chopped

3 —— garlic cloves, finely chopped

1 —— cup/60 g finely chopped cilantro or parsley or combination

½ —— cup/120 ml wine vinegar

½ —— cup/120 ml olive oil

1 —— tablespoon/15 ml hot sauce

Coarse kosher salt to taste

Freshly ground pepper to taste

12—— small red bliss potatoes, peeled

1. Combine the onion, garlic, cilantro and vinegar in a bowl. Whisk in the olive oil and hot sauce, thoroughly mixing. Season with salt and pepper. Let stand for ½ hour. Do not chill.

2. While the dressing flavors are melding, put the potatoes in a pot and cover completely with water. Bring to a boil, reduce the heat to medium-low and simmer until fork-tender, about 25 minutes. Drain and transfer the potatoes to a serving bowl. Spoon the herb sauce over the hot potatoes, turning gently to coat completely, and serve.

Tomato, Onion and Potato Salad

Salada de Tomate, Cebola e Batata

SERVES 4

This salad is perfect for late summer or early fall, when the tomatoes and potatoes are freshly harvested.

---

4 ——— freshly boiled and cooled all-purpose or Yukon gold potatoes, cut into thick rounds

2 ——— meaty tomatoes, thickly sliced or cut into large wedges

1 ——— green bell pepper, thinly sliced into rounds

1 ——— sweet onion, thinly sliced into rounds

1 or 2 — garlic cloves, finely chopped

Coarse kosher salt to taste

Ground black pepper to taste

Olive oil as needed

Cider or wine vinegar as needed

1 ——— tablespoon/4 g chopped fresh cilantro or parsley

1. Arrange the potatoes, tomatoes, peppers and onions, alternating them, on flat salad plates. Scatter the garlic over. Season the vegetables with salt and pepper, then drizzle the olive oil and vinegar over. Garnish with chopped cilantro.

Note: For a large platter, create great eye appeal by combining a rainbow of various colorful bell peppers in the salad.

Garlic, Chile and Wine Simmered Potatoes

Batatas Cozidas em Vinho e Alhos

SERVES 4

Why boil potatoes in plain water when you can make them more flavorful? If you prefer not to use wine, use vegetable, chicken or beef stock, depending on what you are serving the potatoes with. The chile pepper paste has salt, so any additional salt is not really necessary, but go with your preference.

¼ ——— cup/60 ml olive oil

½ ——— cup/80 g finely chopped onion

2 ——— garlic cloves, finely chopped

1 ——— bay leaf

1 ——— teaspoon/3 g sweet paprika

1 ——— teaspoon/5 g Chile Pepper Paste (page 365)

4 to 6 — large boiling potatoes, peeled

1 ——— cup/235 ml white wine or stock as needed

Coarse kosher salt as needed

1. In a medium saucepan, heat the olive oil until hot but not smoking. Add the onion and sauté until lightly golden, about 5 minutes.

2. Toss in the garlic, bay leaf, paprika and Chile Pepper Paste, stirring to blend.

3. Mix in the potatoes. Pour in the enough wine to cover the potatoes. Cover and set over medium-high heat. Bring the contents to a boil, reduce the heat to medium-low and simmer, giving them an occasional turn, until the potatoes are tender, about 25 minutes. Drain the potatoes.

4. Taste for salt and adjust to your preference. Serve with any well-seasoned meat dish.

Fried Polenta with Kale Croutons
Milho com Couves Fritas

SERVES 6 TO 8

Tender polenta croutons speckled with kale and fried in olive oil make a great accompaniment to fish and stews. Patience is needed to make the cornmeal from scratch as well as constant stirring to prevent burning. Using a wooden spoon works well, but a whisk is great in the beginning to prevent lumps. You can use medium-grain white or yellow cornmeal. In some parts of Portugal, yellow cornmeal was most often used for the pigs. Depending on the dish I am serving, I like to sometimes use defatted broth from cooking a boiled dinner or stock made from beef, shrimp or chicken for extra flavor. The amount you get depends on the size you cut.

EQUIPMENT

Heavy-bottomed pot

Wire whisk

Long-handled wooden spoon with flat edge

1 ——— 9 x 12–inch/23 x 30.5–cm sheet pan with 1-inch/2.5-cm sides or large wooden cutting board

6 ——— cups/1410 ml water, broth or stock

2 ——— tablespoons/28 g butter

2 ——— teaspoons/12 g coarse kosher salt or to taste

2 ——— cups/280 g medium-grain white or yellow cornmeal (not instant)

1 ——— cup/70 g finely julienned kale, trimmed of heavy middle rib, washed, well drained, then chopped into ½- to 1-inch/1.3- to 2.5-cm pieces

Olive oil or corn oil, for frying

1. In a 3½-quart/3.2-L pot, bring the water with the butter to a boil over medium-high heat. When it is at a full rolling boil, reduce the heat to medium and gradually stir in the salt. Using a whisk, stir briskly while gradually pouring in the cornmeal in a thin stream. While continuing to stir, break up any lumps that occur. When it starts to get a little thicker, switch to the wooden spoon. Stir in the shredded kale and continue stirring for 25 to 30 minutes. Stir a little less now so the heat will build up underneath and create the steam that will cook the cornmeal, evaporating the liquid. Soon it becomes thick like oatmeal and will pull away more easily from the sides of the pot as you cook, stirring, for about 10 to 15 more minutes.

2. As it thickens, it will form bubbles that will burst and hiss. Be careful not to get burned by the spits. Cornmeal takes a lot of stirring to prevent burning, but it also takes a long time to thicken. It is done when you drag the flat edge of the wooden spoon across the bottom of the pot and any liquid has evaporated and the polenta pulls away from the sides of the pot. At this point, when it is thickened and the liquid has evaporated, turn it out onto a lightly oiled sheet pan or baking dish, spread to an even depth of 1 inch/2.5 cm or your preference and allow it to cool completely.

3. Cut into 1- or 2-inch/2.5- or 5-cm squares and pan-fry in olive oil until golden. The interior texture will be tender. You can also cut them larger and grill over hot coals for about 2 minutes on each side. The polenta can be served on the side with fried squid, shrimp or fish and even incorporated into a finished stew. This makes about one hundred 1-inch/2.5-cm square pieces, but cut to the size you want.

Rice with Herbs and Prosciutto
Arroz com Presunto

SERVES 4

The rice from Peniche on the mainland is said to be the best, but your favorite long-grain rice will work fine. This recipe is one of the most basic and you can build on it with a little creativity.

---

1 ——— tablespoon/14 g butter

1 ——— tablespoon/15 ml olive oil

1 ——— small onion, finely chopped

¼ ——— cup/20 g coarsely chopped prosciutto or chouriço or bacon

3 ——— cups/705 ml water or vegetable stock

¼ ——— cup/15 g finely chopped parsley

¼ ——— cup/15 g finely chopped cilantro

1 ——— bay leaf

1 ——— garlic clove, finely chopped

1 ——— teaspoon/6 g coarse kosher salt

1 ——— cup/190 g long-grain rice

1. Preheat the oven to 350°F/180°C, or gas mark 4.

2. In a 3-quart/2.7-L pot, heat the butter and olive oil over medium heat until hot but not smoking. Throw in the onion and chopped prosciutto and sauté until lightly golden, about 4 to 5 minutes. Mix in the remaining ingredients except the rice. Cover and bring the contents to a boil.

3. When the stock is boiling, add the rice, stir, cover and reduce the heat. Cook the rice until half done, about 10 minutes. Transfer to a 9 x 13–inch/23 x 33–cm baking dish, cover tightly with foil and bake for another 10 to 20 minutes, until the rice is tender and the water has been absorbed. Remove the bay leaf, fluff up the rice and serve.

Variation: I like to use coarsely chopped linguiça or chouriço sausage in place of bacon or *presunto*. Instead of finishing it in the oven, finish cooking it on the stove using just 2¼ cups/530 ml of broth instead of 3 cups/705 ml. Stir a spoonful of softened butter into the pot and remove the bay leaf before serving.

About Rice

In addition to onions and potatoes, rice is another constant pantry staple in a Portuguese kitchen that lends itself to a variety of dishes. It doesn't matter whether we cook plain buttered rice, seafood rice, elaborate Valencia rice and of course our rice pudding—we just love rice. With the wide variety of rice on the market, you will not be at a loss to find a favorite or two. For soups and rice puddings, the medium-grain rice is perfect, and the short-grain Arborio-style rice adds extra creaminess to rice pudding. Various long-grain rices result in a fluffier texture as individual grains stand out. Brown rice, which requires longer cooking, has the whole grain to give more fiber and vitamins. Be sure to rinse rice in a sieve before using unless you are making rice pudding. I do not recommend instant rice for the recipes in this book. Simmering times for rice is 20 minutes on average but can vary a little depending on the variety of rice that is used and the method of preparation. If you choose to use stock instead of water, match it to the protein you are cooking—chicken stock with chicken, seafood stock for seafood dishes and so on—to complement the dish and not confuse the taste buds. Use a heavy-bottomed pot for boiling rice to help prevent sticking and burning.

Roman Beans with Rice

Feijão Romão com Arroz

Serves 4 to 6

Not just for vegetarians, a meal of beans and rice is a great staple for lunch or Saturday supper. Adding some chopped kale or whatever greens I have on hand makes it tasty and completes the dish. Roman beans resemble the cranberry beans. Use freshly shelled beans whenever possible; otherwise, precook reconstituted dried beans or use drained canned beans.

FOR THE RICE

2¼	cups/530 ml water
1	cup/190 g long-grain rice
1	tablespoon/15 ml olive oil
1	teaspoon/6 g coarse kosher salt

FOR THE BEANS AND GREENS

3	tablespoons/45 ml olive oil
½	cup/80 g finely chopped onion
½	large green or red bell pepper, coarsely chopped
1	garlic clove, finely chopped
2	cups/500 g precooked Roman beans, drained
1	cup/235 ml water
1	tablespoon/15 ml vinegar
1	bay leaf
¼	teaspoon ground black pepper
¼	teaspoon cumin
1	teaspoon/6 g coarse kosher salt as needed
2	cups/140 g chopped leafy greens (kale, spinach or beet greens), heavy stems removed, rinsed
½	cup/50 g finely crosswise sliced scallion

FOR THE RICE

1. Bring the water to a boil in a 3-quart/2.7-L pot over medium-high heat. Stir in the rice, olive oil and salt. Cover, reduce the heat to medium-low and simmer for about 20 minutes, until the rice is tender. Set aside and keep warm.

FOR THE BEANS AND GREENS

1. While the rice is cooking, separately, in another pot, over medium heat, heat the olive oil and sauté the onion for 3 minutes. Add the chopped pepper and garlic. Stir in the beans, water, vinegar, bay leaf, black pepper and cumin. Taste for salt and add if needed. Cover and simmer for 10 minutes over medium heat.

2. Mix in the chopped leafy greens of your choice, recover and simmer over medium-low heat for 10 minutes. Cook until the beans are heated through and the greens still have a tiny bite to them. If you use kale, it will take about 5 minutes longer to cook than beet or spinach greens. Transfer the rice to a serving plate and ladle the saucy beans and greens over the rice and gently mix. Sprinkle the top with the thinly sliced scallion. Don't forget to discard the bay leaf.

Rice with St. Jorge Cheese

Arroz com Queijo de São Jorge

SERVES 3 OR 4

It goes without saying, we Portuguese love our cheese. Being a cheese lover, this is one of my favorite ways to enjoy rice and St. Jorge cheese at the same time. St. Jorge cheese has a distinct, indescribable flavor. We pair cheese with fruit, bread and wine, so it makes sense to pair it with rice. This is more of a contemporary rice dish inspired by Chef Jose Cerqueira. If you prefer a different and milder cheese, such as Havarti, use it.

2	tablespoons/30 ml olive oil
¼	cup/40 g finely chopped onion
2¼	cups/530 ml water or stock (see Note)
½	teaspoon coarse kosher salt
1	cup/190 g long-grain or converted rice
½	cup/60 g shredded St. Jorge cheese or other soft cheese

1. In a 2½-quart/2.3-L pot, heat the oil over medium heat until hot but not smoking. Toss in the onion and sauté just until translucent, about 2 to 3 minutes.

2. Pour in the water, cover and bring to a boil over medium-high heat. Stir in the salt and the rice. Recover and reduce the heat to medium-low. Simmer the rice for about 20 minutes, until tender.

3. Toss in the shredded cheese and stir gently to melt and distribute well. Serve immediately.

Note: Remember if you are using stock to match it to the protein you are cooking; i.e., chicken stock for a chicken dish, beef stock for beef and so on.

Variation: Sauté ½ cup/55 g diced chouriço sausage with the onion for a great flavor. This rice is great to serve with grilled shrimp, or it can be used to stuff and bake chicken breasts, fish fillets, and whole hot or bell peppers.

Rice with Spring Greens

Arroz com Grelos

SERVES 4

This is a healthy, flavorful side dish for any main dish, especially fish. You can use baby spinach, young turnip greens, broccoli rabe, young beet greens and even young escarole.

---

4 —— tablespoons/60 ml olive oil

1 —— tablespoon/14 g butter

1 —— medium onion, finely chopped (about ½ cup/80 g)

1 —— garlic clove, finely chopped

2 —— cups/470 ml water

1 —— cup/190 g long-grain rice

1 —— teaspoon/6 g coarse kosher salt

1 —— cup/70 g tender turnip greens, trimmed, rinsed, and coarsely chopped

1. In a 3-quart/2.7-L saucepan, heat the oil and butter over medium-high heat until hot but not smoking. Toss in the onion and sweat in the butter and oil until translucent, about 2 to 3 minutes.

2. Add the garlic, and when it becomes aromatic, about 30 seconds, add the water. Cover the pan and bring the water to a boil.

3. Toss in the rice and salt, stir and recover the pan. When the water returns to the boil, reduce the heat to medium-low and simmer for 5 minutes.

4. Add the turnip greens, stir and recover. Continue cooking for about another 15 minutes, until the rice and greens are tender and the water has been absorbed.

White Beans, Linguiça Sausage and Beet Greens

Feijão Branco, Linguiça e Folhas de Beterraba

SERVES 2 OR 3

Here is a quick lunch that I like to make. Beet greens, another wonderful leafy green, mingle with flavorful saucy beans and garlicky sausage. Change this up and use chicken or another meat instead of the sausage.

¼ —— cup/60 ml olive oil

½ —— pound/227 g linguiça sausage, cut into ¼-inch/6-mm rounds

1 —— medium onion, peeled, quartered

½ —— cup/90 g coarsely chopped peeled tomato

½ —— green bell pepper, coarsely chopped

2 —— teaspoons/6 g paprika

2 —— garlic cloves, finely chopped

3 —— cups/210 g chopped beet greens, heavy stems removed

2 —— cups/500 g cooked white kidney, butter or lima beans

1 —— teaspoon/6 g coarse kosher salt or to taste

¼ —— teaspoon ground black pepper or to taste

1 to 2 — tablespoons/4 to 8 g finely chopped parsley

1. Heat the oil in a skillet over medium-high heat until hot but not smoking. Toss in and sauté the linguiça sausage until it starts to pick up some color, about 3 minutes. Add the onion and sauté until translucent, about 2 to 3 more minutes.

2. Mix in the tomato, green pepper, paprika and garlic. Cook, covered, until the tomatoes are almost married to the onions and the peppers are tender, about 10 minutes.

3. Stir in the greens and beans and then recover. Simmer in the sauce until the greens are just wilted and the beans are heated through, about 5 minutes more. Adjust the seasoning of salt and pepper to your taste. Transfer to a serving dish and garnish with the parsley.

Green Fava Beans with Chouriço Sausage
Favas Verdes com Chouriço

SERVES 4 TO 6

May 1st is known as Fava Day, a day when, in Portuguese kitchens, pots of meaty green or brown fava beans (also known as broad beans) can be found on stove tops, simmering in an onion and tomato base. Fresh green favas can be difficult to get, but sometimes you need to go with the next best thing. Look for them in the frozen food section of some supermarkets or at a Portuguese market. Although fresh cooked and frozen ones give you control over the level of sodium, some jarred ones or canned varieties are great in a pinch. Here I have adapted this recipe, which my friend, Maria Coimbra, originally from São Miguel (St. Michael) island in the Azores, shared with me many years ago. Pair this with a refreshing glass of wine or beer and bread, of course, to sop up the juices. If you don't wish to use sausage, use chopped *presunto* or prosciutto. Serve as a side or main dish.

½ —— cup/120 ml olive oil, divided

½ —— cup/80 g coarsely chopped onion

½ to ¾ —— pound/227 to 340 g chouriço sausage, casing removed, sliced into ¼-inch/6-mm rounds

1 —— tomato, peeled, seeded, coarsely chopped (about 1 cup/180 g)

2 or 3 —— garlic cloves, finely chopped

2 —— tablespoons/8 g finely chopped cilantro or parsley

1 —— teaspoon/3 g sweet paprika

½ —— cup/120 ml white wine

4 —— cups (about 2 pounds/908 g) frozen green broad beans (do not thaw) or substitute kidney beans, chickpeas, lima beans (butter beans) or edamame

½ —— tablespoon/19 g coarse kosher salt or to taste

¼ —— teaspoon freshly ground white pepper

1. Heat ¼ cup/60 ml of the olive oil in a 3-quart/2.7-L pan over medium-high heat until hot but not smoking.

2. Toss in the onion and sauté until soft and translucent, about 2 to 3 minutes.

3. Add the sausage slices and cook until they take on a bit of golden color, about 2 minutes more.

4. Stir in the remaining ¼ cup/60 ml olive oil, tomato, garlic, cilantro and paprika and cover tightly. Reduce the heat and cook over medium-low heat for 10 minutes, until the tomatoes are married with the onions. Pour in the white wine, recover and bring the *refogado* (base) back to a simmer.

5. After a minute or two, add the unthawed beans and stir. Season with salt and pepper, adjusting to taste. Recover tightly and continue to simmer over medium-low heat for about 25 more minutes, pulling the pot back and forth across the burner to stir without opening the cover. Serve hot or at room temperature.

Fava Bean Stew

Favas à Moda da Olivia Cabral

SERVES 6 TO 8

Unlike the recipe for Fava Ricas on page 223, after soaking the beans, some cooks give each bean a slit to allow some starch to be released into the broth, giving more body to this stew. Delightful Delia, as I know her, shares her grandmother, Olivia Cabral's, recipe for favas. As always, read the recipe through first. If you use canned ingredients, taste for salt before adding any. I did not find the need for it, but you may.

4	cups/1000 g canned favas or 1 pound/454 g dried fava beans (see Note)
½	cup/120 ml olive oil
½	cup/112 g butter
2	large onions, coarsely chopped
1	pound/454 g linguiça sausage, sliced or coarsely chopped
¾	cup/45 g finely chopped parsley
1	tablespoon/6 g crushed dried red chile pepper
5	garlic cloves, smashed
½	teaspoon ground black pepper
½	teaspoon sweet paprika
¼	teaspoon wild marjoram or oregano
¼	teaspoon cumin
1	8-ounce/227-g can tomato sauce
1	4-ounce/112-g can tomato paste

Coarse kosher salt to taste

1. Drain the beans from the cooking water or from the cans.

2. Heat the oil and butter in a 4-quart/3.6-L pot over medium-high heat until hot but not smoking. Add the onions and sauté until translucent, about 2 to 3 minutes. Toss in the linguiça and all the seasonings. Reduce the heat to low and simmer for a few minutes to release the essence of the sausage and spices.

3. Mix in the tomato sauce and tomato paste and stir well. Simmer for a few more minutes over medium heat. Add the cooked or canned drained beans to the sauce. Taste for salt and adjust as needed. Stir again, cover and heat through. Let stand for about 20 minutes before serving.

Note: To prep dried fava beans, soak them overnight completely covered by at least 2 inches/5 cm of water. The next day, if making a slit, make the slit in the dark edge of each fava bean. You can slit them before soaking but they will be harder to cut. Transfer to a pot, cover with water and bring to a boil over medium-high heat. Reduce the heat and simmer for 1 hour, until soft. Drain. Use as needed.

We often hear, especially from the men in our Portuguese culture, va'damos, meaning "let's go." With tongue in cheek it is said, if not for the restlessness of the Portuguese male, then for the discoveries that would have been made by someone else or not at all.

Sautéed Beet Greens with Garlic

Folhas de Beterraba com Alho

SERVES 4

This is not only easy and healthy but also quick to make. Keep in mind the greens will shrink in volume just as spinach does. Use the brightest green and freshest leaves. As with any fresh greens, rinse well in cold water, especially the backs of the leaves, and discard any discolored or bruised leaves.

---

8 —— bunches beet greens (about 2 pounds/ 908 g) (reserve beet roots for another recipe)

¼ —— cup/60 ml olive oil as needed

2 or 3 —— garlic cloves, thinly sliced

Pinch of crushed dried chile pepper

1 —— tablespoon/15 ml vinegar (red wine, apple cider or even balsamic) or to taste

Coarse kosher salt to taste

Freshly ground black or white pepper to taste

1. Prepare the greens by removing the leaves from any heavy stems. Coarsely chop, then rinse the greens. Drain well.

2. In a large skillet, warm the olive oil over medium heat until hot but not smoking. Toss in the garlic and the crushed chile pepper. Cook just until the garlic is aromatic, about 30 seconds. Do not allow the garlic to brown. Remove the garlic slices and reserve.

3. Add the greens, give them a quick turn in the garlic and chile–infused olive oil and cover tightly. Cook over low heat just until the greens are tender and slightly wilted, about 5 minutes. Drizzle with vinegar to taste and season with salt and pepper. Turn the greens out onto a serving dish and garnish with the sautéed garlic slices. Additional olive oil may be drizzled over to taste.

Variation: Some vegetables are best roasted in their skins. Beets are one of those vegetables, and roasting them is less messy than other preparations. Preheat the oven to 425°F/220°C, or gas mark 7. Remove the roots and stems. Rinse and place in a roasting pan and seal tightly with foil. Roast for 45 minutes to 1 hour, depending on the size. They are done when easily pierced with a knife or fork. Cool, peel, dice into large cubes and mix into the seasoned sautéed greens.

Sautéed Kale with Pine Nuts and Onions
Couves com Pinhões e Cebola

SERVES 4

My family has always sautéed greens—spinach, kale, broccoli rabe, mustard greens, beet and turnip greens, even slivered green beans—for as long as I can remember. With garlic and bay leaf infusing the olive oil, and a touch of flour and apple cider vinegar, this method is simple, and simple works for many cooks. In this recipe, kale, one of my father's favorite greens, incorporates caramelized onion and pine nuts. The sweetness of the onions softens any harshness of the greens. You can also substitute almond slivers if you prefer. Toasting the nuts first gives another dimension to the dish.

½ —— cup/65 g pine nuts or almond slivers

2 —— pounds/908 g fresh kale or collard greens, rinsed, well drained, sliced into fine julienne (see Note)

¼ —— cup/60 ml olive oil, divided

1 —— garlic clove, smashed

1 —— bay leaf

½ —— cup/80 g chopped sweet onion

1 —— tablespoon/8 g flour or as needed

2 —— tablespoons/30 ml wine or cider vinegar

Pinch of crushed dried peppers

Coarse kosher salt to taste

Freshly ground pepper to taste

1. Place the nuts in a large, dry nonstick skillet over medium heat. Keep the nuts moving in the pan until they pick up some color; keep pulling the pan back and forth across the burner and occasionally tossing the nuts in the pan. Be watchful, as they can start to burn in the blink of an eye. Remove the nuts from the pan when lightly golden, about 2 to 3 minutes, and transfer to a cup.

2. Bring a pot of water to a boil and dump the cut kale into the water. Reduce the heat and cook the kale, uncovered, for about 5 to 7 minutes. Drain well. Set aside.

3. Heat 2 tablespoons/30 ml of the olive oil in a nonstick skillet over medium-high heat until hot but not smoking. Toss in the garlic and bay leaf, heating them until the garlic is lightly golden, about 1 to 2 minutes. Remove the garlic and discard the bay leaf. (The garlic is a treat for the cook.) Add the onion and sauté until medium golden, about 5 to 6 minutes.

4. When the onions are ready, add the remaining 2 tablespoons/30 ml olive oil. Incorporate the kale, turning it in the oil and onions, cooking for a minute or two. Sprinkle or sift the flour over the kale, tossing and turning the greens to distribute it evenly. Keep turning the greens over as they cook, about 1 minute. Splash the vinegar over the greens and add the crushed dried peppers. Season with salt and ground pepper and turn and toss again, about 30 seconds. Pull the pan across the burner, making the greens roll back and forth. Roll them out onto a serving dish. Scatter the toasted pine nuts over and cover to keep warm until needed.

Note: To prepare kale, remove the heavy ribs. Place one leaf on top of another and roll tightly like a cigar. With a sharp knife, slice the kale crosswise into very fine chiffonade rounds. Then cut the rounds crosswise to shorten the lengths of kale, otherwise, you will have green spaghetti-like strands.

Pulled Pork–Stuffed Kale Rolls
Couve Recheadas com Carne de Porco

SERVES 6 TO 8

This recipe puts good use to any leftover or even first-overs of Pulled Pork Shoulder with Onions and Peppers, page 36, and the cooking broth. Chill the broth and skim off the fat. The amount of kale is subject to the amount of pulled pork you have.

1 to 2	—	pounds/454 to 908 g kale or collard leaves, trimmed of heavy stems
3 to 4	—	cups/750 to 1000 g pulled pork (page 36)
1	—	1-pound/454-g can chickpeas, drained
½	—	cup/30 g finely chopped parsley
¼	—	cup/60 ml olive oil
3	—	garlic cloves, finely chopped
1	—	teaspoon/3 g paprika
3	—	tablespoons/24 g cornstarch
4	—	cups/940 ml defatted, cooled, reserved broth from cooking the pork shoulder or vegetable stock

1. Preheat the oven to 350°F/180°C, or gas mark 4.

2. Bring a large pot of water to a boil. Add the kale leaves, reduce the heat and simmer for 20 to 25 minutes, until flexible. Drain.

3. On your workspace, open one of the leaves and spoon about ⅓ cup/ 80 g or so of freshly made or leftover pulled pork about one-third in from the bottom edge, adjusting the amount to enable rolling. Roll the bottom over, then fold in the sides and roll up the stuffed green leaf. Repeat with the remaining leaves.

4. Line a 9 x 13–inch/23 x 33–cm casserole pan with small or torn leaves. Place the rolled ones, seam side down, onto the kale leaves. Scatter the chickpeas over the rolled kale leaves.

5. In a small bowl, whisk together the parsley, olive oil, garlic, paprika. Blend the cornstarch with the broth, then stir into seasoning mix.

6. Pour seasoned broth over the chickpeas and stuffed kale. Cover tightly with foil. Bake for 30 minutes, until the kale is tender.

Easy Green Beans

Feijão Verde Ràpido e Fàcil

SERVES 4

Snapping the ends of green beans is the first kitchen task I, my children and grandchildren learned. The fresh green beans are well complemented with the sweetness of squash or sweet potato. Spritzed with a little vinegar adds tang on the palate. If you are short on time, have the kids or hubby snap the beans and use frozen cut squash as a short cut.

---

1 ——— cup/120 g peeled, diced squash or sweet potato

2 or 3 — scallions, trimmed of roots and heavy green ends

¼ ——— cup/60 ml olive oil

1 or 2 garlic cloves, finely chopped

1 ——— pound/454 g fresh green beans, rinsed, tips snapped off

½ ——— cup/120 ml water

2 ——— tablespoons/8 g finely chopped cilantro

2 ——— tablespoons/30 ml cider or wine vinegar

1 ——— teaspoon/6 g coarse kosher salt or to taste

½ ——— teaspoon ground pepper or to taste

2 ——— tablespoons/16 g toasted pine nuts or almonds slivers (optional)

1. Put the cut squash or potato in a 2-quart/1.8-L pot with water to cover. Bring to a boil over medium-high heat. Reduce the heat and simmer the squash until tender, about 5 to 10 minutes. Drain and reserve.

2. Slice the scallions crosswise, forming narrow ¼- to ½-inch/6-mm to 1.3-cm rings. You should have about ⅓ cup/35 g.

3. Heat the olive oil in a 3-quart/2.7-L pot set over medium heat until hot but not smoking. Toss in the scallions and garlic. When the garlic is aromatic, about 30 seconds, add the green beans and water. Cover, reduce the heat to medium-low and cook the beans for about 6 to 10 minutes, or to the desired firmness.

4. Stir in the drained cooked squash, cilantro, vinegar, salt and pepper, tossing well, and simmer for 1 or 2 more minutes, leaving a little crunch, or cook to the desired tenderness. Remove from the heat and transfer to a serving bowl. Garnish with the nuts.

Stewed Peas with Linguiça Sausage

Ervilhas Guisadas com Linguiça

SERVES 4 TO 6

Introduced to Portugal by the Arabs during the time of their occupation, this is a dish that just may convert a non-pea eater to a pea lover. The concentrated flavor of garlic sausage infuses the onion and tomato base and complements the sweetness of the peas. Peas seasoned and stewed with garlic, tomato, white wine and onion are a flavorful change from the usual plain peas. This aromatic dish can also be made with baby green fava beans or even chickpeas. Using frozen tender peas makes this dish a snap to prepare in short order.

¼ —— cup/60 ml olive oil

2 —— ounces/56 g salt pork, cut into ¼-inch/6-mm cubes (optional)

4 —— ounces/112 g linguiça or chouriço sausage, cut into ¼-inch/6-mm slices

1 —— small onion, coarsely chopped (about ½ cup/80 g)

½ —— cup/90 g chopped seeded tomato or 1 tablespoon/15 g tomato paste

1 —— teaspoon/3 g paprika

1 or 2 — garlic cloves, finely chopped

1 —— bay leaf

½ —— cup/120 ml white wine

¼ —— cup/15 g finely chopped parsley or cilantro

¼ to ½ — teaspoon ground nutmeg or ground cumin

3 —— cups/450 g frozen tender peas

1 —— teaspoon/6 g coarse kosher salt or to taste

¼ —— teaspoon ground black or white pepper

4 to 6 — eggs (1 per person)

1. Heat the oil in a 2½-quart/2.3-L saucepan over medium-high heat until hot but not smoking. Add the salt pork and lightly brown, rendering the fat from it, about 5 minutes. Reduce the heat to medium. Stir in the sausage pieces and onion. When the sausage slices start taking on some color, about 2 to 3 minutes, add the tomato, paprika, garlic and bay leaf, and bring to a simmer.

2. Pour in the wine and stir in the parsley and nutmeg. Add the peas, season with salt and pepper and give everything a stir. Cover tightly. Reduce the heat to medium-low and simmer for about 15 minutes.

3. Make 4 to 6 wells in the peas, one for each egg. Crack the eggs and drop one raw egg into each well. Recover the pan and continue to simmer over medium-low heat for about 5 to 10 minutes, until the eggs are soft poached or to the desired doneness. You can also poach them separately; just cook the peas for 20 minutes and garnish each serving with a poached egg.

Peas Stewed with Lamb and Rice

Ervilhas Guisadas com Cordeiro e Arroz

SERVES 4

Anything with lamb was one of my father's favorites. I can still see him sniffing the mint leaves. He made this old family recipe with lamb, but you can also use pork as a variation. The flavor of lamb surrounds the peas without a strong gamy flavor. Infused with the essence of mint and garlic and the smokiness of the bacon, the peas are the center of this dish. This recipe is adapted so that you can use frozen peas. If you wish to use fresh ones, you must remember to add about 1 cup/235 ml of water. Cuts of meat with bone add extra flavor. Older cooks added a touch of lard as well, and though it does make a difference in the taste, I suggest using olive oil.

FOR THE LAMB AND PEAS

½ —— pound/227 g lamb shoulder or pork chops with bone (have the butcher cut it into 1- to 2-inch/2.5- to 5-cm pieces, especially if you get the blade cut) or use boneless

1 —— tablespoon/18 g coarse kosher salt or to taste

½ —— teaspoon freshly ground pepper or to taste

¼ —— cup/60 ml olive oil

4 —— slices smoked bacon, lean salt pork or Canadian bacon, cut into pieces

1 —— medium onion, finely chopped

1 —— teaspoon/3 g paprika

1 —— garlic clove, smashed or finely chopped

2 —— mint leaves, divided, 1 whole, 1 finely chopped

1 —— 1-pound/454-g bag frozen tender peas, unthawed

1 —— tablespoon/8 g cornstarch

1 —— tablespoon/15 ml water

FOR THE RICE

2¼ —— cups/530 ml water

1 —— cup/190 g long-grain rice

1 —— tablespoon/15 ml olive oil

1 —— teaspoon/6 g coarse kosher salt

1 —— tablespoon/15 ml cider vinegar or to taste (optional, can also be served on the side)

FOR THE LAMB AND PEAS

1. Season the pieces of lamb with the salt and pepper.

2. Heat the oil in a 3-quart/2.7-L saucepan until hot but not smoking. Toss in the lamb and smoked bacon and brown the meat evenly on all sides, about 4 minutes. Add the onion, paprika, garlic and chopped mint. Stir to blend the seasonings well with the meat. Sauté for 2 minutes. Stir in the peas.

3. Blend the cornstarch with the water and stir into the peas and onions. Cover tightly and simmer over medium-low heat until the peas are tender, about 15 minutes. Set aside.

FOR THE RICE

1. In a separate pot, bring the water to a boil over high heat. Add the rice, olive oil and salt. Reduce the heat to medium-low and simmer for 20 minutes, or until the rice is tender and the water is absorbed. Fluff the rice with a fork. Mix the stewed peas and lamb into the rice. Stir in the vinegar and remove from the heat. Serve with bread and olives. Garnish with the remaining whole mint leaf.

Chickpeas with Chouriço Sausage

Grão de Bico com Chouriço

SERVES 4 TO 6

What could be easier than this quick chickpea dish? Full of flavor and protein, this is perfect as a light lunch or a side dish. The nuttiness of the chickpeas comingles nicely with the concentrated base of onions, tomatoes and cumin. If omitting the sausage, add 1 teaspoon/3 g of sweet paprika. You can embellish this dish by mixing in fresh chopped greens during the last few minutes of cooking.

¼ — cup/60 ml olive oil

1 — pound/454 g chouriço sausage, sliced into ¼-inch/6-mm rounds

1 — large onion, coarsely chopped

2 — medium tomatoes, peeled, seeded, coarsely chopped

1 or 2 — garlic cloves, finely chopped

½ — teaspoon cumin or to taste

½ — cup/120 ml white wine

3 to 4 — cups/750 to 1000 g fresh cooked or well-drained canned chickpeas

1 to 2 — tablespoons/4 to 8 g finely chopped cilantro or parsley

1 — teaspoon/6 g coarse kosher salt or to taste

¼ — teaspoon ground pepper or to taste

1. Warm the olive oil in a large skillet over medium-high heat until hot but not smoking. Add the chouriço sausage and sauté until it starts to take on some color, about 2 to 3 minutes. Transfer the sausage slices to a dish and reserve.

2. Add the chopped onion to the pan drippings and sauté over medium heat until lightly golden, about 5 minutes. Mix in the tomatoes, garlic and cumin. Cover and cook over medium-low heat for about 10 minutes. Stir in the wine and bring to a simmer.

3. Toss in the chickpeas, cilantro, salt and pepper. Return the sausage to the pan. Reduce the heat to low and heat through, about 5 minutes, and serve.

Carrots with Cumin and Cilantro
Cenouras com Cominhos e Coentros

SERVES 4 TO 6

North Africa's influence on Portugal's food, especially in the Alentejo, is evident in this flavorful carrot dish. The use of almonds, spices, pomegranates and fruits, and the art of frying, are just a few examples of how Portugal's foodways were shaped. I use a touch of cream to give a bit of richness to the dressing.

FOR THE CARROTS

1 ——— pound/454 g carrots, peeled, cut crosswise into 1- to 2-inch/2.5- to 5-cm pieces or larger if desired

2 ——— tablespoons/30 ml olive oil

FOR THE SAUCE

½ ——— teaspoon cumin seeds

1 ——— teaspoon/6 g coarse kosher salt or to taste

4 ——— black or white peppercorns or a generous pinch of ground white pepper

Pinch of crushed dried chile pepper (optional)

2 ——— garlic cloves, finely chopped

1 ——— teaspoon/3 g sweet paprika

Juice of 1 lemon

2 ——— tablespoons/30 ml olive oil

½ ——— cup/30 g finely chopped cilantro or parsley

2 ——— tablespoons/30 ml heavy cream

½ ——— cup/65 g toasted pine nuts or almond slivers, for garnish

FOR THE CARROTS

1. Preheat the oven to 400°F/200°C, or gas mark 6.

2. In a bowl, coat the carrots with the olive oil. Transfer to a sheet pan and roast in the oven for 20 minutes, or to desired tenderness.

FOR THE SAUCE

1. While the carrots are roasting, make the sauce. Using a mortar and pestle, crush the cumin seeds with the salt until fairly fine. Next, toss in the peppercorns and dried chile pepper, grinding until they are well blended with the cumin and salt. Add the garlic, grinding until a paste is formed.

2. Mix in the paprika followed by the lemon juice. Transfer to a larger bowl. Using a whisk, whip the dressing while gradually drizzling in the olive oil. Stop periodically to taste the amount of lemon juice to your liking. Mix in the cilantro. Drizzle in the cream and stir.

3. Transfer the carrots to a serving bowl. Drizzle the sauce over, tossing the hot carrots to coat. Let stand for 15 minutes and serve garnished with the toasted pine nuts.

Easy Cream Cheese
Requejão Suave

MAKES 3 LARGE ROUNDS

This method may not make sense to cheese-making experts, but it works. This wonderful recipe for homemade cream cheese, from Maria dos Santos, is nothing but heaven to spread on crackers or crusty artisan bread. It is very rich, very decadent and preservative-free. Do not use ultra-pasteurized milk or creams if you can avoid it. Since they sometimes won't coagulate properly, it becomes hit or miss. Search for regular dairy products at smaller local dairies for the best success.

EQUIPMENT

Instant-read thermometer

Fine-mesh "butter muslin" cheesecloth

3 —— perforated cheese molds or baskets (or desired molds and sizes) (see Note

Small bowls or stainless steel shallow rectangular dish or tray with 2-inch/5-cm sides

Long-handled fine-mesh sieve or perforated spoon

1 —— gallon/3.6 L whole milk

1 —— quart/940 ml half-and-half

1 —— quart/940 ml heavy cream

6 —— junket rennet tablets, crushed with small amount of milk, or 1½ teaspoons/4 g powdered rennet

1 —— tablespoon/18 g coarse kosher salt

1. Using a large 8-quart/7.2-L pot, pour in the milk, half-and-half and cream, then stir thoroughly, about 3 to 5 minutes, to evenly blend. Set the pan of milk over medium-low heat and gently warm the milk to 97°F/36°C. Mix in the dissolved rennet and stir for 5 minutes to completely distribute throughout the milk. Stir in the salt. Continue to heat for 30 minutes more. Remove from the heat. Cover the pan tightly.

2. After 1 hour, check and you will find some firmness setting in. Recover tightly and let stand until curds feel fairly firm and are easily separating from the whey, about 30 minutes more if the curds need to firm up a bit more.

3. With a long-bladed knife, make cuts from one side of the curds to the other side, like dividing into hours on a clock. The curds should have a clean edge to them. This allows the whey to be released from within the large curds.

4. Line a large fine-mesh strainer with the fine butter muslin cheesecloth. Set the lined strainer over the sink or large pot. Pour curds into strainer. Pull up corners and edges of cheesecloth. Twist together, gently squeezing out excess whey. Allow most of the whey to drain out. Set the molds or cheese baskets into the small bowls or shallow pan. Using a large spoon, transfer the curds into the molds or baskets, pressing lightly. You can fill them to the top because as the whey continues to drain out, the curds will shrink. Cover with plastic wrap, pressing on the top. Chill for several hours, even overnight, before using. Occasionally, drain out the whey as it accumulates. This will not be a firm cream cheese, though it will become firmer in 4 to 5 days. It will be luscious and easily spreadable.

5. One hour before serving, drain any extra whey that has accumulated. Unmold the cheese and pat dry with paper towels or a clean kitchen cloth. Just before serving, pat dry again and center it on a serving plate with toasted bread rounds and perhaps a drizzle of Roasted Garlic Dressing (*Molho de Alho Assado*, page 370). Cheese should keep for a week or two when properly chilled.

(continued)

Once formed, curds are cut to release whey from within the large curds. Some whey is drained off before scooping curds into cheesecloth to drain off excess whey. A fine sieve can be used as well.

Note: Inexpensive plastic cheese molds and "butter muslin" can sometimes be difficult to find. Look for shops that sell cheese-making supplies. When I was growing up, my father would fashion molds out of empty tuna cans or soup cans. He would remove the top and bottom lids, wash the can rings thoroughly, and place them on a slanted cutting board before filling them. Once filled, the whey would drain out the bottom and flow down the board and into a tray or sink. If you need to do this, just set cans in a shallow sheet pan, fill, press lightly, cover with plastic and slant the board so the whey will drain out from the bottom. After 30 minutes, refrigerate, then tilt the pan to drain excess whey into the sink.

Mixed Meat and Bread Stuffing
Recheio de Carne e Pão

FOR A 20-POUND/9-KG TURKEY

This stuffing requires a little more work, but compliments to the cook make it worthwhile.
This is adapted from my friend Fatima Lima, who generously shared her family recipe. In my adapted version,
I use ground meats and sauté them first before mixing.

½ —— cup/120 ml olive oil, divided, more as needed

2 —— pounds/908 g ground beef

2 —— pounds/908 g ground chicken breast

½ —— pound/227 g linguiça, casing removed

Giblets of turkey (optional), finely chopped

2 —— medium onions, finely chopped

1 —— tablespoon/18 g coarse kosher salt or to taste

2 —— garlic cloves, finely chopped

½ —— teaspoon ground pepper

½ —— cup/112 g butter

1 —— 15-ounce/420-g loaf day-old peasant-style Portuguese, Italian or French bread, heavy crusts removed, shredded

¾ —— cup/45 g finely chopped fresh parsley

1 —— egg, lightly beaten

1 —— cup/235 ml low-sodium or salt-free beef or chicken broth or as needed

1. Heat ¼ cup/60 ml of the olive oil in a large cast-iron skillet over medium-high heat. Separately, brown each of the meats and the onions for about 10 minutes each, using more olive oil if needed, then transfer them as they become brown to a large bowl. To the browned beef, chicken, sausage, giblets and golden chopped onions, mix in the salt, garlic and pepper.

2. Melt the butter and mix into the meats. Stir in the shredded bread, parsley and egg. Pour in just enough broth, in small increments, so that it comes together into a messy ball.

3. Stuff your bird loosely. Don't forget to stuff the neck cavity as well.

Tuna Salad Graciosa Style
Salada de Atum à Moda da Graciosa

SERVES 3 OR 4

Just knowing this style does not include mayonnaise excites me. Onions really make the flavor of this dish. My friend Mary Gil shares this recipe, which calls for one packet of seasoning that contains monosodium glutamate; however, you can add your own amounts of the spices while controlling the sodium. It is so easy and yet it can be used as a filling for today's popular lettuce wraps to serve as small bites, eliminating the bread. Make sure the tuna is solid tuna packed in olive oil.

---

1 —— tablespoon/15 ml olive oil

1½ —— cups/240 g coarsely chopped onion

½ —— tablespoon/4 g sweet paprika

½ —— tablespoon/2 g finely chopped parsley (optional)

1 —— garlic clove, finely chopped

½ —— teaspoon Chile Pepper Paste (page 365)

½ —— teaspoon or generous pinch of saffron, toasted in a dry pan

¼ —— teaspoon ground cumin or to taste

¼ —— teaspoon ground turmeric

1 —— bay leaf

Coarse kosher salt to taste

1 —— tablespoon/15 ml red wine vinegar

1 —— 13½-ounce/378-g can olive oil–packed solid tuna, drained

2 —— hard-boiled eggs, shelled, sliced or quartered

Olives, for garnish

1. Heat the olive oil in a skillet over medium-high heat until hot but not smoking. Add the onion and sauté for about 4 to 5 minutes, until lightly golden. Mix in the seasonings, bay leaf, salt and vinegar. Cook a minute or two over low heat. Transfer to a serving bowl. Discard the bay leaf. Separate the tuna into large flakes. Add to the onions and gently mix. Garnish with the eggs and olives. Serve for sandwiches or on lettuce leaves to serve as a wrap.

Grandmother's Bread and Sausage Stuffing
Recheio da Minha Avó

FOR A 14-POUND/6.4-KG BIRD

My grandmother's stuffing was easy to make. Here I have added my own touches of mixing in linguiça and almonds. When using bacon, she would reserve about 6 slices or so to drape over the turkey before roasting it.

¼ —— cup/60 ml olive oil

¼ —— cup/56 g butter

1 —— onion, peeled, finely chopped

¾ —— pound/340 g chopped bacon, linguiça or chouriço sausage or *presunto* ham

Giblets from the turkey, chopped (optional)

½ —— cup/120 ml white wine

½ —— cup/30 g finely chopped parsley

¾ —— teaspoon ground cinnamon or nutmeg

1 —— teaspoon/6 g coarse kosher salt or to taste

½ —— teaspoon ground white or black pepper or to taste

12 —— cups/1200 g medium-packed day-old Portuguese, Italian, Greek or Spanish bread, heavy crusts removed, torn into 2-inch/5-cm pieces

1 —— cup/235 ml milk

3 —— eggs, lightly beaten

½ —— cup/65 g toasted almonds or pine nuts (optional)

¼ —— cup/25 g pitted, sliced black olives (optional)

1. In a large skillet, heat the olive oil and butter over medium-high heat until hot but not smoking. Toss in the onion and sauté until golden, about 5 minutes. Add the chopped bacon or sausage and giblets. Sauté until they have some color, about 2 to 3 minutes.

2. Pour in the wine, scraping up any caramelized bits from the bottom of the pan. Transfer to a bowl. Add the parsley, cinnamon, salt if needed and pepper.

3. In a second bowl, soak the bread in the milk, turning to coat. Let stand for 5 to 10 minutes. Squeeze out excess milk that hasn't been absorbed and mix the moistened bread, eggs, almonds and olives into the onions and bacon. Mix thoroughly with your hands. Adjust the seasoning to taste.

4. Loosely stuff the cavity of the bird shortly before placing it in the oven. This can also be baked separately from the turkey in a baking dish, for 20 to 30 minutes, in an oven set at 350°F/180°C, or gas mark 4, until the top is golden.

Chickpeas, Rice and Prosciutto Stuffed Peppers

Pimentos, Recheadas com Arroz, Presunto e Grão de Bico

SERVES 6

I love stuffed peppers and tomatoes. The nuttiness of the chickpeas matches well with the prosciutto enveloped with the flavor of jasmine rice. Sometimes, depending on what I have on hand, I use chouriço or linguiça sausage, which gives it a little more of a robust flavor. To make this meatless, skip the meats and add spinach or beet greens to the rice and chickpeas.

¼ —— cup/60 ml olive oil

½ —— cup/80 g finely chopped onion

2 —— garlic cloves, finely chopped

⅓ —— cup/35 g coarsely chopped prosciutto or chouriço sausage

1 —— cup/190 g long-grain jasmine rice

1 —— tablespoon/15 g tomato paste

½ —— cup/120 ml white wine

2 —— cups/470 ml water or vegetable stock

1 —— teaspoon/6 g coarse kosher salt

¼ —— teaspoon ground cumin

¼ —— teaspoon ground white pepper

2 —— tablespoons/8 g finely chopped cilantro, divided

1½ —— cups/375 g cooked chickpeas

1½ —— cups/180 g grated St. Jorge cheese

6 —— medium red bell peppers, cored

½ —— cup/50 g plain bread crumbs mixed with 3 tablespoons/45 g melted butter

1. Preheat the oven to 350°F/180°C, or gas mark 4.

2. Heat the olive oil in a 3-quart/2.7-L pot set over medium heat. Add the onion and sauté until translucent, about 2 to 3 minutes. Toss in the garlic and prosciutto, cooking for 1 minute.

3. Add the rice, stir and let it sizzle in the base. Stir the tomato paste into the white wine and then pour into the rice. Stir until the wine is absorbed by the rice, about 2 minutes.

4. Add the water, salt, cumin, white pepper and 1 tablespoon/4 g of the cilantro. Cover and bring to a boil. Lower the heat and simmer until the rice is almost done, about 15 minutes. Mix in the chickpeas and cheese. Remove from the heat.

5. Stuff the peppers with the rice and set them in a casserole dish that is just big enough to hold them tightly. Pour enough water around the peppers to come halfway up their sides.

6. Top each pepper with some buttered bread crumbs. Cover tightly with foil. Bake for 30 minutes. Remove the foil and bake for 10 to 15 minutes more, until the peppers are tender and the bread crumbs are golden on the top.

Brussels Sprouts with Chouriço
Couve-de-Bruxelas com Chouriço

SERVES 4 TO 6

Brussels sprouts were never one of my favorite vegetables until I cooked them with Portuguese flavors. Roasted or simply boiled, the flavor of Brussels sprouts is beautifully matched with sautéed onions, garlic, chouriço sausage, bell peppers and cilantro, allowing them to take on a new personality. I season cauliflower this way as well.

---

2 —— pounds/908 g Brussels sprouts, whole, trimmed of stems and outer leaves

¼ —— cup/60 ml olive oil

1 —— small onion, peeled, thinly sliced

½ —— red bell pepper, stemmed, seeded, cut into ¼-inch/6-mm strips

½ —— yellow bell pepper, stemmed, seeded, cut into ¼-inch/6-mm strips

4 —— ounces/112 g chouriço sausage, cut like fat toothpicks

½ —— cup/120 ml white wine

¼ —— cup/15 g finely chopped cilantro or parsley or to taste, divided

Coarse kosher salt to taste

Ground black pepper to taste

1. Place the Brussels sprouts in a 3-quart/2.7-L pot with enough water to cover and bring to a boil over medium-high heat. Reduce the heat and simmer until tender, about 20 minutes.

2. In a large skillet, heat the olive oil over medium-high heat. Add the onion, bell peppers and sausage pieces, sautéing until the onions have become lightly golden and the peppers and sausage have taken on some color, about 5 minutes. Pour in the wine and simmer for 1 minute, scraping up the bottom of the pan.

3. Drain the Brussels sprouts when they become tender and add to the pan of onions and peppers. Give the sprouts a turn in the vegetable base, and mix in 2 tablespoons/2 g of the cilantro. Taste for salt and adjust. Simmer for 1 minute. Season with pepper and serve garnished with the remaining 2 tablespoons/8 g cilantro.

Cauliflower with Proscuitto

Couve Flor com Presunto

SERVES 4 TO 6

Cauliflower is one of those vegetables that we like to use in a boiled dinner. My grandmother would cook it in a pot with green beans and salted cod fish. Everything would be drizzled with oil and vinegar with a scattering of garlic.

---

1 —— large head cauliflower, trimmed, separated into florets

¼ —— cup/60 ml olive oil

½ —— cup/40 g proscuitto/presunto, coarsely choppned

1 or 2 — garlic cloves, chopped

Coarse kosher salt to taste

Ground white pepper to taste

1 —— part apple cider vinegar or wine vinegar to taste

1 —— part extra virgin olive oil to taste

1. Preheat the oven to 400°F/200°C, or gas mark 6.

2. Place the cauliflower in a bowl, drizzle with the oil and toss to coat the florets. Transfer to a sheet pan and roast, turning occasionally, for 20 minutes, until fork-tender.

3. Transfer the cauliflower to a serving bowl and add the proscuitto and garlic. Season with salt and pepper to taste and drizzle with equal parts vinegar and extra virgin olive oil, adjusting to taste. Serve.

Spaghetti Squash Preserves
Doce de Gila/Chila

MAKES 4 TO 5 CUPS/1000 TO 1250 G

Gila, also known as *chila*, falls into the family of pumpkins and squashes, particularly the spaghetti squash. At one time in Portugal, the cream and emerald green speckled oval squash would be thrown on the stone floor to break open, rinsed and placed in a pot to cook, with the explanation that cutting it with knives would cause it to turn black (most likely from carbon knives). No need for that today; just a really strong, stainless steel knife and a little muscle is all that is required to cut the squash open. The Portuguese *gila* is the cousin to the pale yellow spaghetti squash here in the United States. Both shred into flax-colored spaghetti-like strands after cooking. Teresa Gonçalves Baker shares her Tia Isaura's recipe that was described in the typical Portuguese manner to her. I have adapted the recipe here and hopefully streamlined it enough for the adventurous cook. This preserve almost has the texture of marmalade and is wonderful on toast as well as incorporated into desserts. If you are going to use this within a week or two, follow the directions below. For longer keeping purposes, see the note at the end of the recipe.

EQUIPMENT

Sterilized canning jars of 1 to 2 cups/225 to 450 g capacity

TWO DAYS AHEAD

| 1 | ——— | spaghetti squash, about 4 to 5 pounds/ 1.8 to 2.3 kg, rinsed, cut in half, stem, seeds and fibrous threads removed, left unpeeled |
| 3 | ——— | lemons, quartered, divided |

TWO DAYS AHEAD

1. Place the squash, cut side down, into a large pot. Add enough water to cover. Bring to a boil, reduce the heat to medium-low and cook until quite tender, about 30 to 40 minutes. You should be able to see the peel pulling away from the meat of the squash when poked with a butter knife. Drain and set in a large bowl; cool a little and then cover with ice cold water.

2. When cool enough to handle, remove the peels. They should come off easily. Pull apart the strands of the squash and place in a separate bowl. Squeeze the juice from 1 lemon over the squash strands and add just enough cold water to cover. Add the squeezed lemon rinds to the bowl and toss with the squash strands to coat. Place in the refrigerator for 24 hours, changing the water two more times, adding the juice and rind of 1 fresh lemon each time.

THE NEXT DAY

1. Drain the squash, pressing out the water. Allow the squash to set in a sieve over a bowl for several hours for any excess water to drain. Hand-shred any pieces that have not separated into strands. Remove the lemon quarters. Makes 4½ to 5 cups/1150 to 1275 g.

(continued)

FOR THE PRESERVES

6½ —— cups/1300 g sugar (see Note)

¾ —— cup/180 ml water

Zest of 1 lemon or orange

4-inch/10-cm piece of cinnamon stick, broken in half, or 1 teaspoon/3 g ground cinnamon

FOR THE PRESERVES

1. Stir the sugar with the water in a 5-quart/4.5-L pot. Toss in the lemon zest and the cinnamon stick. Bring to a boil over high heat and cook until the sugar dissolves. Mix in the strands of squash, reduce the heat to medium-low and simmer for about 20 to 30 minutes, stirring frequently. It will have the consistency of thick marmalade. You will briefly see the bottom of the pot when you draw a spoon through it. It will not be mushy but will have some texture, like short al dente spaghetti pieces. Remove the cinnamon stick and cool completely. It will thicken more as it cools. If you cook it too long you will evaporate the syrup and the mixture will be too dry. When done it should have a loose marmalade texture.

2. Pack into sterilized canning jars and cover with rounds of wax paper that are cut larger than the jar's opening. Place the metal caps on and tighten. Refrigerate until needed.

Note: For long storage, you need to follow the canning process, which requires you to wash jars and lids and place them in boiling water to sterilize. Fill the jars with the hot mixture using a sterilized canning funnel. Put the lids on, then loosely screw on the jar rings. Set the jars on a rack in a large pot of boiling water, with enough water to cover by 1 to 2 inches/2.5 to 5 cm, and simmer for 15 minutes to process. Canning instructions and equipment are available at kitchen and housewares stores.

Sweet Tomato Jam
Doce de Tomate

MAKES 2 CUPS/500 G

Harvesting a plethora of meaty ripe tomatoes, I can make multiple savory dishes. In addition to the savory dishes, I make a sweet, cinnamon-infused tomato jam. It is so delicious, not only on toast but also as a filling for cakes and pastries. The flavor is the very best from freshly harvested, very ripe, meaty tomatoes, which makes me looked forward to harvest time every year. Although plain canned tomatoes could be used, they really are not worth the effort for this recipe.

EQUIPMENT

Flat-edged wooden spoon

2 ——— 8-ounce/227-g sterile jars with tight-fitting lids

3 ——— pounds/1362 g very ripe, meaty tomatoes

1 ——— cup/200 g sugar (1 cup/200 g for every 2 pounds/908 g of drained tomatoes)

1 ——— 3-inch/7.5-cm piece of cinnamon stick

Peel of 1 lemon

1 ——— teaspoon/6 g table salt

1. Bring a large pot of water to a boil over high heat. Have ready a bowl of ice water.

2. Remove the stems from the tomatoes. Make a slight crosshatch score with a knife at the base of the tomatoes. Plunge the tomatoes into the boiling water for 1 minute. Remove the tomatoes (the skin should be starting to separate) and plunge into the ice water. Peel off the skins, remove the seeds and coarsely chop the tomatoes. Don't worry if you still have some seeds; they add flavor. Let the tomatoes sit in a sieve set over a bowl, covered, for several hours or place in the refrigerator overnight to drain. After draining, the weight will be about 2 pounds/908 g.

3. Combine the tomatoes with the sugar, cinnamon stick, lemon peel and salt in a medium pot. Place over medium-high heat and bring to a boil, boiling for 5 to 10 minutes. Reduce the heat to medium-low and simmer the tomato jam for about 45 minutes, stirring frequently, until thickened and reduced by about two-thirds. You should be able to see the bottom of the pot when you draw the flat edge of the wooden spoon through the jam. It will thicken more as it cools.

4. Discard the lemon peel and cinnamon stick. Pack into small jars and use within 3 weeks, stored in the refrigerator. For longer storage, use the canning process (see page 214).

Tomatoes, sugar, lemon and cinnamon are slowly simmered until reduced. When ready, a spoon drawn across the bottom will leave a visable line.

Little Tastes
Petiscos e Salgadinhos

No matter the meal, our "little taste" starters are considered appetizers by non-Portuguese. What might have been served as a typical lunch or light dinner at home has graduated to outside the box. No longer are the restaurant starters of *petiscos* and *salgadinhos* (usually saltier fried savory pastries) limited to salt-brined lupine beans, pickled vegetables, sautéed linguiça, fried fish cakes and the like. Smaller plate versions of lunch or dinner dishes are now popping up on menus as "little tastes," or even as a main meal for the light eater. The use of starters has become more and more popular as creativity and variety have grown, especially in Portuguese restaurants. However there isn't any need to go to a restaurant to enjoy them. Here I have included the traditional as well as some newer ones.

Shrimp with Goat Cheese
Camarão com Queijo de Cabra

SERVES 2 TO 4

Serving this starter, which happens to be one of my husband's favorites, with crusty Portuguese or artisan bread is a must to sop up the sauce. This is a spin-off of my father's peel-and-eat shrimp dish, where soft goat cheese gives just the right counterpoint to the spiciness of the sauce. The flavorful garlicky sauce envelopes the shrimp and goat cheese, with the bell peppers balancing the acidity of the tomatoes. It teases the taste buds in the end with a spicy little kick. Having guests? Double the recipe and serve this over rice and you have a special meal.

---

2 ——— tablespoons/30 ml olive oil

2 ——— tablespoons/28 g butter

¼ ——— cup/40 g finely chopped onion

½ ——— green bell pepper, chopped into 1-inch/2.5-cm chunks

1 ——— cup/180 g chopped, seeded tomato

1 ——— garlic clove, finely chopped

1 ——— teaspoon/3 g paprika

Generous shake or two of hot sauce

¾ ——— pound/340 g (21/26 count) large shrimp, shelled and deveined

½ ——— teaspoon coarse kosher salt or to taste

Pinch of ground white pepper

½ ——— cup/75 g goat cheese, chilled, then crumbled or cut into medium pieces

1 ——— tablespoon/4 g finely chopped cilantro or parsley

1. Heat the olive oil and butter in a medium skillet over medium heat until hot but not smoking. Toss in the onion and sauté just until soft and translucent, about 2 to 3 minutes. Mix in the chopped pepper, tomato, garlic, paprika and hot sauce. Cover and bring to a boil over medium-high heat. Reduce the heat to medium-low, stir, recover and simmer until the sauce starts to come together and the tomatoes are married to the onions, about 10 minutes.

2. Add the shrimp, season with salt and ground pepper, stir and simmer for 3 minutes, just until the shrimp are no longer translucent, start to curl, turn pink and are cooked through. If you use larger shrimp, adjust the cooking time.

3. Transfer to a serving dish and garnish with the goat cheese scattered over the top followed by the cilantro. Serve with crusty bread to dip in the sauce.

Cilantro Garlic Dipping Oil
Azeite com Alho e Coentros

MAKES ABOUT 1½ CUPS/355 ML

This is perfect dipping oil for fresh Portuguese or artisan bread to start off your meal accompanied by your favorite wine or beer. The blending of fruity extra virgin olive oil, aromatic garlic and heady cilantro with a touch of heat perks up the taste buds. Warm your bread ahead of time in the oven and enjoy!

---

1 ——— cup/235 ml good-quality Portuguese or Italian extra virgin olive oil

¼ ——— cup/15 g finely chopped very fresh cilantro

½ ——— teaspoon coarse kosher salt or to taste

1 or 2 — garlic cloves, finely chopped

Dash or two of ground white or black pepper to taste

Splash or two of hot sauce

1. Combine all the ingredients in a small bowl and let stand for 1 or 2 hours so all the components have infused the olive oil. Serve with fresh bread or brush onto toasted slices of Portuguese corn bread, or other crusty artisan bread.

Zesty Linguiça Spread
Picadinho de Linguiça

MAKES 1 CUP/225 G

Although this isn't traditional, the creamy spread works great with toast points or just fresh Portuguese or crusty artisan bread. Keeping simplicity in mind, I thought the cream cheese worked well as a binder and downplayed the garlic without hiding the heady flavor of the linguiça sausage. Chouriço sausage works equally well. Accompanied with a little wine, some olives and crusty bread, this tasty starter always settles us while we are waiting for dinner.

½ —— pound/227 g linguiça or chouriço sausage, casing removed

1½ —— teaspoons/7.5 ml olive oil

¼ —— cup/40 g finely chopped onion

4 —— ounces/112 g softened or whipped cream cheese

1½ —— tablespoons/6 g finely chopped parsley

Dash or two of hot sauce to taste

1. Cut the linguiça into small pieces.

2. Heat the oil in a skillet and add the pieces of linguiça and the onion. Sauté until the sausages get some color and the onions are soft and lightly golden, about 4 minutes. Cool completely, then transfer to the bowl of a food processor.

3. Process for about 20 to 30 seconds, or until the meat and onions are fairly fine. Transfer to a bowl and fold in the cream cheese and parsley, mixing thoroughly. Add the hot sauce, blending well. Serve immediately or cover and chill. Bring out ½ hour before using. Spread on toast points or fresh bread.

Variation: Get creative and spread this over a sheet of puff pastry dough. Roll the dough up and bake on parchment-lined sheet pan at 350°F/180°C, or gas mark 4, until golden. Slice and serve warm. Or you can add rounded teaspoons to miniature filo cups and serve as an appetizer at a gathering.

Creamy Sardine Spread
Picadinho de Sardinhas Cremosas

MAKES ABOUT ¾ CUP/180 G

In Portugal, many little restaurants, especially sidewalk cafés, place a little tin of sardine pâté on the table. My version is easy to make using cream cheese and scallions to tone down the flavor of the sardines while giving it some spirit with Dijon mustard. Although you may enjoy whole char-grilled or broiled sardines as part of a meal, this simple recipe is definitely a keeper for those times when there is a sardine or two left over (I know, hard to believe). Sardines can also be cooked specifically for this recipe or if you don't have any fresh or frozen ones, drain a tin of canned ones. If you use grilled sardines, the spread will have a smoky flavor. The flavor can also be as subtle or as strong as you like by the amount of cream cheese you mix in.

---

1 — generous cup/225 g flaked sardines, grilled or broiled, skin, innards and bones removed, or one 4-ounce/112-g can, packed in olive oil, drained

3 — tablespoons/45 g regular cream cheese, softened

2 — tablespoons/12 g finely chopped scallion

1 — tablespoon/4 g finely chopped parsley

1½ — teaspoons/6 g Dijon mustard or to taste

1 — garlic clove, finely chopped

1 — teaspoon/5 g tomato paste

½ — teaspoon hot sauce

½ — teaspoon coarse kosher salt or to taste

Ground white pepper to taste

1. Transfer the fish to a bowl and flake into small pieces using the flat side of a fork. If you use the canned, drain well and pat dry, gently removing most of the skin, main bones and heads. Mix in the cream cheese, scallion, parsley, mustard, garlic, tomato paste, hot sauce, salt if needed and white pepper. Mix well, thoroughly blending for about 1 minute. Chill until needed and serve on toasted bread points or crackers.

Puréed White Kidney Beans with Chouriço

Picadinho de Feijão Branco com Chouriço

MAKES 1 CUP/240 G

A mix of garlicky sausage, fruity olive oil and scallions married to puréed kidney beans is perfect for toast points or for garnishing soups. This can be made vegetarian friendly with great success by eliminating the sautéed smoked sausage. Both ways are great. It just depends what you like. If you use a smoked linguiça or chouriço, the flavor of the beans is less pronounced. You can choose to purée the beans and leave some texture or push through a sieve for a smoother mouthfeel.

---

1 —— cup/250 g cooked white kidney beans, well drained

1 or 2 — scallions, finely chopped

1 —— garlic clove, finely chopped

½ —— teaspoon Chile Pepper Paste (page 365) or hot sauce

¼ —— teaspoon ground cumin

¼ —— cup/25 g finely chopped chouriço or linguiça sausage

1 —— tablespoon/15 ml extra virgin olive oil as needed

1 —— teaspoon/6 g coarse kosher salt or to taste

2 —— tablespoons/8 g finely chopped cilantro or parsley, divided

1. Drain any cooking water from the beans. Purée the beans by hand using a food mill, removing the skins at the same time, or use a food processor to process the beans until smooth, then press through a sieve into a medium bowl. Add the scallion, garlic, Chile Pepper Paste and cumin and mix well. Set aside.

2. Sauté the chopped sausage in a skillet with the olive oil over medium-high heat until the sausage picks up some color and releases some juices, about 2 minutes. Remove from the heat. Mix the sausage with the seasoned puréed beans. Taste for salt and season to taste as needed. Toss in 1 tablespoon/4 g of the cilantro and mix well. To use, plop a tablespoon or two in the middle of a bowl of soup as a garnish or transfer to a small serving bowl, scattered with the remaining 1 tablespoon/4 g cilantro, and serve with toast points as a starter.

Salt Cod Croquettes of St. Michael Island
Croquetes de Bacalhau de São Miguel

MAKES ABOUT 3 DOZEN

Are these croquettes better than the traditional mainland codfish cakes, *bolinhos de bacalhau*, made with salt cod, potato, eggs, onion and seasonings (recipe in *Portuguese Homestyle Cooking*)? "Better" is a matter of preference. Both are equally delicious and flavorful. I love them both. It was on the island of São Miguel that my friend Margarida Bettencourt Carvalho generously shared her recipe. These croquettes have a creamy rich mouthfeel with a denser texture than the mainland counterpart. The trick to these is to have the nutmeg-infused béchamel sauce as thick as possible and use only what is absolutely necessary in small increments. If you use too much sauce, you will have a gloopy mess that will prevent shaping the croquettes. Preparing the batch a day ahead and refrigerating it helps in shaping the croquettes.

FOR THE FISH

TWO DAYS AHEAD

1 ———— pound/454 g salt cod, soaked in several changes of water for 24 to 36 hours, refrigerated (see page 102)

FOR THE WHITE SAUCE

4 ———— tablespoons/56 g butter

2 ———— large onions, finely chopped (about 1 cup/160 g)

½ ———— cup/30 g finely chopped parsley

½ ———— teaspoon ground white pepper

¾ ———— cup/90 g flour

Pinch of ground nutmeg

1 ———— cup/235 ml whole milk or as needed

Coarse kosher salt to taste

COOKING THE FISH

1. After soaking, bring 2 quarts/1.8 L of water to a boil in a 4-quart/3.6-L pot over high heat. Drain and rinse the fish from the soaking water. Add the fish to the hot water, cover and turn off the heat. Let the fish poach in the water for 15 minutes.

2. With a slotted spoon, transfer the fish to a bowl. When it is cool enough to handle, blot dry and remove any skin and bones. Using a meat grinder, process the fish into small pieces or finely chop the fish using a chef's knife and cutting board. Transfer the fish to a large bowl and reserve.

FOR THE WHITE SAUCE

1. Melt the butter in a large skillet. Add the onions and sauté until translucent, about 2 to 3 minutes. Stir in the parsley and white pepper. Gradually, with a whisk, mix in the flour and nutmeg. Cook for 1 minute, until the flour is emulsified into the butter and onions. When the flour-butter emulsion starts to bubble, gradually, while whisking quickly, pour in just enough of the cold milk to make a very thick white sauce. Stirring constantly, cook over medium-low heat until it is very thick and starts to bubble, about 10 minutes. Remove from the heat.

2. Mix in the shredded fish. If the mix is too thick to stir, add just a little milk, about ¼ cup/60 ml at the most. Do not go over 1¼ cups/295 ml of total milk. The batter should be thick enough to hold a shape once the fish is added. Taste to make sure the batter has enough salt. Add a very small amount if it is needed. Allow the mix to cool completely. I like to cover and chill this for several hours or overnight to stiffen it.

TO COOK

Corn oil or grapeseed oil, for frying

1 ——— egg, beaten with 1 tablespoon/15 ml water for wash

Plain bread crumbs as needed

Hot sauce (optional)

TO COOK

1. Heat 5 inches/12.5 cm of oil in a deep saucepan to 350°F/180°C.

2. Take a tablespoon/15 g of the well-chilled croquette mix and gently shape with your hands into a thumb-size log. Dip quickly into the egg wash and then roll in the bread crumbs, coating evenly. Place on a plate or sheet pan. Repeat with the remaining croquette mix.

3. Carefully lower 3 or 4 croquettes into the hot oil to fry. Do not crowd the pot because it will lower the temperature of the oil and they will become greasy. Fry until golden and remove to drain on paper toweling. (These can also be frozen on tightly wrapped parchment-lined sheet pans for future use.)

Chestnuts with Anise

Castanhas com Anis

MAKES 2 POUNDS/908 G

In Portugal, earthy aromas filling the fall air signal street vendors are nearby selling chestnuts hot off the roasting cart. Portuguese cooks know full well the wonderful sweetness of chestnuts, whether they are roasted or boiled with salt alone or together with anise. Try serving these up with a nice glass of tawny port or sweet wine. If you don't care for the flavor of anise, just omit it. The boiling method used here results in a more tender texture. Chestnuts peel easiest while still fairly hot. Be careful not to burn your fingers.

---

2 —— pounds/908 g chestnuts, rinsed

1 —— tablespoon/18 g coarse kosher salt as needed

½ —— teaspoon anise or fennel seeds (optional)

1. Carefully, with a sharp paring knife, make a horizontal slit, about ⅛ inch/ 3 mm deep, completely around the middle of each chestnut. Be sure to cut the skin to the meat but not into the meat of the chestnut. Some cooks make a deep crosshatch slit on the top point of the chestnut.

2. Dump the chestnuts into a pot and cover completely with water. Add the salt and anise seeds. Cover and bring to a boil over medium-high heat. Reduce the heat to medium-low and simmer for 18 to 20 minutes, until tender.

3. Remove from the heat, drain and start peeling away for a great treat. These get harder to peel as they cool off. Traditionally, these are served on the feast of São Martin, November 11, along with fried fish drizzled with a traditional Villain Sauce (page 115).

Variation: Without a roasted chestnut vendor in your neck of the woods, prepare them at home. They will have a dry, nutty texture without the smokiness. Preheat the oven to 400°F/200°C, or gas mark 6. Prepare the chestnuts as in step 1 and place on a sheet pan. Roast for about 25 to 30 minutes, until the shell is split.

Salt-Brined Lupini Beans

Tremoços

MAKES ABOUT 2 QUARTS/1.8 L

Snack on *tremoços*, a traditional tavern or home snack while kicking back a couple of cold beers. Here is our family recipe from cousin Tony. Everyone makes them pretty much the same. The texture will be just a hair more than al dente. Bite off the tip and give them a squeeze, popping them in your mouth. The skin will slide off for you to discard. Plan ahead because these take about a week before they are ready to eat. Once they are, chase them down with your favorite beverage. Read the directions through carefully before beginning.

---

1 —— 2-pound/908-g bag dried lupini beans

1 —— cup/288 g coarse sea or kosher salt as needed

Finely chopped pickled red chile peppers, for garnish

Finely chopped parsley, for garnish

Finely chopped garlic, for garnish

DAY 1

1. Empty the beans into a large bowl and cover with plenty of cold water by at least by 4 inches/10 cm. Let soak for a good 24 hours.

DAYS 2, 3, AND 4

1. Strain the beans from the water. Rinse and place them in a deep pot. Cover again with fresh cold water by about 2 inches/5 cm. *Do not cook them in salted water.* Cover, bring to a boil, then reduce the heat to medium-low. Cook the beans for about 2 to 2½ hours, even as long as 3½ hours. It varies depending on the age of the beans. Sometimes during the cooking period you may have to add more water to keep the beans submerged at all times. You can tell the beans are ready when the skins slide from the bean after it is given a slight squeeze between your thumb and index finger. The beans will be a tiny bit chewy.

2. Drain the beans from the cooking water, rinse and place in a large bowl. Add enough cold water to just cover them. Keep them soaked in cold water for 2 days, changing the water a couple of times each day. This is done to remove the bitterness of the beans.

DAY 5

1. Again drain the beans. Return them to the bowl with fresh water and a generous handful of coarse salt (about ¼ cup/72 g; this has always been done by eye so it is approximate). It is important that you use coarse sea or coarse kosher salt.

(continued)

DAY 6

1. Repeat Day 5, rinsing the beans after draining and then adding fresh water and a fresh dose of salt.

DAY 7

1. Repeat Day 6.

DAY 8

1. Repeat Day 6 again.

These beans should not end up salty, but the process is necessary to remove the bitterness of the beans.

To use: Always remove the beans with a spoon, *never* with your hands, which could cause contamination.

To store: For long-term storage, pack into jars with the salted water and refrigerate. They will keep for a month or two. You can store them at room temperature, however, but you *must* change the water and re-salt them *every 2 days* or the water will get mucky. If you refrigerate them, you must change the water and re-salt them about once a week.

To serve: Remove from the brine with a slotted spoon. You can garnish the top with finely chopped pickled chile peppers, parsley and garlic.

Note: Some home cooks only rinse in cold water once after cooking and start the salting process on Day 2, but this is a personal preference.

Broad Beans

Favas

One ingredient that is a particular favorite, especially among folks from the Azores, is fava beans. The Portuguese love, love, love their fava beans almost as much as sardines. These beans are available fresh, dried, canned, jarred and frozen. When you use raw baby favas, less water is needed to cook the beans thoroughly. The dried ones, which are creamy beige in color, require prior soaking overnight. After soaking, they are rinsed, given a slice across the top and then may be cooked ahead depending on a given recipe for a stew or braise. Today, with canned favas available, with and without the skin, it saves a lot of prep work. If you are using canned or jarred favas, you only need to drain them, then add to the dish and heat through so the beans are hot. The baby green ones I have found in glass jars are pretty good. With frozen favas, water isn't needed provided the heat is on medium-low and the pot is tightly covered. This creates condensation in the pot, which will provide any necessary moisture. Some canned ones have slits and others do not. For a dish like *favas ricas*, the bean is not sliced because it needs to stay intact. Whatever you choose in favas beans, pick what is easiest for you.

Easy Rich Brown Fava Beans with Vinegar Sauce

Favas Ricas

SERVES 4 TO 6

My uncle Ilidio smiles as he remembers buying cone-filled servings of fava beans in a garlicky onion vinegar dressing from street vendors as one would buy roasted chestnuts. Even the pickiest eater just might enjoy this bean dish, which also works well on a buffet table, as a "little taste" before dinner or as a snack with ice cold beer while you watch the game of the week.

Cooking with dried large fava beans requires soaking overnight in water. Brighten the color with a sprinkling of finely chopped aromatic parsley or cilantro. As for substituting other beans, like butterbeans or red kidney beans, you can, just don't overcook them because their skin is thinner, and their integrity needs to hold up well.

For this recipe, the body of the bean needs to be maintained and not turned into mush, so you can pick it up with a toothpick if you choose. Therefore, do not slice the beans; keep the skin intact. Here the method for the favas is to soak them, leave them whole, rinse and then cook as directed.

This version is adaptable for quick preparation using canned brown fava beans, if desired. There are good-quality canned ones that in a pinch work well. Testing revealed no significant difference in using a shortcut with frozen or canned favas that have skins intact.

IF USING DRIED BEANS, START THE DAY BEFORE

1 ——— 1-pound/454-g bag dried fava or broad beans with skin

IF USING DRIED BEANS, START THE DAY BEFORE

1. Rinse the beans, pour into a bowl, and cover with water by 4 inches/ 10 cm. Soak overnight.

THE NEXT DAY

1. Drain, rinse and place the beans in a 4-quart/3.6-L pot. Cover with fresh water by 3 inches/7.5 cm and bring the beans to a boil over medium-high heat. Reduce the heat to medium-low and simmer the beans for 45 minutes. When the beans are tender to the bite, but still holding their shape, drain and set aside. Do not salt the beans during the cooking process as this will toughen them. If you feel you must add some salt, do so in the last 5 minutes of cooking.

(continued)

FOR THE VINAIGRETTE

½ ——— cup/120 ml olive oil or to taste

1 ——— medium onion, coarsely chopped (about ½ cup/80 g)

2 or 3 — garlic cloves, finely chopped

¼ ——— teaspoon crushed red chile pepper or to taste

¼ ——— cup/15 g finely chopped cilantro or parsley, divided

½ ——— cup/120 ml red wine vinegar or to taste

4 to 5 — cups/1000 to 1250 g cooked fava beans, drained (see Note)

½ to 1 — tablespoon/9 to 18 g coarse kosher salt or to taste

FOR THE VINAIGRETTE

1. In a 3-quart/2.7-L pot, heat the olive oil over medium heat. Toss in the onion and garlic. When the garlic becomes aromatic, about 1 minute, stir in the crushed chiles and 2 tablespoons/8 g of the cilantro. Stir in the vinegar last. Taste the sauce. Add a little more vinegar if you like more or if it is too much, tone it down with a touch of olive oil. Mix in the fava beans and heat through. Season the beans with salt to your taste, keeping in mind that the canned beans already contain salt. Heat through for 1 minute to flavor the beans.

2. Transfer the beans to a serving dish. Garnish with remaining 2 tablespoons/ 8 g chopped cilantro. Serve warm or at room temperature.

Note: If using canned beans, use two or three 14-ounce/ 392-g cans. Open and drain the liquid from the beans, rinse if desired, and set the beans aside.

Dried favas are sold packaged in supermarkets. Some Italian or Spanish markets may have them packaged or loose as well.

Beef-Filled Puff Pastry Pillows
Almofadas com Recheio de Bife

MAKES 1½ QUARTS/1.4 L FILLING FOR 3 TO 4 DOZEN PILLOWS

The combination of spiced beef, bell peppers and onions in a delectable, flaky blanket makes this a perfect party appetizer. Although I have made this with regular pastry dough, I like using puff pastry. Short of making your own puff pastry, buy the best that you can find.

¼ ——— cup/60 ml olive oil

1 ——— pound/908 g lean ground or finely chopped beef

½ ——— cup/80 g finely chopped onion

1 ——— green bell pepper, stemmed and coarsely chopped

1 or 2 — garlic cloves, chopped

1 ——— teaspoon/3 g sweet curry

1 ——— teaspoon/6 g coarse kosher salt or to taste

1 ——— teaspoon/5 ml hot sauce or to taste

1 ——— teaspoon/3 g paprika

½ ——— teaspoon ground black pepper

¼ ——— teaspoon ground cumin

½ ——— cup/50 g soft bread crumbs

2½ ——— pounds/1135 g puff pastry dough

1 ——— egg beaten with 1 tablespoon/15 ml water

1. Preheat the oven to 425°F/220°C, or gas mark 7.

2. Heat the olive oil in a large skillet over medium-high heat until hot but not smoking. Add the beef, onion, bell pepper, garlic, sweet curry, salt, hot sauce, paprika, pepper and cumin, blending well, and sauté until the beef is browned and the onion and pepper are soft and lightly colored, about 5 to 10 minutes. Allow to cool completely. Mix in the bread crumbs.

3. Open out the pastry dough and if need be use a rolling pin to roll it to a scant ⅛ inch/3 mm thick, then cut the pastry into 4 x 3–inch/10 x 7.5–cm rectangles. Place some of the filling in the middle of each piece, brush the edges with the egg wash and fold the pastry over short edge to short edge, pressing to seal. Transfer to a baking sheet. Repeat with the remaining dough. The number you get depends on the size you make them. Cover and chill for 30 minutes. Bake for 15 to 20 minutes, until richly golden.

Variation: Make it easier and skip the baking. Use prebaked miniature filo pastry shells and just drop a tablespoon/15 g of freshly made filling into the shells. This will make about 4 dozen miniatures. Chicken or leftover meat from beef pot roasts will also make a great filling.

Braised Beef and Chicken Sandwiches
Picadinho de Bife e Galinha

MAKES ABOUT 4½ CUPS/1080 G SPREAD

Picadinho means "finely chopped." Sometimes I have roast beef or chicken left over and wonder, "How can I use this other than just heating up leftovers?" Well, the Portuguese try very hard not to waste anything. Of course, versions differ, but essentially the braised meats are finely chopped or ground up with a meat grinder or food processor, combined with other ingredients and turned into a flavorful spread for sandwiches. Leftovers are fine for a small batch but you also don't need to wait for leftover meat to make this recipe. However, these sandwiches are frequently served on a buffet at social events. So if you have a crowd to serve, this will work well. You can use all beef or all chicken as well. Even leftover roast turkey would work. I find the best flavor comes from combining the two. The spread can also be used to fill savory little turnovers made with puff pastry. The number of sandwiches depends on the bread size and amount placed in each sandwich.

2	pounds/908 g chuck roast with bone or 1½ pounds/680 g boneless
1 to 4	boneless chicken thighs (optional)
¼ to ½	pound/112 to 227 g linguiça or chouriço sausage
1	medium onion, peeled, quartered
1	cup/235 ml water or as needed
1	cup/235 ml red or white wine or as needed
1	tablespoon/8 g paprika
1	tablespoon/15 g tomato paste
3	garlic cloves, finely chopped
1	bay leaf
6	tablespoons/84 g softened butter or butter substitute, plus extra for assembling the sandwiches
¼ to ½	teaspoon cinnamon
2	teaspoons/12 g coarse kosher salt or to taste

Ground pepper to taste

Sliced sandwich bread

1. Preheat the oven to 325°F/170°C, or gas mark 3.

2. Combine the meats, sausage and onion in a Dutch oven. Mix the water with the wine, paprika, tomato paste, garlic and bay leaf. Pour over and around the meats, adding more wine and water in equal amounts as needed to come halfway up the side of the meats.

3. Slow cook in the oven for nearly 2 hours uncovered. As the meats become fork-tender, remove them from the pan. Set aside to cool and reserve the pan juices.

4. When the meats are cool enough to handle, remove and discard the bones, tendons and skins from the chicken, the casing from any sausage, and the bones, fat and gristle from the beef.

5. Using a grinder or food processor, process the meats until a consistency of shredded tuna fish is reached. Mix in the softened butter and cinnamon. Add a small amount of the reserved pan broth as needed if it seems a little dry. I use about ½ cup/120 ml of the pan broth. Season the *picadinho* with salt and pepper, only if needed. Butter the bread slices before filling. Depending on how much you fill them, you should get 16 to 24 sandwiches. Arrange on a platter for serving.

Veal Croquettes

Croquetes da Vitela

MAKES ABOUT 3 DOZEN

This makes a great starter, as well as a light meal when accompanied with a salad and rice or potato. These have a light, delicate flavor with a creamy texture. Make sure your white sauce is very, very thick, then chill it for several hours to firm up. With a few changes to the sauce, I adapted this from a cousin, Mary Ortins. These can be shaped, breaded and frozen ahead on parchment-lined sheet pans. Just pop the number you want into hot oil when needed.

FOR THE WHITE SAUCE

4 tablespoons/56 g butter

⅓ cup/40 g flour

½ cup/120 ml whole milk

Pinch of ground nutmeg

FOR THE MEAT

2 tablespoons/28 g butter

½ onion, finely chopped

1 garlic clove, finely chopped

1 pound/454 g ground or finely chopped veal (beef, chicken or rabbit can be alternatives)

1 teaspoon/6 g coarse kosher salt or to taste

¼ teaspoon ground white pepper

1 egg yolk, lightly beaten

1 tablespoon/15 ml lemon juice (optional)

ONE DAY BEFORE OR EARLY IN THE DAY, MAKE THE SAUCE

1. Melt the butter in a saucepan over medium heat. Whisk in the flour and cook for about 1 minute, until the flour is completely emulsified into the butter and it starts to foam. The roux should fall like wet sand when lifted with the whisk. While continuously whisking, gradually stream in the cold milk and add the nutmeg. Still stirring with the whisk, simmer until quite thickened and just starting to bubble, about 5 minutes. Remove from the heat to a bowl. Cover with plastic wrap pressed against the surface, and cool completely in the refrigerator for several hours or overnight.

ONE DAY BEFORE OR EARLY IN THE DAY, PREP THE MEAT

1. Melt the butter in a medium skillet over medium-high heat. Add the onion and garlic and sweat until they are translucent, about 2 to 3 minutes.

2. Crumble the veal into the skillet and toss with the onion. When the veal has lightly browned, about 2 to 3 minutes, remove the skillet from the heat and cool completely. Season the veal with salt and pepper, then mix in the egg yolk and lemon juice. Transfer to a bowl, cover and chill for several hours or overnight.

(continued)

TO COOK

All-purpose flour as needed

2 ——— eggs, slightly beaten with
2 tablespoons/30 ml of water for egg
wash

Plain dry bread crumbs

Corn oil, grapeseed oil or light olive oil, for frying

TO COOK

1. Combine just enough of the chilled white sauce, 1 tablespoon/15 ml at a time, into the cold meat, mix and bring it together into a stiff ball. If it isn't well chilled, wait a few hours longer. Take about 2 tablespoons/30 g of the veal mix and shape into little logs, almost like cigar stubs or your index finger, about 2 to 3 inches/5 to 7.5 cm long and 1 inch/2.5 cm in diameter. Place on a lightly floured or parchment-lined sheet pan. Repeat with the remaining veal mix. Cover and keep chilled for about 1 hour, to firm up until needed.

2. When ready to cook, set up the breading: a small tray or plate of all-purpose flour, a bowl of the beaten egg and a bowl of fine plain bread crumbs. You can use wax paper for the flour and bread crumbs if you wish. Heat 5 inches/12.5 cm of oil in a deep saucepan to 350°F/180°C.

3. Dip a croquette into the flour, shaking off the excess. Dip it quickly into the beaten egg followed by a roll in the bread crumbs, coating it thoroughly but shaking off the excess. Fry in the oil until golden. Drain on paper toweling. Repeat with the remaining croquettes. Breaded croquettes can also be frozen on tightly wrapped, parchment-lined sheet pans and then fried from frozen, when needed. Serve hot or at room temperature.

Beef Croquettes

Croquetes de Bife

MAKES ABOUT 2 DOZEN

This savory treat, from my cousin Lili Ferreira of Lisbon, Portugal, gives you an opportunity to use up any leftover roast beef. It's flavorful like beef stew, and the sweetness of the carrots and garlicky sausage come through. If you like, prepare these ahead and freeze them without cooking. For best results, make these the day before cooking to give them sufficient time to firm up. Serve with a salad for a light lunch or as a starter for another meal.

---

2 or 3 — slices day-old bread, heavy crusts removed

¾ —— cup/180 ml whole milk, hot

2½ —— cups/565 g previously roasted or braised beef (alternatively lamb, pork or chicken)

½ —— cup/60 g cooked carrot

4 —— ounces/112 g chouriço sausage

3 —— tablespoons/45 ml olive oil

¼ —— cup/40 g finely chopped onion

1 —— tablespoon/14 g butter, softened

1 —— tablespoon/8 g flour

1 —— egg yolk

2 —— tablespoons/30 ml beef broth

2 —— teaspoons/12 g coarse kosher salt or to taste

Corn oil, for frying

2 —— eggs beaten with 2 tablespoons/30 ml water

Dry bread crumbs

1. Hand-shred the bread into small pieces and transfer to a medium bowl. You should have about 1 cup/100 g packed shredded bread. Pour the hot milk over the bread in a bowl. Let stand for a few minutes until the bread is soft and the milk is absorbed. Squeeze out and discard the excess milk. Add the moistened bread with the meat and carrot to the bowl of a food processor. Peel the casings from the sausage and crumble the sausage into pieces. It should measure about ½ cup/55 g. Add to the bread, beef and carrot. Cover and process the ingredients, pulsing for about 30 seconds, until it is ground into very small pieces, like ground beef. You can also pass the ingredients through a meat grinder. Set aside in the bowl.

2. In a 3-quart/2.7-L pot, heat the olive oil over medium-high heat until hot but not smoking. Toss in the onion and sauté until soft and translucent, about 2 to 3 minutes. Reduce the heat to medium-low. Mix in the ground meats and bread. Stirring occasionally, brown the ground ingredients, about 5 minutes.

3. Separately, in a small bowl, mix together the butter, flour, egg yolk and beef broth. Stirring quickly, add to the pan with the beef and onion. Season with salt if needed. Continue to cook over medium-low heat until the moisture is evaporated and the ingredients come together, pulling away from the sides of the pot, about 3 minutes. Transfer to a bowl, cover and allow the mix to cool completely, chilling in the refrigerator to firm up, several hours or overnight.

4. Make the croquettes by compressing 2 to 3 tablespoons/30 to 45 g of the mixture in the palm of your hand, shaping into index finger lengths or shorter and 1 inch/2.5 cm thick. Lay out on wax or parchment paper. Repeat with the remaining mixture.

(continued)

5. Heat 5 inches/12.5 cm of corn oil in a deep saucepan to 350°F/180°C.

6. Dip each croquette into the egg wash, then roll in the dry bread crumbs. Fry immediately in the corn oil until golden and then drain on paper toweling. Alternatively, freeze, well wrapped with plastic, on parchment-lined sheet pans. Once frozen, just transfer to freezer bags, pushing out any air to avoid freezer frost. When the occasion calls, just remove the amount you need and deep-fry. Serve with a salad of black-eyed peas, red onion, some chopped garlic and a drizzle of olive oil and vinegar. You can serve these with the Garlic Cream Sauce with Cilantro, page 373, to dip in.

Cleaning Squid

It is great if you can get squid already prepped, but sometimes you cannot. To do it yourself, grab and pull the tentacles and head from the body. Reserving the tentacles, separate them by cutting the tentacles from the eyes, entrails and ink sack, which you can then throw out. In the middle where the tentacles come together, there is the mouth/beak of the squid, which is small but hard. This can be removed by simply squeezing the tentacles together around it and it should pop out. Throw the mouth out as well. Hold the body of the squid with one hand and use your other hand to feel for the long, single flat cartilage bone that runs through the middle of the body. Once located, push the bone forward toward the opening. At this point, I usually turn the body of the squid inside out by pushing the point of the body together with the bone toward the opening. This also makes it easier to clean the inside. The bone should come out fairly easily, although you sometimes need to give it a little pull. Clean the inside of any remaining entrails, rinse and then turn it back inside. Sprinkle the outside of the squid with salt. Rub the salt over the outside, peel off the skin and rinse.

Fried Wine and Garlic Marinated Squid

Lulas em Vinho d'Alhos

SERVES 4

This is a tasty little recipe from the island of Madeira and makes a great starter. The combination of garlic and cilantro, with a vinegar and wine fusion, adds brightness to the squid and tingles the taste buds. Just add cooked legumes on the side and this dish becomes lunch.

1	——	pound/454 g cleaned squid (see page 242), cut crosswise into 1-inch/2.5-cm rings
¾	——	cup/180 ml white wine
½	——	cup/30 g finely chopped cilantro or parsley
¼	——	cup/60 ml wine vinegar
¼	——	cup/40 g finely chopped onion
2	——	garlic cloves, coarsely chopped
1	——	teaspoon/5 ml hot sauce, plus more for serving
1	——	teaspoon/6 g coarse kosher salt or to taste
¼	——	teaspoon ground white pepper or to taste
1 to 2	——	cups/120 to 240 g all-purpose flour or as needed
2	——	eggs, lightly beaten
1 to 2	——	cups/100 to 200 g plain bread crumbs or as needed

Corn oil or grapeseed oil as needed

1. In a nonreactive bowl, combine the squid, wine, cilantro, vinegar, onion, garlic, hot sauce, salt and pepper, cover and marinate the squid for about 30 minutes.

2. Reserving the marinade, strain out the squid to a separate dish.

3. Set up a plate of flour, a small bowl with the beaten eggs and a plate with bread crumbs. Heat 4 to 5 inches/10 to 12.5 cm of oil in a 3-quart/2.7-L pot over medium-high heat to 350°F/180°C, or gas mark 4. Lightly coat the squid in flour, shaking off the excess. Next, dip the squid rings into the beaten egg and then coat with the bread crumbs. Working in small batches, fry them for about 3 minutes; do not overcook or they will be tough. Transfer the squid to a serving dish.

4. Pour the reserved marinade into a small pot. Reduce slightly over medium heat, about 2 minutes. Serve on the side or drizzle over the fried squid. Serve hot sauce on the side.

Squid and Polenta with White Wine Sauce
Lulas com Milho Frito

SERVES 2 TO 4

Frying cornmeal on the island of Madeira is almost as commonplace as cooking polenta is in Italy. Here it is pan-fried in butter and olive oil to accompany the squid in a lemon wine sauce. This recipe is my interpretation inspired by Atasca Restaurant in Cambridge, Massachusetts. Make sure you have extra bread to sop up the sauce.

FOR THE CROUTONS

1 ——— tablespoon/14 g butter

2 ——— tablespoons/30 ml olive oil

1 ——— cup/100 g Fried Polenta with Kale Croutons (page 173), cut into 1-inch/2.5-cm cubes

FOR THE SQUID

1 ——— tablespoon/15 ml olive oil

3 ——— tablespoons/42 g butter, divided

2 ——— garlic cloves, coarsely chopped

1 ——— red bell pepper, seeded, chopped into 1-inch/2.5-cm pieces (optional)

2 ——— medium squid, about ½ pound/ 227 g each, cleaned (see page 242), sliced crosswise into 1-inch/2.5-cm rings

½ ——— teaspoon coarse kosher salt

¼ ——— cup/60 ml lemon juice

¼ ——— cup/60 ml white wine, such as Portuguese vinho verde

2 ——— tablespoons/8 g finely chopped parsley, divided

Dash of hot sauce (optional)

FOR THE CROUTONS

1. Heat the butter and olive oil together in a medium skillet. Add the polenta croutons and fry until lightly golden on each side, about 3 to 4 minutes each. Transfer the polenta to a paper towel–lined dish and reserve.

FOR THE SQUID

1. In the same pan, heat the olive oil and 1 tablespoon/14 g of the butter over medium-high heat until hot but not smoking.

2. Toss in the garlic and chopped pepper and sauté until the garlic becomes aromatic, about 30 seconds. Reduce the heat to medium. Season the squid rings with salt, add the squid rings to the pan and cook for 2 minutes. Transfer the squid rings to a dish.

3. Pour in the lemon juice and wine to deglaze the pan. Bring to a boil over medium heat. Reduce the volume of the sauce by half. Lower the heat to medium-low. Return the squid to the pan with 1 tablespoon/4 g of the parsley. Cook the squid in the sauce for about 2 to 3 minutes, until just tender. Turn off the heat. Swirl the remaining 2 tablespoons/28 g butter and hot sauce. Do not overcook, or the texture will be like rubber bands. Serve, topped with cubes of freshly fried polenta. Garnish with the remaining 1 tablespoon/4 g parsley. Don't forget to serve with bread to mop up the sauce.

Breads
Pães

Sometimes there just isn't anything as rewarding, not to mention relaxing, as making your own bread by hand. The breads in this book are for the most part handmade rustic country style.

One thing about Portuguese country breads and Portuguese cooking in general is that religious and sometimes quirky traditional foodways can still be found in methods of preparing bread and meals. When I was young, I was taught to always bless the bread dough to ensure that it would rise. Three days of marinating foods or three days of letting dough sponge rise was akin to Jesus rising from the dead on the third day. The source of some culinary habits is long forgotten. Only remembered is when mother did it this way or that way, and she did so because her mother or mother-in-law did it with or without an explanation. Ingrained in me, I still bless any bread dough when I set it to rise. And it does.

Old-Style Leavening

Whether it is for regular bread or sweet bread, what we now know as yeast was not used years ago in the fermentation process. The simple combination of potato and some flour and potato water, mixed and left for days to ferment, or leftover bread dough formed the leavening for the breads. Through trial and error, many people had their own concoctions for the slower rise of breads. Although these methods impart wonderful flavor, it requires a lot of patience with today's commercial bread makers, who need a quicker production. Once the bread dough was formed, a part of it was saved to make the next batch of bread dough. Sometimes a neighbor would ask another, "Hey, Maria, do you have any *fermente*?" Be it professional bakers or just between friends and neighbors, helping is at the heart and camaraderie of the Portuguese, and they would share the starter dough to help each other out.

Today's yeasts come in the forms of cake and granulated. The granulated yeast can be quick acting and regular. Unless the granulated yeast is being sprinkled on the flour, granulated and cake yeasts need to be proofed. For the recipes requiring yeast in this chapter and the desserts, it is important to use an instant-read thermometer to make sure the water is not above 112°F/44.4°C. Too often, dough fails to rise because the water is too hot and kills the yeast. Mix a small amount of tepid water and yeast and let it stand for 10 minutes to make sure the yeast is active to start the fermentation process. After 10 minutes, if no bubbles and foam appear at the top of the solution, the water temperature and freshness of the yeast should be questioned and replaced. To save time, always check the freshness dates before you begin and store yeast in the refrigerator.

EQUIPMENT

- 5- to 7-quart/4.5- to 6.3-L standing mixer (optional)

- Dough rising bucket

- Instant-read thermometer

- Assorted size whisks

- Standard measuring cups and spoons

- Square oven stone like those for making pizza

- Large wooden cutting board approximately 24 x 22 inches/61 x 56 cm

- Wooden oven peel (shovel)

- Sheet pans

- Parchment paper

- One or two inexpensive bath towels or small blankets, reserved just for baking

- Digital kitchen scale

- Large mixing bowl or two

A few tips

- Never add salt to a proofing solution. Like hot water, it will kill the yeast as well.

- When baking bread, remember to give your dough a great start by having your ingredients at room temperature and not straight from the refrigerator.

- When working with bread dough, use a wooden surface for direct contact with the dough. The cooler ceramic or stone surfaces are better suited for pastry dough.

- I find that dough rises better in non-metal bowls but does especially well in food-safe dough rising buckets with lids, which are available at restaurant supply stores. If you use metal bowls, rinse them in hot water, dry them and place a towel under them before you start. Save clean old towels, tablecloths or small blankets just for covering the plastic-sealed rising dough, keeping it warm and draft-free.

Flatbread of Pico Island
Bolo do Pico

MAKES TWO 16-INCH/40.6-CM LARGE BREADS OR 6 TO 8 SMALL

When this bread is baked on the island of Pico, in keeping with tradition, it is baked on *tijolho* clay bricks. Here in the United States, the oven bricks used to bake pizza in home ovens work nicely as a substitute. This is a dense flatbread, perfectly suited to serve warm with stews, cheese and sautéed Portuguese sausages like chouriço or linguiça. While this unleavened bread can be made in one bowl, dividing the mix allows for faster cooling and easier handling of the dough. Conceição Silva, who is from the island of Pico in the Azores, uses a preheated sheet pan as a substitute for her old stone oven, yielding a softer texture on the bread's bottom crust than that baked on a stone. I use an oven stone like that for making pizza and a cornmeal-sprinkled oven shovel (peel). The interior texture is moist and dense. The bread can be sliced and placed in a toaster to reheat if desired. It is best eaten on the day it is made.

---

2 ——— pounds/908 g white corn flour, divided

2 ——— tablespoons/36 g table salt, divided

10——— cups/2350 ml boiling water, divided

2 ——— cups/240 g all-purpose flour, divided

Cornmeal as needed

1. Mix 3 cups/360 g (measured by pouring, not scooping) of the white corn flour and 1 tablespoon/18 g of the salt in a bowl. Blend well. Repeat with a second bowl. You should have some corn flour left for dusting the workspace later, about ½ to ¾ cup/60 to 90 g.

2. Pour 5 cups/1175 ml of the rapidly boiling water into the first bowl and over the corn flour, then use a wooden spoon to mix fast and furiously. Quickly stir the water as fast as you can into the flour until you have the consistency of thick mashed potatoes. If you work too slowly, the consistency will be lumpy.

3. After mixing well, cover with a kitchen towel and set aside until cool enough to handle with your hands, about ½ hour. Meanwhile, repeat with the second bowl of corn flour, salt and remaining 5 cups/1175 ml rapidly boiling water (reheat if needed). Set the second bowl of dough aside to cool as well. (In winter you can set it on a cool enclosed porch.) Give the dough in each bowl an occasional turn or two with the wooden spoon, which helps hasten the cooling.

4. At this time, if you are using an oven stone, place it in a cold oven. Depending on your oven, set it to 500°F/250°C, or gas mark 10 (max) or at the highest it will go; adjust the baking time to more or less as needed.

5. When the corn flour "mashed potatoes" is cool enough to handle with your hands, take one of the bowls and knead the corn flour mash really well with a closed fist for 1 minute. Scatter 1 cup/120 g of the all-purpose flour over the corn flour mash and knead it in, incorporating the flour thoroughly and bringing the dough together until it pulls away from the sides of the bowl, about 5 minutes. If needed, in small increments, sprinkle ¼ cup/60 ml maximum additional water over the dough and knead it in. If using the sheet pan instead of a stone, set it in the oven at this time to preheat and leave in the oven until needed.

(continued)

Corn flour is scalded with boiling water mixed and cooled. After mixing with regular flour, kneaded and shaped into a ball, it is patted into a smooth flat shape then baked.

6. Sprinkle your workspace with about ¼ cup/60 g of the remaining corn flour. Fill a small bowl with some cool water and dip your hands into it. (Conceição, showing her years of experience, lifts the dough, in one mass, out of the bowl and by tossing and turning the dough in her hands, shapes it into one large, fairly wet, smooth ball.) With your wet hands, pick up a ball of dough and shape it by turning and slightly tossing in your hands or divide the dough into 3 or 4 smaller equal amounts before shaping into balls. Smaller ones are easier to toss. You also can shape it in a dampened bowl by swirling it around in the bowl.

7. Place the ball of dough onto the corn flour–dusted workspace. Again, barely wet your dominant hand with water and pat the dough down; keep patting and slightly pushing with your palm all over, shaping it into a large 16-inch/40.6-cm disk, or 3 or 4 smaller ones, with a thickness of ½ to ¾ inch/1.3 to 2 cm. Lightly remoisten your hand as needed to smooth and pat the dough into shape. Repeat with the second bowl of dough.

8. Because this dough is moist it doesn't slide off the oven shovel very well. The parchment paper is great for this bread, especially if you are making large rounds.

Using the sheet pan: Preheat the sheet pan in the oven. Make sure your patted shape fits within the size of the sheet pan. Open the oven door and dust the sheet pan with flour and then carefully pick up the flat dough and lay it on the dusted sheet pan to bake, or place the dough on parchment paper first, then transfer to the sheet pan. I find the parchment paper makes for easier transfer of the larger sizes, whether baking on the sheet pan or stone.

Using the oven stone: Place the stone in a cold oven, then preheat. Sprinkle the wooden peel with cornmeal, place the shaped flat dough on the shovel and slide onto the stone, or place the dough on parchment paper, trimming excess paper, and transfer to the wooden oven peel. Slide onto the hot stone.

9. Bake for about 35 to 45 minutes, until the bottom is richly golden.

Sweet Raised Muffins

Bolos Levedos

MAKES 18 MUFFINS

The ultimate treat for breakfast instead of regular toasted bread is one of these sweet muffins that look like an oversized English muffin. Whether you slather them with butter or marmalade, top them with a poached egg or just spread them with peanut butter as my son-in-law does, you will enjoy these muffins. Remember to have your ingredients lined up in order of use.

2	——	¼-ounce/7-g packages yeast
½	——	cup/120 ml warm water, 100° to 110°F/37.8° to 43.3°C
1¼	——	cups/250 g sugar, divided
6¾	——	cups/810 g bread flour or as needed, divided
½	——	teaspoon table salt
4	——	large eggs, lightly beaten
1¼	——	cups/295 ml warm whole milk
½	——	teaspoon cinnamon
Grated peel of 1 lemon		
½	——	cup/112 g melted butter, warm

1. In a cup or small bowl, sprinkle the yeast over the water and add a teaspoon/5 g of the sugar. Stir, cover and let stand for 10 minutes to proof.

2. Sift together into a large bowl 3 cups/360 g of the flour, the remaining sugar and the salt.

3. Make a well in the center of the flour, then add the beaten eggs, proofed yeast, milk, cinnamon and grated lemon peel. Next, pour in the warm melted butter. Using your hands, mix the ingredients together, adding in the remaining 3¾ cups/450 g flour, in increments, until all the ingredients are thoroughly blended. If the texture is stiff or a little dry, add a bit more warm milk, or a little more flour if the dough seems too sticky, until you have the texture and feel of a medium bread dough. Knead the dough until it is smooth and elastic, about 10 to 15 minutes.

4. Transfer the dough to a dough-rising bucket or cover the bowl with plastic wrap followed by a clean towel and set aside in a warm, draft-free place to rise until doubled, about 1 hour. Do not set on a stone surface.

5. Divide the dough into 12 to 18 equal portions about the size of 3 inches/ 7.5 cm in diameter, or 3 to 4 ounces/84 to 112 g in weight. Shape each piece by rolling into a ball. Cover and let rest for 10 minutes. Then use the palm of your hand and gently flatten them into a disk a scant ½ inch/1.3 cm thick. (If they are too thick they will burn before the center is done.) Repeat with the remaining dough. Place the disks on a lightly floured table or dish cloth, several inches apart. Cover them lightly with another kitchen towel and let them rise again, free from drafts, until almost doubled in size, about 25 minutes.

(continued)

Divided dough is shaped into rounds before flattened by hand. After a second rising the discs of dough are "baked" in a non-stick skillet.

6. Preheat a heavy, nonstick, dry skillet over medium-low heat. Do not grease the pan. Do not use a cast-iron pan, as any residual fat in the pan will burn the muffins before they are done. Brush off any residual flour on the muffin dough and then place one *bolo* in the pan and cook on each side for about 6 to 12 minutes, until medium golden, top and bottom. Keep an eye on them to make sure they do not burn. The sides should be slightly firm when pressed with your finger. Repeat with the remaining disks of dough. These freeze very well.

Note: Although traditionally regular cast-iron skillets or cement tiles would be used, if you happen to have today's nonstick skillets, they are excellent for this recipe.

Brindes

Someone once told me that when she was young, her mother would make *brindes* (gifts) for the children. She described them as baked bread with pieces of sausage and/or *presunto* (similar to prosciutto) hiding in the middle. I told her that what she had been given was a *bolo*, which can be as large as a casserole or as small as sandwich roll. If it were Easter, someone might give *folares* as a *brinde*. For Easter, however, the *folares de páscoa* might be as simple as a small cake, but today a small sweet bread with a colored egg on the top is popular. A gift of a *bolo* or *folar* is a tasty one indeed!

Linguiça and Presunto/Prosciutto Bread

Bolos ou Folares de Linguiça e Presunto

MAKES FOUR 8-INCH/20-CM BREADS

A perfect addition to tailgate parties or picnic baskets, or sliced thin for appetizers, this bread is a winner. My brother likes to add some soft cheese. I suggest Portuguese cheese like St. Jorge or Topo. I like to add caramelized onions. This recipe, which I make with sausage, *presunto*, cheese and caramelized onions, can be made on a lightly oiled sheet pan, but I find the best results come from using an oven stone and wooden oven peels, like those used in pizza shops. Before preheating the oven stone, cut a sheet of parchment to the size of the stone. Place the paper on the wooden peel. When you slide the *bolos* into the oven on the peel, the paper will slide with it and keep your stone clean. As always, read the recipe through before beginning.

EQUIPMENT:

Oven stone

Wooden peel

Parchment paper (optional)

½	ounce/14 g dry yeast or two ¼-ounce/7-g packages dry yeast
½	cup/120 ml warm water, 100° to 110°F/37.8° to 43.3°C
1	teaspoon/5 g sugar
3½	cups/420 g bread flour, divided, as needed
½	teaspoon table salt
4	large eggs, lightly beaten
3 to 4	tablespoons/45 to 60 ml olive oil, divided
1	cup/160 g chopped onion (optional)
1½	pounds/680 g linguiça sausage, cut into ¼-inch/6-mm rounds, or thinly sliced *presunto*, or ¾ pound/340 g each, if combining
1	large egg beaten with 1 tablespoon/ 15 ml water
1	cup/120 g grated St. Jorge, Topo or other soft cheese (optional)

Fine cornmeal for dusting

1. In a small cup or bowl, sprinkle the yeast over the warm water (not hotter than 110°F/43.3°C), add the sugar, stir and cover. Let stand for 10 minutes to proof.

2. Mix 3 cups/360 g of the flour with the salt in a large bowl, distributing the salt evenly throughout the flour, about 1 minute. Make a well in the middle of the flour. Into the well pour the lightly beaten eggs, yeast sponge and 2 tablespoons/30 ml of the olive oil. Use your hands, blending well, to form a shaggy dough, incorporating enough of the remaining ½ cup/60 g flour until a medium dough (not sticky or loose) is formed, about 2 to 3 minutes. The dough should leave the sides of the bowl clean.

3. Turn the dough out onto a lightly floured board and knead for 10 minutes, until the dough is fairly smooth and gives a light spring when pressed with your index finger. Shape into a ball, give it a light dusting with flour and cover with a clean kitchen towel or place in a dough-rising bucket. Set in a warm, draft-free spot to rise until doubled in size, about 1 hour. The dough is ready when you poke your finger into it and the indentation remains.

4. While the dough is rising, in a skillet set over medium heat, sauté the chopped onion in the remaining 1 or 2 tablespoons/15 or 30 ml olive oil just until they pick up some color, about 4 to 5 minutes, then add in the sausage slices and/or *presunto* and sauté for 2 more minutes. Set aside.

(continued)

5. When the dough has doubled, without punching the dough, use a dough scraper or knife to divide it into 4 equal parts. Stretch by hand or roll out each part on a lightly floured work surface, to an approximately 6 x 8–inch/15 x 20–cm rectangle. Brush a 1-inch/2.5-cm border around the edges with the egg wash. Spread the onions and sausage plus any sautéed juices over, leaving the 1-inch/2.5-cm border all around. Add some grated soft cheese. With the long edge facing you, fold in the short sides, then roll it like a jelly roll. Brush the edges with egg wash, then pinch the edges together to seal. Place on a lightly floured surface or on individual sheets of parchment paper. Cover with a towel and let rest for about 30 to 45 minutes. Set a baking stone in a cold oven and preheat the oven to 425°F/220°C, or gas mark 7.

6. When the *bolos* are almost double in size, they are ready. Dust a wooden oven peel with fine cornmeal. Generously brush the egg wash over the bolos, place them on the wooden peel, and transfer them to the preheated oven stone. If using parchment paper, you can omit the cornmeal and just slide the bolos with the parchment paper onto the wooden peels and place on the stones. These can also be baked on a parchment-lined sheet pan.

7. Bake for about 25 minutes, until richly golden. The bottom should give a fairly hollow sound when tapped. Do not overbake.

Variation: Some cooks make these with very small sardines, trimmed of innards and heads, scattering the shredded fish over the dough. Olive oil is drizzled over the fish followed with a scattering of salt and covered with a top dough or rolled up and baked.

Egg Rich Chouriço Sausage and Presunto/Prosciutto Bread

Folar Rica

MAKES 1 LARGE BREAD

Think of this as a Portuguese-style calzone. Everyone has his version. Whether it calls for two, three or a dozen eggs, the recipes include butter, olive oil, flour and yeast. This version isn't an exact recipe but a formula. Once you make the dough, all you have to add is the chouriço and the *presunto*/prosciutto. This version, considered *rica*, or rich, because of the immense amount of eggs and butter in the dough, comes from a friend, Dalila Martins. The instructions follow a typical dough method as in the previous recipe. This can be doubled. If you choose not to use *presunto*, increase the chouriço to 2 pounds/908 g. You can also use linguiça.

---

3 — ¼-ounce/7-g packages dry yeast or 3 cubes of yeast cake (yeast cakes needsto be dissolved in the warm water)

1 — cup/235 ml warm water, 100° to 110°F/37.8° to 43.3°C

1 — teaspoon/5 g sugar

12 — large eggs

1 — teaspoon/6 g table salt

2½ — pounds/1135 g bread flour

8 — tablespoons/112 g butter, melted

½ — cup/120 ml olive oil or as needed

1 — 1½-pound/680-g chouriço sausage, cut into ¼-inch/6-mm round slices

1 — pound/454 g *presunto*/prosciutto, cut into pieces

1 to 1½— cups/120 to 180 g grated St. Jorge or Havarti cheese (optional)

1 — egg beaten with 1 tablespoon/ 15 ml water

1. In a cup or small bowl, sprinkle the yeast over the warm water. Add the sugar, stir and cover. Let stand to proof, about 10 minutes.

2. If you have a stand mixer with a dough hook, use it if the mixing bowl is large enough to accommodate all of the ingredients. Otherwise, in a large bowl, using a whisk, beat the eggs with the salt until foamy. Dump in the proofed yeast and flour. With one hand mixing, use the other hand to gradually pour in the melted butter and mix until a medium dough (not sticky or loose) is formed. The dough should leave the sides of the bowl clean.

3. Knead for 10 to 15 minutes, until the dough is fairly smooth and gives a slight spring when lightly pressed with your index finger. Shape into a ball, give it a light dusting with flour and cover with a towel. Set in a warm draft-free spot to rise until doubled in size. To test if the dough is ready, poke your finger into it; an indentation should remain.

4. Grease a sheet pan with the olive oil or line the pan with parchment paper. Without punching the dough, use a dough scraper to scoop it out onto a lightly floured work surface. Divide the dough in half. Roll half into a rectangle large enough to line the sheet pan. Spread slices of sausage and *presunto* over it, leaving a 1-inch/2.5-cm border all around. Sprinkle the grated cheese over all. Roll out the second half of the dough and cover the filling. Pinch the edges together to seal. Cover with a towel and let rest for about 30 to 45 minutes. Preheat the oven to 425°F/220°C, or gas mark 7.

5. Brush the top of the *folar* with the egg wash and put the pan in the oven. Bake for 30 to 45 minutes, until richly golden.

Madeiran Corn Bread
Pão de Milho à Madeirense

MAKES 1 LARGE OR 2 MEDIUM BREADS

The people of Madeira set their corn bread apart with the inclusion of sweet potato in their dough. This bread has a fairly dense crumb with a slightly crunchy crust.

EQUIPMENT

Oven stone

Wooden oven peel (shovel)

Sheet pan and parchment paper

3½ —— cups/822 ml water

1 —— medium sweet potato, unpeeled, scrubbed

3½ —— cups/420 g corn flour

3 —— tablespoons/36 g baker's yeast cake or three ¼-ounce/7-g packages dry yeast

1 —— teaspoon/5 g sugar

3½ —— cups/420 g whole wheat or unbleached bread flour

1½ —— teaspoons/9 g table salt

Cornmeal as needed

1. Bring the water and potato to a boil in a medium pan. Reduce the heat to medium-low and cook the potato until it is very tender and nearly falling apart, about 20 to 25 minutes. Reserving the water, transfer the potato to a sieve set in a bowl and let drain any excess water for about ½ hour to cool down a bit. Peel the potato when it is cool enough to handle. Purée the potato, with a potato ricer or masher, until fairly smooth, then press through a sieve to remove any lumps. You should have about 1 cup/225 g.

2. Dump the corn flour into a medium bowl. Pour 2½ cups/588 ml of the boiling potato water (reboil if needed) over and around the flour. Using a wooden spoon, quickly mix until it resembles cooked mashed potatoes. Set aside to cool for 30 minutes.

3. Check to see that the temperature of the remaining potato water has cooled to 100° to 110°F/37.8° to 43.3°C (if it is too hot, it will kill the yeast). Transfer ¾ cup/180 ml of the warm water to a cup or small bowl. Sprinkle the yeast over the water, then stir in the sugar. Cover and let stand for 10 minutes to proof.

4. Pour the bread flour into a large bowl. Add and distribute the salt throughout the flour. Make a well in the middle of the flour. Into the well, mix in 1 cup/225 g of the puréed potato, corn flour mash and yeast, incorporating the ingredients until the dough is pulling away from the sides of the bowl and a medium dough is formed, about 3 to 5 minutes. Knead for 10 minutes. When it has been sufficiently kneaded, the dough should spring back slightly when lightly pressed with your index finger. Cover and let rise until doubled in size. Punch down and shape into one large or 2 medium balls. Cover and let rise again to almost double, about 30 to 45 minutes. (This dough can also be made into rolls rather than loaves. Just roll pieces of dough into 2- to 3-inch/5- to 7.5-cm balls, cover, let rise until double, and then bake.) Preheat the oven to 400°F/200°C, or gas mark 6. If using the oven stone, place the stone in the cold oven to preheat it.

5. Place the rounds of dough upside down on a cornmeal-dusted oven shovel or a parchment-lined sheet pan. Just before putting the bread dough in the oven, with a very sharp knife, razor blade or lamé blade, give the top a shallow slash, about ¼ inch/6 mm deep from one side to the other. Immediately place in the oven to bake.

Using the oven stone: Place the stone in the cold oven to preheat it. When the dough has risen sufficiently as directed above, transfer the shaped dough upside down on the cornmeal-dusted oven peel or on parchment paper. Then, using the oven peel, slide it onto the hot stone, shuffling the peel's tip at the far edge of the stone and sliding the dough onto its hot surface.

Using the sheet pan: Place the rounds of bread dough upside down on a parchment-lined sheet pan, then transfer the pan to the preheated oven.

6. Bake the bread for 30 to 35 minutes. The bread should have a hollow sound when thumped on the bottom. If not thumping, bake for about 5 minutes longer, especially for the sheet pan. Let the bread cool for at least 15 minutes before slicing. Adjust the baking time for smaller loaves to 25 to 30 minutes.

* * *

The humidity of the Azores encouraged rapid growth of mold. About three days after baking bread, especially corn bread, any leftover bread would sometimes develop mold. The amount of mold varied from one loaf to another. My friend Marguerite's mother would scrape off the mold from any salvageable loaf. She would then sprinkle it with water and refresh it in the oven. Looking back, she smiles, recalling those memories. "It wasn't funny at the time, it was an unappetizing necessity."

Madeiran Homestyle Bread
Pão Caseiro à Madeirense

MAKES 2 LARGE OR 4 SMALL BREADS

The people of Madeira Island and the Azores use a great deal of sweet potatoes. Where you might not expect it is in their breads. The added flavor, moistness and nutrition of sweet potatoes make the extra steps worthwhile.

1	———	medium yellow sweet potato, unpeeled, scrubbed
4	———	cups/940 ml water or as needed
2	———	¼-ounce/7-g packages dry yeast or 1½ ounces/42 g baker's yeast cake
1	———	teaspoon/5 g sugar
2¾	———	pounds/1250 g (about 7½ cups) unbleached bread flour (12% protein), poured not scooped to measure, divided
2	———	teaspoons/12 g table salt

Note: An oven stone and peel (oven shovel) can be purchased at kitchen stores or restaurant supply places. Alternatively, line the peel with parchment paper or bake on a parchment-lined sheet pan as in the previous recipe.

1. Drop the potato into a pan with the water. Cover, bring to a boil, reduce the heat to medium-low and cook until the potato is very tender and nearly falling apart, about 20 to 25 minutes. Reserving the water, transfer the potato to a dish and peel it when it is cool enough to handle. Purée the peeled potato with a masher or ricer until smooth and press through a sieve to remove any lumps.

2. Meanwhile, let the potato water cool to about 100 to 110°F/37.8 to 43.3°C. Transfer ½ cup/120 ml of the water to a cup or bowl. Sprinkle the yeast over the potato water, stir in the sugar, cover and let stand for about 10 minutes, until the yeast has proofed (you will see foam and bubbles forming on the surface).

3. Pour 6 cups/720 g of the flour into a large bowl. Make a well in the center of the flour. Dump the warm puréed potato into the well along with the proofed yeast. Scramble the potato with the yeast, gradually pulling in the flour. Alternating with only 2 cups/470 ml of the remaining warm potato water, mix in just enough of the remaining 1½ cups/180 g flour to form the dough. Sprinkle the salt over. If necessary, add more of the flour in small increments, until the dough is no longer sticking.

4. Knead the dough on a lightly floured board for about 10 minutes, until it is fairly smooth and elastic. You can keep the dough on the board or place it back in the bowl. Cover with a towel. Let it rise until doubled in size, about 1½ hours.

5. Divide the dough into 2 or 4 portions depending upon the size you want to make and shape into rounds. Let them rise a second time until almost doubled in size, about 30 to 45 minutes.

6. While the dough is rising, set the oven stone into the cold oven and preheat to 400°F/200°C, or gas mark 6. When the dough is ready, place each round upside down on a cornmeal-dusted wooden oven peel (shovel). Bring the oven shovel or pan next to a spot closest to the oven. With a very sharp knife, give a few angled shallow slashes, about ¼ inch/6 mm deep, over the top and transfer the dough immediately to the preheated oven stone. Bake the large rounds for 45 to 50 and the smaller ones for 25 to 30 minutes. Let the bread cool for at least 15 minutes before slicing.

Madeiran Stone Baked Bread
Bolo de Caco

MAKES 6 TO 8 LARGE OR 2½ DOZEN SMALL

Traditionally baked on hot clay slabs, this Madeiran flat bread isn't quite as flat as the flat bread of Pico Island. With a touch of yeast, this puffed-up bread is made using an equal amount of flour and sweet potato by weight. A pizza stone preheated in the oven makes a great substitute for the clay slab. Its ingredients are the same as the Madeiran homestyle bread but with a different ratio of potato to flour. Like the flat bread of Pico Island, these breads are best the day they are baked, so serve them with stews, soups, cheese or just butter if desired.

1	pound/454 g yellow sweet potato, unpeeled, scrubbed
4	cups/940 ml cold water
1	¼-ounce/7-g package dry yeast
½	cup/120 ml warm water, 100° to 110°F/37.8° to 43.3°C
1	teaspoon/5 g sugar
1	pound/454 g (about 3½ cups) bread flour
2	teaspoons/12 g table salt

1. Bring the potato and cold water to a boil in a medium pan over medium-high heat. Reduce the heat to medium-low and cook until the potato is almost falling-apart tender, about 20 to 25 minutes. Reserving 1 cup/240 ml of the cooking water, transfer the potato to a dish until cool enough to peel. Discard the peel and then mash the potato thoroughly, puréeing with a ricer or masher and then pressing through a sieve to ensure no lumps remain.

2. While the potato is cooling, in a small bowl or cup, sprinkle the yeast over the warm water (be sure to test the temperature). Stir in the sugar. Cover and let stand for 10 minutes, until proofed.

3. Dump the flour into a large bowl, mix in the salt and then make a well in the middle. Add the somewhat cooled puréed potato to the well followed by the proofed yeast. Mix well with your hands, making sure there are no lumps.

4. Drizzle in the reserved warm potato water, beginning with ½-cup/120-ml increments, to make a light dough, being careful not to add too much water or you will need to add back some additional flour. It should not be a sticky dough. Knead well for about 10 to 15 minutes. The dough is ready when it springs back after pressing lightly with your index finger. Alternatively, use a stand mixer with a dough hook and mix until you are able to stretch a walnut-size piece of dough without tearing, thin enough to almost see through. This is what we call the windowpane test. Once done, shape the dough into one large round, cover and set aside to rise in a warm, draft-free spot until doubled in size, about 1 hour.

5. Divide the dough into 6 to 8 medium rounds or 28 to 30 fairly even pieces. Lightly dust your workspace with flour. Roll each piece into a ball and then flatten each with the palm of your hand, making them about ¾-inch/2-cm disks. Set each one on a lightly floured kitchen towel, cover and let rise again until almost but not quite doubled, about 30 minutes.

6. To bake use one of the following methods:

Method 1

Like *bolos levedos* (page 253), this bread was typically cooked on a flat cement or stone tile with a wood fire beneath it. Today you can use your stove top with a dry, grease-free cast-iron or a nonstick pan.

Preheat a nonstick skillet over medium heat. Do not add any fat. Since nonstick skillets are free of any seasoning, the bread is less likely to burn as easily. Place the individual dough top side down onto the skillet. Cook for 5 minutes, then turn over and cook for 10 to 15 minutes more. Be careful not to burn the bottom. These are best on the day they are made. They also freeze well.

Method 2

Set an oven stone in a cold oven and preheat to 400°F/200°C, or gas mark 6. Dust a wooden oven peel with cornmeal. When the *bolos* are almost double in size, place them upside down on the wooden peel and slide them onto the heated oven stone to bake. Bake for about 5 minutes, then flip over and continue to bake for 15 to 20 minutes.

Homestyle Wheat Bread
Pão Caseiro de Centeio

MAKES 4 LOAVES

Although this bread is not the traditional *broa* made with cornmeal, Clara Santos and her husband Jose Antonio call their bread
"*broa*" because of the shape they make it. She mixes, he kneads, and their cooperative labor of love yields a flavorful bread with a
lightly dense texture sought out beyond the usual family and friends. With deep roots from Arganil, in northern Portugal, they
sometimes put in corn flour and other times a touch of barley and set the dough to rise just once before baking. You can mix
up the flours as they do, using whole wheat in combination with all-purpose or different ratios of corn, whole wheat, barley and
regular flour. While I tend to make my breads by hand, if it is easier on your hands, use a stand mixer if you have one.

EQUIPMENT
Kitchen scale

Oven stone or sheet pan

2 ————	¼-ounce/7-g packages dry yeast
5 ————	cups/1175 ml warm water, 100° to 110°F/37.8° to 43.3°C, divided
2½ ———	pounds/1135 g all-purpose flour
1¼ ———	pounds/568 g hard red wheat flour
2 ————	teaspoons/12 g table salt

Cornmeal, for sprinkling

Note: When I say "cover your dough well," I mean in addition to the cover of the dough-rising bucket, plastic wrap or kitchen towel, cover completely with an additional heavy bath-size towel reserved just for baking to keep the dough warm from winter drafts and summer air conditioning.

Note: You can also cut a round of parchment paper to fit the shovel and transfer the rounds of dough onto the parchment, then slide the dough onto the shovel, then onto the hot stone.

1. In a cup or small bowl, sprinkle the yeast over ½ cup/120 ml of the warm water. Cover and let stand for 10 minutes to proof.

2. Combine the flours in a large bowl, or the bowl of your mixer, blending well to aerate. Add the proofed yeast and 4 cups/940 ml of the warm water and mix well, forming a medium dough. Mix in the remaining ½ cup/120 ml water. When the dough is pulling away from the sides of the bowl it is ready.

3. Turn out the dough onto a lightly floured workspace (not stone) and sprinkle the salt over. Knead well for 10 to 15 minutes until the dough springs back when pressed lightly with your index finger. Transfer to a dough-rising bucket if you have one. Cover well (see Note) and let rise in a draft-free spot until doubled in size, about 1½ hours.

4. Preheat the oven to 425°F/220°C, or gas mark 7. If using an oven stone, place it in the cold oven to preheat it.

5. When the dough has doubled, gently without punching down, divide the dough into 4 equal parts. Gently shape into rounds on a floured workspace, pulling the rounds across the work surface. Bake as follows:

Using the oven stone: Transfer the rounds of dough upside down onto a cornmeal-sprinkled wooden oven shovel (peel) and dust with flour (see Note). Bring the rounds close to the oven, score the tops, angled ¼ inch/6 mm deep, from one side to the other, if desired (Clara doesn't) and immediately and carefully slide the rounds onto the hot stone. Bake for about 30 minutes.

Using the sheet pan: With the pans, transfer a round of dough upside down onto cornmeal in the middle of the sheet pan and dust with flour. With a very sharp knife, razor blade or lamé blade, give the top a shallow slash, if desired, about ¼ inch/6 mm deep, and immediately put in the oven. Bake for 30 minutes (adjusting for size if larger), or until the bread is hollow sounding when tapped on the bottom.

Vienna Bread
Pão de Viena

MAKES 3 OR 4 (APPROXIMATELY 1-POUND/454-G) LOAVES

When my father owned his bakery, one of the breads he would make was Vienna bread. His style of Vienna bread did not contain milk. He would check the temperature of the room, the flour, water and then the resulting dough, which he would bake into an elongated oval-shaped bread that had a fluffier texture than most Portuguese breads. His recipe has been downsized for the home baker. Make sure the flour is at room temperature and don't place bowls or yeast containers on cold granite or stone surfaces. Read the recipe through before beginning.

EQUIPMENT
Oven stone or sheet pan
Wooden oven peel (shovel)
Instant-read thermometer

FOR THE SPONGE
½ —— ounce/14 g (4½ teaspoons) baker's yeast cake or two ¼-ounce/7-g packages dry yeast

½ —— cup/120 ml warm water, 80° to 90°F/26.7° to 32.2°C maximum

1 —— cup/120 g bread flour

FOR THE DOUGH
3½ —— cups/823 ml warm water, 100°F/37.8°C

2½ —— pounds/1135 g (about 7 cups) bread flour (12% protein), plus extra for dusting

1 —— teaspoon/6 g table salt

FOR THE SPONGE

1. In a small bowl, dissolve the yeast cake in the warm water or sprinkle the granulated yeast over the water. Give a brief stir, cover and let stand for about 10 minutes, until the yeast is proofed. You will see foam form on the surface.

2. Gradually, mix in the flour, cover tightly and set in warm spot to rise until doubled in size, about 1 hour.

FOR THE DOUGH

1. Transfer the yeast sponge to a warmed extra-large mixing bowl. Place the warm water in a small bowl. Gradually, while mixing with one hand opened like a claw, pour in just enough of the warm water, about 1 cup/235 ml, to scramble up the yeast sponge into a loose slurry. Dump in the flour and sprinkle the salt over the top. Use one hand in the beginning because you will need the other to add water. With your fingers spread wide, mix in the flour until you form a dough. It will be mushy. With the one hand, keep pressing down, mixing and kneading, while turning the bowl with the other hand.

2. The dough should come together into a ball, pulling away from the sides of the bowl. It is almost ready as it pulls away from the sides of the bowl. Clean around the sides of the dough and under the dough with a sprinkle of water. Dip a closed fist into the bowl of warm water, just to get it wet. Using your fist, press down, twisting it into the dough, kneading the water in. Pull up the sides of the dough and fold the dough over onto itself. Keep dipping your fist into the water and repeat the method of pressing down into the dough and pulling and folding it over until the water is used up. You should see the texture in the dough change. This will take about 20 minutes for this hand method. You need to develop the elasticity in the dough. When it has been sufficiently kneaded, the dough should spring back slightly when pressed lightly with your index finger.

(continued)

Take a walnut-size piece of dough, dust with flour and stretch it to the point of almost seeing through it like a windowpane without tearing it. When you can do this, it is sufficiently kneaded. Cover well. I generally use a dough-rising bucket that has a lid, then I place several kitchen towels over to protect it from drafts. If I am not using a bucket, I cover the bowl with plastic wrap and then place towels over, around and under the bowl. (Old-timers would use clean bath towels or blankets to cover bowls because they were thick and warmer. Some still use that method or multiple kitchen towels and aprons.) Let the dough rise in a warm, draft-free place (not on a stone surface) until doubled in size, about 1 hour to 1 hour 15 minutes.

3. Without punching down, divide the dough into 3 or 4 equal parts or the sizes you want. Roll into rounds if making a round loaf, or if making the Vienna, just take one part of the dough, then gently form into about a 10-inch/25-cm log, rolling your hands back and forth and slightly stretching lengthwise into an oval. Elongate and taper the ends into a slight point. Place the shaped dough on floured kitchen towels or a tablecloth, spaced 4 inches/10 cm apart. Cover well with towels and let rise until almost doubled in size, about 30 minutes. If you let the dough rise to fully double again, the yeast will lose its power in the oven.

4. Meanwhile, preheat the oven to 400°F/200°C, or gas mark 6. Place a pan of water in the lower or highest rack of the oven. If using a stone, place it in the cold oven to preheat. When the dough is ready, transfer the loaves of dough, upside down, onto a wooden oven peel (shovel). Bring the shovel over to the oven. Using the sharp edge of a lamé razor or knife, make a shallow slice (about ¼ inch/6 mm) at a slight angle from one end to the other (see Note). Immediately shuffle the peel to the farthest edge of the preheated stone, lightly jerk it and slide the dough onto the preheated stone, or bake on parchment-lined sheet pans instead. Do not open the oven door, especially during the first 15 minutes. Bake for about 35 minutes. The breads should be golden and have a hollow sound when thumped on the bottom. You will want to have the butter waiting.

Note: Scoring bread dough can take some practice. It is important to do it near the oven door and just seconds before placing the dough in the oven. My father would have the oven door open just before scoring. After closing the oven door, do not open it during the first 15 minutes of baking.

Crusty Puffed-Up Rolls

Papo-secos

MAKES ABOUT 2 DOZEN

Adapted from *Portuguese Homestyle Cooking*, one of the most popular breads for the Portuguese are these crusty rolls. The day's batch never lasted long in my father's bakery. Like my father, I believe good bread cannot be rushed. However, today's yeast speeds the old three-plus days of making sponges and dough starters. Here, my father's recipe is converted back to a smaller size batch that is made in our home, and without preservatives. It still calls for patience so the dough will rise with a developed flavor. If possible, use a hard red spring wheat flour with a high protein content (14%). A strong, high-protein flour requires more water and an extra yeast boost. Otherwise, regular bread flour can be used.

EQUIPMENT

Sheet pan or oven stone and wooden oven peel

Digital kitchen scale

Shallow pan to fit on rack

Free-standing mixer

4 broadcloth kitchen towels

Instant-read thermometer

FOR THE SPONGE

1 ——— cup/235 ml water, 80°F/26.7°C

1 ——— ¼-ounce/7-g package dry yeast

1 ——— cup/120 g high protein flour (about ¼ pound)

FOR THE DOUGH

6 ——— cups (about 1¾ pounds/795 g) high-protein (14%) spring hard red wheat flour, scooped

2 ——— scant tablespoons/28 g lard or shortening

2 ——— scant tablespoons (1 ounce/28 g) table salt

2 ——— scant tablespoons (1 ounce/28 g) sugar

1 ——— ¼-ounce/7-g package dry yeast

2 ——— cups/470 ml lukewarm water, 80°F/26.7°C, divided

½ ——— cup/60 g rice flour, for dusting

FOR THE SPONGE

1. Pour the water into a bowl and scatter the yeast over it, then stir to dissolve. Mix in the flour until blended. Cover with plastic and set aside at room temperature, covered, in a warm spot, until doubled in size, about 1 hour.

FOR THE DOUGH

1. Dump the hard wheat flour into the bowl of a stand mixer. Rub the shortening with your hands or fingers with the flour to distribute evenly. Mix in the salt, sugar and dry yeast, mixing with flour for about 1 minute to make sure everything is well blended. A stand mixer really helps to develop the gluten in a high-protein flour.

2. Make a well in the middle of the flour and add the sponge with 1½ cups/295 ml of the warm water. Using the dough hook on the highest speed, mix for 15 minutes, developing the gluten. After mixing for just 5 minutes, if needed, pour in small increments of the remaining ½ cup/120 ml water. Mix and knead until the dough comes together, pulls away from the sides of the bowl and becomes smooth and elastic. The dough, when it has been sufficiently kneaded, should slightly spring back when pressed lightly with your finger. Do the windowpane test, stretching a small piece of dough without tearing, so thin you can almost see through it. If it tears, knead a few minutes longer until it stretches. Cover tightly with plastic wrap, then cover completely with large towels.

3. Set aside in a warm, draft-free spot to rise until doubled in size, about 1½ hours. Punch the dough down to redistribute the gases and recover. Set the dough aside to rise for 45 minutes more.

4. Turn out the dough onto a floured large wooden cutting board. Divide the dough into 22 to 24 equal-size pieces, about 2.5 ounces/73 g in weight.

(continued)

Rounds of dough are flattened, folded over and given a slight stretch. The ends are punched and rolled into a point. After second rise they are baked.

5. Place the palm of your hand, curling your fingers like a claw, over a piece of dough, then move the piece of dough in a circular motion against the work surface. Rotate the dough inside the cage of your hand, rolling, until each piece is a fairly tight and smooth ball. Repeat with remaining pieces. Set aside each rolled piece of dough, about 3 inches/7.5 cm apart, on a floured board, cover with a towel and let relax for about 15 minutes.

6. Lightly dust your work surface with flour. Use your open palm to flatten each ball into a disk about 4 inches/10 cm in diameter. Give a light dusting of rice flour to the top of the disks. Make a deep impression across the center of the disks with the side of the palm of your hand, as though you were dividing it in half.

7. Place one thumb at each end of the impression and slightly stretch the dough disks lengthwise to make it slightly more oval. Fold the dough on the impression and pinch the ends to secure the fold, giving the ends a slight roll to a point. Only roll the points.

8. Transfer each roll upside down (fold side up) onto lightly floured kitchen towels, 3 inches/7.5 cm apart, in rows. Cover each row as you complete it to keep the dough warm. Follow with a larger towel. Now just let the rolls rise until almost doubled in size, about 30 to 45 minutes, because you want it to finish springing in the oven.

9. Set an oven stone on the center shelf of the cold oven and an empty shallow pan on the top shelf. Preheat the oven to 400°F/200°C, or gas mark 6.

10. Remove enough rolls from under the toweling that will fit on the wooden shovel. Turning them right side up, set the rolls in rows on the shovel. Pour water into the preheated empty pan on the shelf to create steam. Quickly bring the tip of the shovel onto the oven stone. With small jerks, pull back the shovel while sliding the rolls onto the oven stone. Make sure the rolls are upright. Bake for about 20 minutes, until lightly golden and hollow sounding when tapped on the bottom. Use the shovel to scoop them up. Repeat with the remaining rolls. *Papo-secos* do not have fluffy, cottony interiors. The crust should be crispy and the crumb should be slightly dense, with substance to it.

I am dedicating this next recipe to one of my dearest friends, Marguerite. We met when she was a young mother and I was a teenager. In those early years, I babysat for her and often just visited, where we bonded. Every holiday she would make—or I should say, attempt to make—sweet bread, or massa, *as the Azoreans call it. Time after time, her breads exited the oven, dense, rubbery and heavy like bricks. We laughed every time. At the end of one baking session, during the Vietnam War, her husband quipped, "Perhaps, we should send these to the president so he can use them as bullets for the war." To this day, she has trouble. Once or twice, we all thought she was making progress. We even tried to fool her family with one of mine, but they knew by just looking at it. Although mine are becoming more regular on her table, she continues to bake her "bread" because her family feels it would not be the same if she didn't. She often relates to me how she jokingly tells folks she is upset with me because I didn't ask her for her recipe to add to this book. I tell her that I would not want her secret recipe to get out.*

***

Ana's Sweet Bread
Pão Doce d'Ana (A Minha Moda)

MAKES 4 OR 5 BREADS

I never gave much thought as to why I made my sweet bread with a potato and its water. When asked why, I really didn't have an answer other than it was a handed-down method, made in our family bakery. So I tested it without potato and found that although the bread still tasted good, the rise and texture of the bread wasn't as moist and tender. Over the years I have tweaked this family recipe here and there to get a lighter, moister texture. Some regions make a heavier bread, while others, especially on the mainland, can be fluffy. I like to think mine falls somewhere in between. My use of a potato and a low baking temperature results in a moister, somewhat dense but lighter crumb that won't fall apart in the toaster. It will seems like it has a lot of sugar, but the sugar is what makes this bread soft and moist with a tender crumb. It is what some might call *meia cozida*, or half baked. I assure you it is baked, but just enough to prevent dryness. I hope you will enjoy it as much as my Alentejo family and friends do. For those of you who are avid bakers, this recipe follows a straight dough method. Before you begin, make sure all ingredients are at room temperature and your yeast is good. Check the date of your yeast. Allow yourself, from beginning to end, approximately 5 to 7 hours for this recipe. This recipe can also be cut in half. Read the recipe thoroughly before beginning.

EQUIPMENT
2-quart/1.8-L container with tight lid (optional) or bowl
12-quart/10.8-L dough-rising bucket or warm bowl
Instant-read thermometer

FOR THE SPONGE

1 ——— medium potato, peeled, cut into large chunks

3 ——— cups/705 ml water

3 ——— ¼-ounce/7-g packages (6¾ teaspoons) dry yeast or SAF brand Gold yeast (great for sweet doughs)

2 ——— large eggs, at room temperature, lightly beaten

1 ——— tablespoon/12 g sugar

1 ——— cup/120 g unbleached bread flour, sifted

FOR THE DOUGH

2 ——— cups/470 ml whole milk

1 ——— pound/454 g butter, at room temperature, divided

4½ ——— cups/900 g sugar

Peels of 2 whole lemons, without pith

10——— large eggs, at room temperature

1 ——— teaspoon/3 g ground cinnamon

5 ——— pounds/2270 g unbleached bread flour (12% protein)

1 ——— teaspoon/6 g table salt

Notes: Using a food server glove for this sticky dough will prevent dough from sticking to your hands.

Not all brands of flour come in a 5-pound/2270-g weight. Some all-purpose Canadian brands are 5½ pounds/2500 g, which would need a little more milk.

If you forget to remove your eggs from the refrigerator to bring them to room temperature, simply fill a bowl halfway with warm water and submerge the eggs until the chill is gone.

If you have overheated your milk, just wait 15 minutes or so, until it has cooled. Check with an instant-read thermometer if you have one.

FOR THE SPONGE

1. Boil the potato in the water in a covered pot until easily falling apart with a fork, about 20 to 25 minutes. Reserving the cooking water, remove the potato to a plate or bowl and use a couple of tablespoons/30 ml of cooking water to help mash with a fork until a smooth purée is formed (you don't want it to be watery). You should have about 1 cup/225 g fairly thick puréed potato. Strain through a mesh sieve to remove any lumps. Set aside to cool to 110°F/37.8°C.

2. When the cooking liquid has cooled to 100° to 110°F/37.8° to 43.3°C, pour 1 cup/235 ml of the remaining warm potato water into a 2-quart/1.8-L container or bowl and sprinkle the yeast over it. Mix slightly, cover, and let stand for 10 minutes to proof. Stir the lightly beaten eggs, the sugar, warm (not over 100°F/37.8°C) puréed potato and flour into the yeast, blending well, to make a loose dough. Cover tightly and let rise until doubled in size, approximately 15 to 20 minutes. It should nearly fill the 2-quart/1.8-L container.

FOR THE DOUGH

1. While the potato is cooking, pour the milk into a medium saucepan. Cut ¾ pound/340 g of the butter into 2-inch/5-cm pieces. Add the cut-up butter, sugar and lemon peels to the milk. Stir to blend and set the pan over medium-low heat. Do not allow the milk to boil, but heat until the butter is melted and the sugar is dissolved, about 15 minutes. Remove the lemon peels. Cool to about 100° to 110°F/37.8° to 43.3°C, or cool enough so it won't curdle the eggs or burn your hand.

2. Beat the eggs in a medium bowl using an electric mixer until frothy, about 1 minute. Set aside.

3. Separately, in a small pan, melt the remaining ¼ pound/112 g (8 tablespoons) butter and keep warm.

4. Combine the cinnamon, flour and the salt in an extra-large bowl or the 12-quart/10.8-L dough-rising bucket. Stir to evenly distribute the cinnamon and salt. Make a well in the middle. Pour in the beaten eggs along with the yeast sponge, which should be doubled by now. Butter your mixing hand. While holding the bowl with the other hand, use the buttered hand, your fingers outstretched, to mix the beaten eggs and yeast sponge with the flour. With your clean hand, pour half of the sweetened, somewhat cooler but still warm flavored milk into and around the mix. Knead it in. (If you are making the *bolo rei* [see page 278], add the fruits and nuts at this time.) Gradually incorporate the remaining warm sweetened milk to form a semisoft dough. Knead with a closed fist, punching the dough all around the mixing container, then pulling the edges of dough up, over and on top of itself. Keep kneading this way until the dough pulls away from the sides and is getting smooth, about 5 minutes. Do not add additional flour.

Breads (*Pães*) — 275

(continued)

TO SHAPE

2 to 4 — tablespoons/28 to 45 g butter, for buttering hands during shaping

1 ——— large egg beaten with 1 tablespoon/ 15 ml water for egg wash

Variation: For Easter *folares*, nicknamed *brindes*, meaning a present: To make about 25 to 30 buns, use a kitchen scale to divide the dough into 6-ounce/ 168-g rounds. Although years ago the eggs sported their natural color, today the *folares* are made with colorful eggs embedded in the bread dough after they have been shaped, but before rising the second time. The colorful dough, once risen, has strips of extra dough brushed with egg wash and crisscrossed over each colored egg to "glue" them securely before baking. To add the eggs, color them raw and let dry. Carefully place in the dough, pressing very lightly. Uncooked eggs are less likely to burst or crack open than precooked ones. Keep in mind the addition of colored eggs will hold down the rise of the dough where they are placed. Once baked with eggs, keep refrigerated. Some folks may even brush the baked bread with melted butter after removing from the oven. Even today, grandmothers, mothers and others make little ones with a single colored egg as a *brinde* for beloved children.

5. Pour the reserved melted butter over, under and around the dough, kneading it in. With your buttered hand, knead well for 10 minutes, until the dough is fairly smooth and pulls away from the sides of the bowl. This dough is kneaded in the bowl, not on a workspace. It should spring back slightly when pressed lightly with your index finger. The dough will be smooth but slightly sticky and buttery. Cover with plastic wrap if you are using a bowl, or transfer to a dough-rising bucket, if you have one, and cover with the lid. Then cover the sealed bowl or container with towels and place in a warm, draft-free spot until doubled in size. Try not to rush the rising. Do not place the bowl or container on a cold surface like a stone counter. Put it on a wooden board or on top of a doubled-up dish towel. The 12-quart/10.8-L dough-rising bucket with a lid works extremely well. They are available at restaurant supply stores. When the dough reaches the top of my bucket, I know it is ready. The dough should double in about 1½ to 2 hours.

TO SHAPE

1. Clean your kitchen counter for a workspace before handling the dough. Whether your workspace is stone, Formica, enamel or stainless steel, give a generous coating of butter on the surface. Butter your hands to prevent sticking. Divide the dough into 4 or 5 equal parts. Shape each part into free-formed rounds, ovals, rectangles or rings.

To make a twisted ring: Pull the dough into a slightly rough rectangle. Grab each end and give a slight lengthwise stretch, flapping it on the workspace and then twisting each end in the opposite direction of the other. Bring the ends together, overlapping them to form a ring. Place on a parchment-lined sheet pan or round aluminum pie pans. (You can also use parchment-lined loaf pans, cutting the parchment to fit for formed rectangular loaves, to slice evenly for the toaster.) After shaping all the dough, cover and let them rise to almost doubled in size, about 45 minutes. (They will finish rising in the oven.)

2. Preheat the oven to 325°F/170°C, or gas mark 3.

3. When the breads have risen until nearly double on the second rising, make 4 evenly spaced slashes on the ring shape; for other shapes, slash the tops, about ½ inch/1.3 cm deep, in the shape of a cross. Brush the tops and slashes with the egg wash. Bake for about 35 minutes, until a wooden skewer comes out clean when inserted into the thickest part of the bread. If the breads are larger, bake a couple of minutes longer, until the skewer comes out clean. The color will be lightly golden. Any longer baking and the dough will not be as moist. Do not overbake.

King's Bread
Bolo do Rei

MAKES 4 OR 5 BREADS

During Christmastime, for Epiphany Sunday, make king's bread with the additions listed below. Tradition has it that whoever finds the broad bean in his or her bread will have good luck for the year. These, of course, can be altered to suit your taste. My family prefers that I just decorate the top before placing in the oven.
Caution: if swallowed accidentally, the broad bean can cause a choking hazard.

---

1 ——— recipe Ana's Sweet Bread (page 274)

¼ ——— cup/60 ml brandy of choice

¼ ——— cup/35 g raisins

¼ ——— cup/30 g chopped dried apricots

¼ ——— cup/35 g finely chopped walnuts

¼ ——— cup/30 g chopped dried fruit of choice

5 ——— dried broad/fava beans, as needed, see headnote

1 ——— large egg beaten with 1 tablespoon/ 15 ml water

Crystalized fruit, as desired

¼ ——— cup/35 g pine nuts, toasted

Coarse non-melting sugar (optional)

1. Make the sweet bread recipe, incorporating the brandy, raisins, dried apricots, walnuts and chopped dried fruit in step 4. Continue with step 5 and then shape as directed. Push one bean into each of the breads, if using. Brush with the egg wash, cut the crystallized fruit as desired and arrange decoratively on the dough and scatter the toasted pine nuts over. If you have non-melting coarse sugar, a sprinkling here and there on top gives the finishing touch. Bake as directed on page 277.

God's Bread

Pão de Deus

These delightful buns are thoroughly enjoyed in the north of Portugal, especially by my friend Laureen Andria, when she visits her husband's family in Vila Real of the Trás-os-Montes and Alto Douro regions, and in Marco de Canaveses, near Porto. These sweet little buns with the crowning finish of crunchy, toasted coconut won me over— and I was never a fan of coconut. Here I have adapted the recipe using potato. You don't have to use the potato and potato water, but I find it gives a tender crumb to the bun. If you prefer, just use regular water or milk and eliminate the puréed potato.

EQUIPMENT

Instant read thermometer

1 ———— quart/1-L container with cover

FOR THE SPONGE

3 ———— ¼-ounce/7-g packages dry yeast

½ ———— cup/120 ml warm potato water or plain water, 100° to 110°F/37.8° to 43.3°C

1 ———— cup/120 g all-purpose flour

½ ———— cup/120 g warm puréed boiled potato

½ ———— cup/120 ml warm whole milk, 100° to 110°F/37.8° to 43.3°C

1 ———— teaspoon/5 g sugar

FOR THE DOUGH

5 ———— cups/625 g all-purpose flour

½ ———— teaspoon ground cinnamon

⅓ ———— cup/75 g butter

1 ———— cup/200 g sugar

3 ———— large eggs, at room temperature, lightly beaten

1 ———— teaspoon/6 g table salt

Grated orange or lemon peel (optional)

¼ ———— cup/60 ml orange or lemon juice

FOR THE SPONGE

1. In a small bowl, dissolve the yeast in the warm potato water or plain water, making sure it isn't too hot or it will kill the yeast. Use your thermometer to check the temperature. Cover and let stand for 10 minutes to proof; it will form a bubbly foam on top.

2. In a 1-quart/1-L container, preferably with a lid, combine the proofed yeast, flour, puréed potato, warm milk and sugar. Mix well, cover and allow to stand in a warm place until doubled in size, about 15 to 20 minutes.

FOR THE DOUGH

1. Dump the flour into a large bowl. Add the cinnamon and stir well to distribute throughout, about 1 minute.

2. In a small saucepan over medium heat, combine the butter and sugar and heat until the butter is melted and the sugar is almost dissolved, about 10 to 15 minutes. Cool slightly.

3. Make a well in the middle of the flour and pour in the eggs, salt, grated orange peel, orange juice and yeast sponge. Mix with one hand while drizzling in the sweetened warm butter with the other. Then use both hands to knead until all is well incorporated, about 10 minutes. It will be a soft dough. Transfer the dough to a buttered bowl or dough-rising bucket with a lid, turning to coat. If using a bowl, cover with plastic followed by a small blanket on top to keep it warm and keep in a draft-free place until doubled in size, about 1 hour.

(continued)

FOR THE TOPPING

1 ——— large egg white, whipped

2 ——— teaspoons/8 g granulated sugar

½ ——— cup/50 g fine flaked sweetened coconut

1 ——— large egg yolk lightly beaten with 2 tablespoons/30 ml water

Confectioners' sugar, for dusting

4. Dump the dough out onto a wooden board (stone is too cold) and divide into 12 to 18 even pieces. Take a piece of the dough and place it on the board. Cover it with your hand, positioned like a claw over it, and move in a circular motion to give it a smooth, round shape. Place on parchment-lined sheet pans and cover with a kitchen towel. Repeat with the remaining dough, moving quickly so the dough doesn't cool off too much. Leave plenty of room between them, placing just 8 on a pan. Cover, keep warm and let rise again until almost doubled in size.

5. Meanwhile, prepare the topping.

FOR THE TOPPING:

1. Beat the egg white and granulated sugar together in a small bowl. Incorporate the coconut, mixing well. Set aside.

2. Preheat the oven to 325°F/170°C, or gas mark 3.

3. When the buns are nearly doubled in size, gently brush the tops of the buns with the egg wash. Use your thumb and gently make an indentation in the top of each bun. Place a generous teaspoon/5 g of the topping in each one. Place the sheet pan in the oven and bake for 20 minutes (or bake at 350°F/180°C, or gas mark 4, for 15 minutes), until medium light golden. A toothpick inserted into the center should come out clean even if the top seems soft. The bottom will be slightly darker, so be careful not to overbake. These do not take very long to bake.

4. Remove from the oven and allow to cool. Dust generously with the confectioners' sugar and have your coffee or tea ready.

Sleeping Sweet Buns
Dormidos de Penalva de Castello

MAKES 3 DOZEN

This recipe gets its name because traditionally the dough was made in the early evening, and after the shaping, the dough was put to bed on towels to "sleep" overnight for the second rising. These buns are infused with orange and have a dense interior crumb, perfect for morning coffee or afternoon tea. I have made them using olive oil as well as melted butter, and they are delicious either way. Olive oil is cholesterol-free and gives it a denser crumb and different taste. Here I have substituted butter for the oil and yeast instead of using baking powder and baking soda, giving it a buttery flavor. These make delicious little *brindes* (presents) for the inner child.

FOR THE SPONGE

2 ——— ¼-ounce/7-g packages dry yeast

½ ——— cup/120 ml warm water, 100° to 110°F/37.8° to 43.3°C

1 ——— teaspoon/4 g sugar

½ ——— cup/60 g flour

FOR THE DOUGH

6 ——— large eggs, at room temperature

1½ —— cups/300 g sugar

½ ——— cup/120 ml whole milk

½ ——— cup/120 ml orange juice

¼ ——— cup/60 ml brandy (optional)

Peel of 2 whole oranges, not grated

6½ —— cups/780 g all-purpose flour, divided

1 ——— teaspoon/3 g cinnamon

½ ——— cup/120 ml warm melted butter or warm olive oil

1 ——— egg beaten with 1 tablespoon/ 15 ml water

Coarse baker's sugar or granulated sugar

FOR THE SPONGE

1. In a small bowl or cup, sprinkle the yeast over the warm water. Stir in the sugar. Cover and set aside for 10 minutes to proof. Mix the flour into the proofed yeast. Cover and let rise until doubled in size.

FOR THE DOUGH

1. Beat the eggs in a small bowl until frothy. Set aside.

2. In a medium saucepan combine the sugar, milk, orange juice, brandy and orange peels. Set the pan over medium heat and bring to a scald, dissolving the sugar, about 15 to 20 minutes. Do not boil. Remove from the heat and discard the peel. Cool slightly.

3. Dump 5 cups/600 g of the flour into a large bowl and add the cinnamon, mixing well to distribute evenly. Make a well in the middle of the flour and pour in the beaten eggs and yeast sponge. Mix while slowly incorporating the warm, orange-infused sweetened milk followed by the warm melted butter. Mix everything thoroughly, forming a dough. If you need to add more of the remaining flour, do so in ½-cup/60-g increments. The dough should be pulling away from the sides of the bowl. It will still be a little sticky, so butter your hands and then knead for 10 to 15 minutes, pulling the sides of the dough onto itself, into a ball. It will be like a cookie dough, just not as stiff. Cover well and set aside in a draft-free spot to rise until doubled in size.

4. Preheat the oven to 325°F/170°C, or gas mark 3.

5. Divide the dough into 36 even pieces. Shape into little rounds on your workspace. Place on parchment-lined sheet pans and cover for a second rise, but only to nearly doubled in size. When ready, turn over, bottom side up, pinch the tops, brush generously with the egg wash and sprinkle with the coarse sugar. Bake for about 25 to 30 minutes, until lightly golden. Check the bottom of the rolls to make sure they are not too dark or burning.

Desserts

Sobremesas

Portuguese desserts go beyond sweet rice pudding, sweet bread and custard tarts. Egg white meringues baked into lusciously light cakes, filo thin dough filled and baked into delicately crisp pastries and a decadent no-bake chocolate dessert are just a few examples of a greater choice for one's sweet tooth. Once upon a time desserts were reserved for special occasions and holidays. Today, social gatherings are sure to be blessed with an array of sweet treats for everyone's pleasure. Lemon, orange and lime peels are the traditional flavoring elements used for puddings and baked goods.

Cinnamon and Sugar Dusted Fried Dough Pastries
Malassadas/Filhós

Depending on whom you are speaking with and where they are from, you will hear *filhós* and *malassadas* referring to basically the same thing (though *malassadas* typically do not have a hole in the middle and will have a soft doughy center): a fried dough pastry that is dusted with sugar. Typically, *filhós* of Graciosa will be shaped like a doughnut and they have been called "Portuguese doughnuts." *Malassadas*, like those of São Miguel, are pieces of dough stretched into triangles, squares or rounds. Quick batter versions of *filhós* from the northern mainland are spoon-dropped into free-form fritters. The shape is really a regional thing. The Alentejo has fritters made with squash and pumpkin called *bêilhós*. The *filhós* of the Alentejo, page 291, an exception to the cake-like textures, are crisp, fried, thin twisted pastries with orange, cinnamon and brandy flavors. A similar pastry with a different shape, called *coscurões*, is found in other regions. I have tasted many, and the following recipes are only a few of the better ones. It would be a book in itself to print everyone's recipe that I have been given. *Filhós* of any variety are quite popular, especially at Christmastime, at Carnival time, for special occasions, and, of course, at street fairs.

Aunt Leta's Carrot Fritters
Filhós de Cenoura da Tia Leta

MAKES ABOUT 2 DOZEN

Teresa Gonçalves Baker's aunt Leta, who lives in New Jersey, makes these wonderful, puffy carrot fritters. They are easy to make and delicious to eat, not to mention loaded with vitamin A. This recipe can be cut in half. They can also be made with pumpkin or squash like the ones in the Alentejo that are yeast raised. These are a perfect treat for getting children to eat their vegetables. The number it makes depends on the size of the spoon and how generously you fill it. Make sure the carrots are well drained because excess moisture will affect their lightness. They are best eaten on the same day.

THE DAY BEFORE

1 ——— pound 10 ounces/735 g carrots, peeled

THE NEXT DAY

1 ——— cup/200 g sugar

3 ——— large eggs, lightly beaten

2 ——— cups/240 g all-purpose flour

2 ——— teaspoons/6 g baking powder

Grated peel of 1 lemon

1 ——— teaspoon/6 g table salt

Vegetable, grapeseed or corn oil, for frying

1 ——— teaspoon/3 g ground cinnamon mixed with 1 cup/200 g sugar

THE DAY BEFORE

1. In a pot over medium-high heat, boil the carrots in water until very tender, about 25 minutes; drain well and purée. Let stand in a strainer set in a bowl overnight to drain completely. You should have about 1½ cups/340 g puréed carrots.

THE NEXT DAY

1. Using the high speed of an electric hand mixer, thoroughly beat the puréed carrots, sugar, eggs, flour, baking powder, lemon peel and salt together in a large bowl for about 5 minutes. Cover and let rest for 20 minutes.

2. Heat 5 inches/12.5 cm of oil in a deep saucepan to 350°F/180°C over medium-high heat. If you have an electric fryer, all the better. Fry the batter by generous teaspoons, into golden puffs. Toss the puffs in the cinnamon sugar mix and serve.

Fried Dough of Graciosa

Filhós da Graciosa

MAKES ABOUT 4½ DOZEN

Dilia Luz, who is from the island of Graciosa in the Azores, likes to use Canadian brands of flour, which contain a dough conditioner that she feels makes a difference. However, she also gets excellent results using regular unbleached all-purpose flour. She makes the *filhós* about 4 inches/10 cm in diameter rather than the typical 6-inch/15-cm ones. Sometimes the larger ones can be heavier and they need to fry longer to be cooked through, ending up a darker golden color. Biting into her version is like biting into a delicately sweet, golden ring of air. They require less frying time, thus absorbing less oil. Dusted lightly with sugar makes it difficult to eat just one. I have cut this recipe in half. Be sure to use a thermometer and make sure your yeast is fresh before starting. It is best to weigh the flour if you can.

EQUIPMENT

Instant-read thermometer

2 ——— 12-inch/30.5-cm ¼-inch/6-mm diameter wooden dowels, for turning the doughnuts over

FOR THE SPONGE

1 ——— ¼-ounce/7-g package dry yeast

¼ ——— cup/60 ml warm water, 100° to 110°F/37.8° to 43.3°C

1 ——— tablespoon/12 g sugar

FOR THE DOUGH

2½ ——— pounds/1135 g Santa Isabella or Five Roses flour (see Note) or unbleached all-purpose flour (8½ to 9 cups)

¼ ——— teaspoon table salt

2 ——— cups/470 ml whole milk

½ ——— cup/120 ml water

½ ——— teaspoon ground cinnamon

1 ——— tablespoon/12 g sugar, plus 1 to 2 cups/120 to 240 g for coating, divided

6 ——— large eggs, at room temperature

1 ——— tablespoon/6 g grated lemon peel or 2 teaspoons/10 ml lemon extract

3 ——— tablespoons/45 ml hot melted butter

Vegetable, grapeseed or corn oil, for frying

FOR THE SPONGE

1. In a cup or small bowl, sprinkle the yeast over the water. Stir in the sugar and cover. Let stand for 10 minutes to proof.

FOR THE DOUGH

1. Dump the flour and salt into a very large bowl and whisk to evenly distribute the salt.

2. In a small pot, heat the milk, water, cinnamon and 1 tablespoon/12 g of the sugar until warm (100°F/37.8°C), not boiling, about 10 minutes. Set aside to cool.

3. In a bowl, beat the eggs until frothy. Make a well in the center of the flour and mix in the beaten eggs, proofed yeast sponge, warm flavored milk and grated lemon peel, forming a dough. Knead the dough for 10 to 15 minutes until it is pulling away from the sides of the bowl and is smooth. When it has been sufficiently kneaded, the dough should spring back slightly when pressed with your index finger.

4. Pour half of the hot melted butter over the dough, spreading it over. Pull up and fold the edges of the dough over the butter, bringing the dough onto itself, repeating around the bowl. Cover and let rise for about 30 minutes.

(continued)

5. Rewarm the remaining melted butter and repeat as before. Punch and turn the dough. Cover the dough well with plastic wrap and towels. Set in a draft-free spot. Let rise until doubled in size, about 1 to 1½ hours longer. You will see some bubbles form under the surface of the dough. Don't rush the rising. This is a softer dough than others I have experienced. It is more of a gloopy, extra-thick batter. There is a temptation to add extra flour but don't because it will make the *filhós* heavy.

6. If you are making these alone, use a wide, deep pot to fry several at a time. (An electric deep fryer works well except you cannot fry more than 4 at a time and if you are alone it is difficult to stop and clean your hands and start again.) Pour about 4 to 5 inches/10 to 12.5 cm of corn oil into the pot and heat to about 350°F/180°C. Set up a sheet pan with the remaining 1 to 2 cups/120 to 240 g sugar.

7. Butter your hands or wet them with water so the dough won't stick to your hands. (I prefer to use melted butter on my hands because any water that hits the hot oil will spatter.) It is a sticky, wet dough. Don't overhandle the dough or stretch it out to have the perfect shape. It all works out in the frying. With one hand grab a fistful of dough about the size of a medium plum. Use the other wet or buttered hand to break it off. Poke your thumbs in the middle from each side and give a very slight stretch, forming a donut. (You cannot rotate this dough as you would other versions because it is softer due to less flour.) Drop into the hot oil, using the wooden dowels to straight them out if necessary and open up the middle. Deep-fry until light golden on one side, then turn them to fry the other side.

8. Remove with a slotted spoon. Drop into the sugar, turning to coat all sides. Place on a serving platter and repeat with the remaining dough.

Note: The Canadian brands, Five Roses or Santa Isabella, are all-purpose flours that contain ascorbic acid and enzymes as a dough conditioner. The flours come in 5½-pound/2500-g packages.

Crispy Orange-Flavored Alentejo Pastries
Filhós à Alentejana

The secret to these delicate, crispy pastries, with the essence of orange and brandy and a light coating of sugar, is rolling the dough as thin as possible. One of my family's favorite treats, especially around Christmas and Carnival, these keep in large tin containers for at least a month, if they last that long. When I was a young girl, my grandfather would give verbal instructions to me so that I would learn how to make these delightful treats. This recipe can be cut in half or doubled. Who would have guessed an Italian ravioli machine would be so handy for a Portuguese recipe?

FOR THE SPONGE

1	¼-ounce/7-g package dry yeast
¼	cup/60 ml warm water, 100° to 110°F/37.8° to 43.3°C
1	tablespoon/12 g sugar

FOR THE DOUGH

6	cups/720 g all-purpose flour, divided, plus extra for rolling
5	large eggs, lightly beaten, room temperature
½	cup/120 ml orange juice, freshly squeezed or store-bought
⅓	cup/80 ml olive oil, warmed
¼	cup/60 ml *aguardente* (whiskey or brandy)
1	teaspoon/6 g table salt

Vegetable, grapeseed or corn oil, for frying

3	cups/600 g sugar mixed with 1 tablespoon/8 g ground cinnamon, for coating

FOR THE SPONGE

1. In a cup or small bowl, sprinkle the yeast over the water, then stir in the sugar and cover. Let stand for 10 minutes, to proof.

FOR THE DOUGH

1. Dump 5 cups/600 g of the flour into a large bowl. Make a well in the center and add the yeast sponge, eggs, orange juice, olive oil, whiskey and salt.

2. Using one hand, with fingers curled like a claw, mix all the ingredients until they come together into a dough. If necessary, add the remaining 1 cup/120 g flour so that the dough is not so soft that it will stretch too easily or too sticky. Knead for 10 to 15 minutes. It should be smooth and spring back when lightly pressed with your finger.

3. Cover the bowl with plastic wrap, then cover completely with a large towel. Place the bowl in a draft-free spot and leave the dough to rise until doubled in size. It will be a slow rise and could take between 2 and 3 hours. The dough is ready when an indentation remains after you have pressed the dough again with your index finger.

4. Lay out kitchen towels near your workspace and lightly dust them with flour. Use some of the remaining flour to dust your workspace and roll out walnut-size pieces of dough into 6- to 8-inch/15- to 20-cm disks (trimming, if necessary) and about ¹⁄₁₆ inch/1.5 mm thick. Better still, if you have a ravioli machine, use it. To roll the dough with a pasta dough machine, flatten a piece of the dough, lightly dust it with some flour and pass it through the cylinders four times, cranking the level thinner each time, to achieve ¹⁄₁₆ inch/1.5 mm. Give the disks a slight stretch and place on the very lightly floured towels.

(continued)

Dough is passed through rollers of a ravioli machine then cut and shaped. Twisted shapes are deep fried and the filhós are coated with cinnamon and sugar.

5. After all the disks have been rolled, or working in batches, place the disks one at a time on a cutting board and, using a sharp knife or baker's razor, cut 4 parallel slits 1 inch/2.5 cm from the edge and evenly spaced about ¾ inch/2 cm apart. Transfer back to the towels. Repeat with the remaining dough. If you have someone helping you, he or she can roll and cut while you fry. Set up the sugar and cinnamon (see below) on a tray or large plate.

6. Heat 5 to 6 inches/12.5 to 15 cm of oil in a medium saucepan to 350°F/180°C. When the oil is quivering, pick up a disk with one hand. With the other hand, take every other loop and pull it away from the center. Then with the first hand, pull the remaining middle loop in the opposite direction, away from the center of the disk. Holding the loops out, horizontally in opposite directions, carefully lower the dough into the hot oil. Fry until golden and crisp. You might like these light golden but there is a richer taste when the pastries are fried to a medium golden. (If they are not crisp and are very golden, the dough is too thick.)

7. As they become done, transfer the pastries to a plate with the cinnamon-sugar topping and gently use your fingers to coat thoroughly. The topping will not stick as well if they are too cool. The shape will look like tangled ribbons. These are fragile and break easily. Stored in large tins, they will keep for at least a month.

Creamy Custard Tartlets
Natércias

MAKES ABOUT 24 (2-OUNCE/56-G) TARTLETS

Maria Pereira Ellis raves about her mom Blandina's *natércias*, and with good reason. They are just a mouthful of joy. Like the following recipe, these pastries are crust-free, and really take little time to prepare. Creamy, with just enough sweetness, they are perfect for a quick dessert.

EQUIPMENT:

24——— tartlet tins (2 ounces/56 g) or 2 miniature muffin pans

2¼ ——— cups/530 ml whole milk

½ ——— cup/112 g butter

2 ——— cinnamon sticks

Peel of 1 lemon

2 ——— large eggs

2 ——— cups/400 g sugar

¾ ——— cup/90 g all-purpose flour

1. Preheat the oven to 350°F/180°C, or gas mark 4.

2. Lightly grease the unlined miniature tins or miniature muffin pans with margarine or butter, then set them on a sheet pan. Heat the milk in a medium pot with the butter, cinnamon sticks and lemon peel until the butter is melted and steam is rising from the milk, about 5 minutes. Do not allow the milk to boil.

3. Using the high speed of an electric mixer, beat the eggs in a bowl with the sugar until they are thick and pale yellow, about 3 to 4 minutes. Reduce the speed to medium and gradually add the flour in small increments while beating. Slowly, while mixing, incorporate the hot milk into the batter, about 1 minute. Discard the lemon peel and cinnamon sticks.

4. Ladle a scant ¼ cup/60 g of custard into each miniature tin, filling them about three-fourths full. Place in the oven and bake until a toothpick inserted into the center comes out clean and they are lightly golden on top, about 30 to 35 minutes. Remove from the oven. They will firm up as they cool. When slightly cool, transfer to a serving dish. Cool completely. Serve cool or at room temperature. Be sure to keep refrigerated if you are not serving immediately.

Sweet Rice Pastries

Pasteis de Arroz

MAKES ABOUT 3½ DOZEN MINIATURES

Baked rice custard, infused with cinnamon and your choice of lemon or orange, has the scrumptious texture of a semi-firm pudding. I would like to say "while on my way to the forum" these little dainties came to be as I was testing a version of rice cakes. This is a perfect one-bite dessert of baked rice pudding in pastry form. Make sure you cool them completely and only just before serving, give them a good dusting of confectioners' sugar. If they stand, covered with plastic wrap with the dusted confectioners' sugar, the sugar will melt from the moisture in the pastry and you will need to re-dust them.

FOR THE RICE

2¼ —— cups/530 ml water

½ —— cup/90 g short-grain rice

EQUIPMENT

24 —— tartlet tins or a miniature muffin pan, preferably nonstick

FOR THE PASTRIES

1 —— cup/200 g granulated sugar

½ —— cup/120 ml whole milk

½ —— cup/112 g butter

Peel of 1 orange or lemon

½ —— teaspoon cinnamon

3 —— large eggs, at room temperature, separated

1 —— cup/120 g all-purpose flour

1 —— teaspoon/3 g baking powder

¼ —— teaspoon table salt

Confectioners' sugar, for dusting

FOR THE RICE

1. Bring the water to a boil in a medium pot over medium-high heat and add the rice. Reduce the heat to medium-low and cook until the rice is very mushy and tender, about 25 to 30 minutes. Remove from the heat. Do not drain. Keep covered and let stand until the residual water is absorbed into the rice. Set aside to cool.

FOR THE PASTRIES

1. Preheat the oven to 350°F/180°C, or gas mark 4. Lightly butter unlined miniature tartlet or miniature muffin tins.

2. In a 2½-quart/2.3-L pot, combine the granulated sugar, milk, butter, orange peel and cinnamon. Set the pan over medium heat and warm the contents until the milk is scalded, the butter is just melted and the sugar is dissolved, about 5 minutes. Do not boil. Discard the orange peel and set aside to cool to almost room temperature.

3. Using a food processor or alternative, purée the cooled cooked rice until fairly smooth, about 30 seconds. Transfer to a bowl.

4. Using the medium-high speed of an electric hand mixer, beat the egg yolks, one at a time, into the bowl of cooled rice. Combine the flour with the baking powder and salt. Alternating with the warm milk, fold the dry ingredients into the rice batter. Mix on low speed for about 30 seconds until well blended.

(continued)

5. Separately, in another bowl, with clean beaters, beat the egg whites to soft peaks. Fold the egg whites into the rice batter, blending until the whites are no longer visible. Fill each cup of the prepared tins three-fourths of the way with batter. Bake for 17 to 19 minutes. Or you can fill 2 dozen regular-size muffin tins and adjust the baking time to 20 to 25 minutes.

6. Remove from the oven and cool for 5 minutes. The centers will sink slightly when cooled. Transfer the pastries to a parchment-lined sheet pan to cool completely. Do not cool completely in the tins or they might be difficult to remove. If you are not serving immediately, store in the refrigerator. When ready to serve, give a generous dusting of the confectioners' sugar then, if you wish, place in paper liners for serving. Repeat with any remaining batter.

Sweet Bishop's Bread

Fatias de Bispo

SERVES 6

I don't know the origin of this bread, but it certainly is fit for a bishop. When I was a little girl, my *avó* would make egg-rich bread, without the sugar syrup. She called them *rabanadas*. Instead of a sugar syrup, she would coat the fried slices of egg-dipped bread with sugar. I called the sugar the poor man's syrup because it is cheaper than maple syrup, which wasn't available in Portugal. The bread needs to be dry to absorb the egg batter. Make these with the syrup or simply dust with confectioners' sugar. If you like French toast, you will surely enjoy these.

EQUIPMENT

Candy thermometer

FOR THE SYRUP

1 ——— cup/200 g sugar

½ ——— cup/120 ml water

Peel of 1 orange (optional)

FOR THE BREAD

8 ——— large eggs

1 ——— teaspoon/3 g ground cinnamon, plus more for sprinkling

Butter, as needed

1 ——— 1-pound/454-g loaf of bread, stale, sliced 1 inch/2.5 cm thick

FOR THE SYRUP

1. Stir the sugar and water together in a small saucepan. Bring to a boil over medium-high heat, reduce the heat to medium and simmer, uncovered, until the thermometer reads 230°F/110°C, about 5 to 7 minutes. If you want, you can add the peel of an orange to the sugar water while it is simmering. Discard the peel before using the syrup.

FOR THE BREAD

1. Beat the eggs with the cinnamon in a shallow bowl. Preheat a skillet over medium-high heat. Reduce the heat to medium. Melt some butter in the pan. Dip the bread slices into the egg, letting them soak up some of the egg batter. Fry them until golden on each side. Transfer to a serving dish and drizzle the sugar syrup over. Sprinkle with additional cinnamon if desired.

Chocolate Salami Roll

Paio de Chocolate

SERVES 8 TO 10

At one time it was rare to see chocolate desserts in Portuguese fare, but of the very few, this one is a true chocolate fix. This is a decadent, dense, fudgy chocolate roll made to resemble a sausage by its shape. It is unusual because with the exception of coddling the egg yolks, it requires basically no cooking. The cookies are crumbled into ½-inch/1.3-cm pieces, more or less. Make sure you pasteurize the eggs before using them. Lucy Rebelo, who is from the island of Terceira in the Azores, rolls her *paio* in granulated sugar. Here I have adapted her recipe, which she shared so many years ago. Mixing by hand can be a messy job, so I suggest using food service gloves. It makes cleanup a breeze.

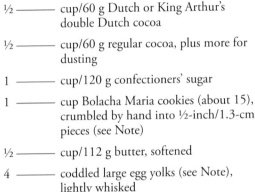

½ —— cup/60 g Dutch or King Arthur's double Dutch cocoa

½ —— cup/60 g regular cocoa, plus more for dusting

1 —— cup/120 g confectioners' sugar

1 —— cup Bolacha Maria cookies (about 15), crumbled by hand into ½-inch/1.3-cm pieces (see Note)

½ —— cup/112 g butter, softened

4 —— coddled large egg yolks (see Note), lightly whisked

2 to 3 —— tablespoons/25 to 38 g granulated sugar, for coating (optional)

Extra confectioners' sugar, for dusting (optional)

Chocolate ganache or your favorite chocolate sauce and whipped cream, for serving (optional)

1. Set a piece of 10 x 10–inch/25 x 25–cm foil on your workspace. Sift the cocoas and confectioners' sugar into a large bowl, mixing well to blend evenly, about 2 minutes. Mix in the cookie pieces, thoroughly blending.

2. Add the soft butter with the coddled egg yolks and use your hand or an electric mixer to disperse them into the dry ingredients until it all comes together into a medium-soft dough. Press the ball of dough together, with your hand, compacting it to push out any air.

3. Place the ball of dough onto a lightly cocoa-dusted workspace. Dust your hands with a small amount of cocoa and shape the dough into a log about 3½ inches/ 9 cm in diameter and 8 inches/20 cm in length. Generously dust a sheet of wax paper with cocoa and roll the chocolate log in it. Make sure it is completely coated with a dusting of cocoa. Transfer the roll to the middle of the foil and wrap it, sealing completely around it, and refrigerate several hours until it is quite firm.

4. About 30 minutes before serving, remove it from the refrigerator and unwrap. Bring to room temperature. Roll it in additional cocoa or granulated sugar, then slice into ¾-inch/2-cm or desired thickness and serve dusted with confectioners' sugar. To update this dessert, especially for festive occasions, serve slices as I do with a drizzle of your favorite chocolate ganache or chocolate sauce and a dollop of whipped cream.

Note: To coddle an egg, bring a small pot of water to a boil. Lower the egg or eggs into the boiling water and simmer for exactly 45 seconds. Remove the egg immediately and submerge in cold water. Peel the tops of the eggshells, scoop out just the yolks, and use as directed.

Note: Bolacha Maria cookies are a very thin, 2½-inch/6.4-cm cookies that the Portuguese love to use for more than just tea. They can be found in Portuguese or Spanish sections of the supermarket under different brand names. It is a popular component to desserts, especially the Bolacha Maria pudding. Tea cookies like Petite Beurre, or even animal crackers, which are similar in taste, can be substituted for this recipe.

Little Christmas Breads
Broinhas de Natal

MAKES ABOUT 4 DOZEN

The first time I tasted this Christmas gem, made with potatoes and carrots and speckled with candied fruit, I had to have another. Maria Cunha, an established cook, was generous to share her recipe. Loaded with vitamin A and potassium, this dessert couldn't be better. I substituted sweet potatoes in place of the regular ones that Maria uses. You will need a kitchen scale for this. In some regions, chopped walnuts, pine nuts, raisins and almonds are combined in this dough instead of candied fruit. On the island of São Miguel, coconut and corn flour are in some versions. Every region has its little Christmas breads. These are best eaten the same day because the texture changes after two days. These holiday treats can be frozen and then rewarmed in a low oven to serve. This recipe can be cut in half.

A DAY AHEAD

2 ——— pounds/908 g sweet potatoes

1 ——— pound/454 g peeled carrots

THE NEXT DAY

5½ to 6— cups/660 to 720 g all-purpose flour, plus more for dusting

3 ——— cups/600 g sugar

2 ——— teaspoons/4 g baking powder

4 ——— large eggs, lightly beaten

1½ —— cups/190 g candied fruit, coarsely chopped into ½-inch/1.3-cm pieces

A DAY AHEAD

1. Boil the potatoes and carrots, separately, until almost falling-apart tender, about 25 minutes. Cool and purée, separately, until smooth and set in a mesh strainer over a bowl to drain completely, preferably overnight in the refrigerator. You should have 3 cups/750 g of sweet potato purée and 1½ cups/365 g of carrot purée. They must be well drained or the breads will be too heavy.

THE NEXT DAY

1. Preheat the oven to 350°F/180°C, or gas mark 4.

2. Combine the puréed potatoes and carrots in a large bowl.

3. Mix in the flour, sugar and baking powder. Make a well in the center and pour in the eggs and candied fruit.

4. Blend the ingredients to thoroughly combine, forming a sticky, soft, medium-heavy dough, about 2 minutes.

5. With your hands lightly floured, gently pat walnut-size pieces of dough into oval shapes about 2 to 3 inches/5 to 7.5 cm long by 1½ inches/3.8 cm wide and a generous ¼ inch/6 mm thick. Set on parchment-lined or lightly greased and floured sheet pans. Let the *broinhas* rest for 10 minutes. Lightly dust with flour.

6. Bake for 20 to 25 minutes, until light golden. The texture will be moist and tender. The bottoms will be golden and have a slight exterior crunch.

Aveiro-Style Sweet Egg Filling
Ovos-Moles

MAKES ABOUT 1½ CUPS/360 G

In several of the recipes that follow, a traditional sweetened egg yolk filling is used. Some cooks rely on water-based sugar syrup while others from the town of Aveiro in northern Portugal use the starchy water from cooking rice instead of plain water to make this egg filling. The starch in the water helps thicken the egg sauce. Some just add 2 to 3 tablespoons/16 to 24 g of rice flour, a method I have not used. I have tried both types of water and it is a matter of preference. Make the filling ahead and cool completely. If you prefer to use other fillings, feel free to do so, just change the recipe name.

EQUIPMENT

Candy thermometer

Wooden spoon

MAKE THE FILLING A DAY OR
SEVERAL HOURS AHEAD

¾ ——— cup/180 ml water

¼ ——— cup/45 g rice

1¼ ——— cups/250 g sugar

12——— extra-large egg yolks (1 cup/235 ml)
         lightly beaten

Peel of 1 lemon or orange (optional)

¼ ——— teaspoon cinnamon

MAKE THE FILLING A DAY OR SEVERAL HOURS AHEAD

1. In a small pot set over high heat, bring the water to a boil. Add the rice, stir, reduce the heat and cook until tender, about 20 minutes. Drain the rice water into a 2½-quart/2.3-L pot. Discard the rice or use for something else. Bring the water back to a boil and stir in the sugar. Reduce the heat to medium. Continue to simmer, dissolving the sugar and forming a light syrup, until the temperature of the syrup reaches 230°F/110°C on the candy thermometer, about 5 to 7 minutes. Remove from the heat and slightly cool for 5 minutes.

2. Beat the yolks in a medium bowl. Mix in the lemon peel. While constantly whisking, in a thread-like stream, very slowly drizzle the syrup into the beaten egg. DO NOT whisk the eggs into the hot syrup or they will curdle. Transfer the warmed eggs back into the syrup pan.

3. Return to the stove and continue to cook over medium-low heat, stirring constantly with a wooden spoon, until thickened like pudding, about 12 to 15 minutes. Do not allow to boil. Stir in the cinnamon. With your finger, draw a line through the filling on the back of the spoon. It is ready when it holds the line and isn't runny. Remove from the heat and discard any citrus peels.

4. Pass the filling through a sieve into a bowl and set the bowl over a larger bowl of ice, stirring frequently. It will thicken more as it cools. Cover with plastic wrap, pressing the plastic wrap against the filling, and chill if you are not using immediately. This can be made a day ahead.

Filo Pastries with Sweet Egg Filling

Tentugals

MAKES 1½ DOZEN

The traditional dough for these delicate flaky pastries, from Poiares, near Coimbra in northern Portugal, is extremely similar to Greek filo dough. Technically, filo dough isn't Portuguese, but it doesn't affect the outcome of the recipe. It is tedious to roll the dough by hand, and unless you are very good at rolling dough to paper thinness, substituting filo is the way to go. With filo you can make them more often. This isn't a dessert you would make all the time, but it is worth the effort. You could make the traditional dough and use a pasta machine to roll it, but filo is so much easier and faster and I use it willingly. Maria Veludo, who is from Poiares, gave me the inspiration of using filo. These can be made small or large depending on your preference. I find it easiest to lightly butter whole sheets of filo dough, placing one on top of the other, and then with a very sharp knife cut them into the desired size before filling. This method takes less time. You can update this old classic by using the Sweet Tomato Jam on page 217, or other fruit preserves.

EQUIPMENT

20-inch/50-cm ruler

Pizza wheel or sharp knife

FOR THE FILLING

1 ———— recipe Aveiro-Style Sweet Egg Filling (page 305)

FOR THE PASTRY

1 ———— pound/454 g filo dough (this recipe will use about ½ box)

½ ———— cup/112 g butter, melted

Confectioners' sugar, for dusting

Note: One box of filo sheets will use a double recipe of the filling. Each set of 3 filo sheets should give you six pastries. One box of filo should be enough for close to 36 pastries depending on the exact number of sheets and the size you decide to cut them.

FOR THE PASTRY

1. Preheat the oven to 350°F/180°C, or gas mark 4. Line two sheet pans with parchment paper.

2. On your workspace, place one sheet of filo dough. With the lightest of hand, brush some melted butter over the dough. Do not saturate the dough. Place a second sheet of dough on top. Repeat with the butter and one more sheet of dough to make a total of three layers. Brush the top layer equally lightly with butter. You do not want too much or it will be greasy.

3. Using the ruler and sharp knife or pizza wheel, cut 6 rectangles 4½ x 6½ inches/11.4 x 16.5 cm. Each rectangle represents one pastry with 3 layers. Place a rounded teaspoon/5 g of filling in the middle, spreading slightly lengthwise. Lightly butter the edges of the rectangle. Bring one long side over by one-third, covering the filling. Then bring the other long side over, overlapping the first side, essentially folding it into thirds. Press lightly. Lightly brush any areas of the openings of the top ends with additional butter to ensure they are sealed, or they may burst open. Fold the short ends upright by about 1 inch/ 2.5 cm and place the pastry on the parchment-lined sheet pan. Repeat with the remaining rectangles. If you wish to fill the pastries with a larger portion of the filling, you will need to double the filling recipe. Beware, too much will cause them to burst open. I use a regular teaspoon, especially for the smaller size and because it is a rich filling. There are approximately 20 sheets in a box of filo. Sometimes a sheet may tear, but if layered correctly, it can still be used. Work quickly before the dough dries out.

4. Bake in the oven for 15 minutes, or until lightly golden. Cool completely, then sift confectioners' sugar over just before serving.

Sponge Cake Roll of Viana
Torta de Viana

SERVES 8 TO 10

This happens to be one of my favorite sponge cakes since I was young. The cake's crumb is ethereal, not just in taste but also in mouthfeel. Luscious and moist, it almost doesn't need any filling. The sponge cake is versatile like jelly rolls. You can add any filling and just roll the cake up. You also can make *lencinhos* (page 311). Start off making the filling so that it will have plenty of time to cool. You can make the filling a day ahead.

EQUIPMENT
Candy thermometer

1	———	recipe Aveiro-Style Sweet Egg Filling (page 305)
6	———	large egg yolks, at room temperature
3	———	large eggs, at room temperature
¾	———	cup/150 g sugar, plus more for sprinkling

Grated peel of 1 lemon or orange

¾	———	cup/90 g cake flour
½	———	teaspoon table salt
4	———	tablespoons/56 g butter, melted

Confectioners' sugar, for dusting

1. Preheat the oven to 400°F/200°C, or gas mark 6.

2. Dot an 11 x 18–inch/28 x 46–cm sheet pan with butter, then butter inside the perimeter of the pan and line the bottom of the pan with parchment paper. Set aside.

3. Whisk the yolks and whole eggs together in a medium-large bowl until frothy, about 1 minute. Tablespoon by tablespoon, whisk in the sugar as you scatter it over the foamy eggs. Using your thermometer to monitor the temperature, set the bowl over a pan of simmering water, to just warm the eggs and sugar to 110°F/43.3°C. Make sure the bottom of the bowl is not touching the surface of the water. (If they get too hot, the eggs will curdle.) Remove the bowl from the heat. Immediately, using the highest speed of your hand mixer, beat the eggs and sugar for 8 minutes. Beat until the batter falls from the beaters like pale thick ribbons onto the batter's surface, without disappearing into the batter. Remove from the heat. Fold in the grated lemon peel.

4. Place the flour and salt in a hand sieve and, in small increments to avoid lumps, gradually sift the flour over the egg batter. With your other hand and a rubber spatula, gently, without deflating, fold in the flour, using a down in the middle and up toward you vertical but circular motion. Turning the bowl as you go, fold in just to incorporate the ingredients. Then, carefully and completely, without overmixing, fold in the melted butter.

5. Immediately pour the batter onto the lined pan, spreading it evenly with an offset. Transfer to the oven immediately and bake for about 8 minutes, until a toothpick inserted into the center comes out clean. The cake will be light in color and spring slightly when pressed with your index finger.

(continued)

6. While the cake is baking, lay out a clean kitchen towel and sprinkle it generously all over with sugar. When the cake is done, remove from the oven and immediately invert the pan onto the towel. The pan should come off easily. Quickly peel the parchment paper off. Starting at the short end of the cake, take the short end of the towel, fold it up over the edge of the cake and carefully, but not too tightly, quickly roll the cake up, like a jelly roll. Let the cake cool in the rolled position. If you cool the cake before rolling, it will crack.

7. Have your filling ready. When cooled, carefully unroll the cake. Quickly spread the filling over three-fourths of the cake to within 1 inch/2.5 cm of the edges. Then quickly roll it back up without the towel. Place on a cake dish, seam side down, and sift confectioners' sugar over the top.

Variation: If you would rather not use the egg filling, spin your creativity using this traditional sponge recipe with other fillings like Sweet Tomato Jam (page 217), Spaghetti Squash Preserves (page 213) or your favorite preserves. Make your favorite chocolate ganache or orange syrup and drizzle over the top. Although it won't be *Torta de Viana,* you can give it a different name, and still it will have the same delicious sponge cake. Don't be shy; be creative.

Hankies

Lencinhos

MAKES 24

With a slight variation, I use the same delicate sponge cake as in the *Torta de Viana* to make these two-bite cream-filled treats. The name comes from the handkerchief fold of the cake squares. The filling is usually the egg filling or preserves, but sometimes the cake is simply perfect with a light drizzle of liquor-infused syrup. Ideally, the cake needs to be a little thinner than the previous recipe to facilitate folding the cake without breaking. Do not overbake or it will make the cake drier and risk cracking.

---

12 to 20–inch/30 to 50–cm ruler

1 ——— recipe Aveiro-Style Sweet Egg Filling (page 305)

1 ——— recipe Sponge Cake Roll of Viana (page 309)

Confectioners' sugar or cinnamon, for sprinkling

1. Make the filling a day or several hours ahead. Preheat oven to 400°F/200°C or gas mark 6.

2. Prepare the cake, following the recipe on page 309, but using just ½ cup/ 60 g cake flour and beat the egg batter for exactly 5 minutes, until thickened. Continue with the recipe, baking for about 8 minutes, until a toothpick comes out clean. The cake will be light in color.

3. Work quickly in these next steps. Turn the pan out onto a generous sugar-coated 11 x 18–inch/28 x 45.7–cm sheet of parchment placed on a cutting board. Quickly and carefully remove the parchment paper that was baked with the cake. If you wait it will be harder to remove. Use your ruler and a very sharp knife to cut the cake into 3- or 4-inch/7.5- or 10-cm squares, without ragged edges, folding them immediately into triangles as you go and pressing at the center point to set the shape. Once all the squares are cut and the triangles shaped, go back and slightly reopen the triangles, fill each with a generous teaspoon of the filling and reclose at the point. Transfer to paper liners and place on a serving tray. If you use a temperature-sensitive filling, such as those containing egg, cream or custard, store these in the refrigerator. Serve at room temperature. Sprinkle with an additional touch of confectioners' sugar or cinnamon just before serving.

Bride's Meringue Mattress

Colchão de Noiva

MAKES 12 TO 24 SQUARES

Some might refer to this dessert as *Torta de Claras*, but because it is so similar, I like the sound of *Colchão de Noiva* better, and it makes a perfect dessert for a bridal shower. Light and airy, sweetened egg whites are baked into a meringue sheet. The meringue is so delicate it nearly melts in your mouth. This meringue is usually plain but you can add a fine grating of lemon or orange peel to the batter, if you wish. This is a recipe that allows you to be a little creative. Switch up and use a different filling in place of the rich egg one. It is still a mattress, but a different brand. You can make this a rolled-up "mattress," but I like it flat and airy as a mattress, especially as a bride's mattress should be. For a shower, I recommend doubling the recipe, making two 11 x 18–inch/28 x 45.7–cm layers.

---

1 ——— recipe Aveiro-Style Sweet Egg Filling (page 305)

FOR THE MERINGUE "MATTRESS"
2 ——— cups/470 ml large egg whites (about 16 large whites)
1 ——— cup/200 g sugar
2 ——— ounces/56 g toasted almond slivers

Nothing is as sweet to a newly married couple as an airy mattress on their wedding night. However, there was a time, and perhaps it still is so today, when the bridesmaids or maid of honor would play a trick on the happy couple. Back then, they would remove some hay from the mattress and replace it with stones.

1. Make the filling a day or several hours ahead.

2. Preheat the oven 325°F/170°C, or gas mark 3.

3. Dot two 9 x 12–inch/23 x 30.5–cm sheet pans with butter and butter inside the perimeter. Line each pan with a sheet of parchment paper to fit.

4. Beat the egg whites in a glass or metal bowl, using the highest speed of an electric mixer, until foamy, about 2 minutes, moving the beaters around the bowl to incorporate as much air as possible. When they are frothy and foamy, continue beating while gradually adding the sugar. Continue to beat until firm stiff peaks are formed, about 3 more minutes.

5. Spread the meringue evenly in the prepared pans, about 1 inch/2.5 cm in depth. Bake for about 15 to 16 minutes. Do not overbake. Keep the meringue flat. Let it cool. Peel off the parchment that lined the pans.

6. Place one layer on a serving tray. Reserving some filling to drizzle over the top, gently spread the rest of the filling over the first layer. Carefully add the second layer of meringue on top. Drizzle the remaining filling over the top layer followed with a sprinkling of the toasted almonds. Cut into squares to serve.

Variation: Take it a step further by adding whipped cream and strawberries for an alternative nontraditional filling. Be creative.

Albufeira Tart with Custard and Spaghetti Squash Preserves

Torta de Albufeira com Natas e Doce de Gila/Chila

SERVES 10 TO 12

This recipe is dedicated to Alice Acker, who described a tart her father enjoyed in the Algarve, near Lagoa de Carvoeiro, as an Albufeira tart. I certainly can see why he enjoyed it. My version, based on her description, uses an almond pastry crust, topped with Spaghetti Squash Preserves on page 213 and finished with pastry cream as an alternative to the richer egg filling, but you can make it to your preference. You will need a tart pan with a removable bottom for this recipe. It is a rich dessert, which gives a wonderful use for spaghetti squash outside the savory dishes. If using the egg filling, it is easier first to coat the pastry base with the egg filling, then top it with the preserves. Read the directions thoroughly.

EQUIPMENT
10-inch/25-cm tart pan with removable bottom

MAKE THE DOUGH SEVERAL HOURS OR ONE DAY AHEAD

1¼	——	cups/150 g all-purpose flour
2	——	ounces/56 g (¼ cup) toasted almond flour
4	——	tablespoons/50 g sugar
¼	——	teaspoon table salt
10	——	tablespoons (5 ounces/140 g) butter, chilled, cut into cubes
1	——	large egg yolk
4	——	tablespoons/60 ml ice water, divided

MAKE THE DOUGH SEVERAL HOURS OR ONE DAY AHEAD

1. In a large bowl, or in the bowl of a food processor, combine the all-purpose flour, almond flour, sugar and salt. Cut in the butter, using a fork or pulsing 8 or 9 times in the food processor, so that it looks like coarse little pebbles. Then, add the egg yolk.

2. Using a fork to mix, drizzle in, to start, about 3 tablespoons/45 ml of the ice cold water. Form a dough, using the remaining 1 tablespoon/15 ml ice water as needed. If using the food processor, use the pulsing method, being careful not to overprocess the dough. Drizzle in the water and pulse briefly a few times, until you see the pebble-like dough pieces form. Remove the cover and press some dough together; it should be fairly soft and pliable. If ready, transfer the dough to your lightly floured workspace and gently shape into a ball.

3. Roll out on lightly floured surface to about 3 inches/7.5 cm more than the diameter of your pan. Line your tart pan, lightly pressing on the sides. Do not stretch the dough too tightly as it will shrink a little while baking. Roll your rolling pin across the top of the edges to trim. Cover the pastry shell with plastic wrap, smoothing it onto the surface so that no air is in direct contact. Place the lined tart pan on a sheet pan and place in the freezer until needed.

(continued)

EQUIPMENT

Double boiler or heavy-bottomed 2-quart/
1.8-L saucepan

FOR THE PASTRY CREAM

3 ——— large egg yolks, at room temperature

6 ——— tablespoons/72 g sugar

3 ——— tablespoons/24 g flour

1 ——— cup/235 ml whole milk, divided

2 ——— tablespoons/30 ml heavy cream

Peel of 1 orange or lemon

1 ——— 2-inch/5-cm piece of cinnamon stick

1 ——— tablespoon/14 g butter

FOR ASSEMBLY

1 ——— large egg, lightly beaten

1 ——— recipe Aveiro-Style Sweet Egg Filling
(page 305, optional)

2 ——— cups/450 g Spaghetti Squash Preserves
(page 213)

1 ——— cup/130 g sliced almonds, toasted in a
dry pan, for garnish

FOR THE PASTRY CREAM

1. Whisk the egg yolks and sugar together in a bowl until light and pale yellow, about 3 minutes. Gradually whisk in the flour. Slowly incorporate ¼ cup/60 ml of the milk. Stir well, making sure there aren't any lumps. Separately, heat the remaining ¾ cup/180 ml milk with the cream in a small pot until steaming hot, but not boiling, about 5 minutes.

2. Whisking briskly, temper the beaten eggs, as you gradually stream the heated milk into the egg mixture. Toss in the orange peel and cinnamon stick, then stir. Stir in the butter, blending well. Transfer the custard to a heavy-bottomed 2-quart/1.8-L pot or the top of a double boiler set over simmering water. (Make sure the bottom of the pot is not touching the water.) Reduce the heat to medium-low and stir constantly with a flat-edged wooden spoon until it becomes a thick pudding consistency, about 10 to 15 minutes. (If you are using a regular saucepan, be sure to stir constantly so the pastry cream doesn't burn.) Remove from the heat. Discard the citrus peel and cinnamon stick. Stir in the butter, blending well. Transfer the pastry cream to a bowl set over ice, stir occasionally and let cool. Press through a fine sieve to remove any lumps. Cover with plastic wrap or wax paper, pressing it to touch the surface to prevent a skin and condensation from forming on the custard. Reserve chilled. Makes 1 cup/235 ml.

FOR ASSEMBLY

1. Preheat the oven to 350°F/180°C, or gas mark 4.

2. Remove the pastry-lined tart pan from the freezer. Brush the pastry with the beaten egg. Prick the pastry all over with a fork to prevent bubbles. Place the cold pastry in the oven and bake for 20 minutes. Remove and allow the pastry to cool completely.

3. Spread the sweet egg filling in the bottom of the pastry shell. Gently, add the squash preserves on top.

4. Carefully spread the cold pastry cream over the preserves, to the edges of the pastry shell.

Garnish with the toasted almond slices across the top. Chill well before serving.

> *Note:* If you unable to obtain the squash or the jam, try substituting orange marmalade. The flavor and texture will be different, but adding a touch of cinnamon to it before using will enhance the flavor.

Sweet Iced Popovers

Cavacas

This delightful popover-like pastry is very popular, especially around the holidays and at Portuguese social events. I have adapted Maria Alice Pais' version here. Dolores Antunes uses a popover pan for easy shaping, and it works very well. Usually, most *cavacas* are crispy, hence the name; here, the use of olive oil makes them tender. A nonstick popover or large muffin tin makes baking these a breeze. Do not use an extra virgin type of oil, as this gives it a heavy flavor. There are many who pour a shot of port wine into the cavity of the *cavaca* and let it soak in before enjoying the popover.

EQUIPMENT

1 or 2 nonstick popover pans or deep muffin pans

FOR THE *CAVACAS*

12	———	large or 9 extra-large eggs
1	———	cup/235 ml light olive oil
2	———	cups/240 g all-purpose flour
½	———	teaspoon table salt

FOR THE ICING

2	———	cups/240 g confectioners' sugar
2 to 3	—	tablespoons/30 to 45 ml water or milk, divided
1	———	teaspoon/5 ml vanilla or lemon extract

FOR THE *CAVACAS*

1. Preheat the oven to 350°F/180°C, or gas mark 4.

2. Using the high speed of an electric mixer, whip the eggs until they are very well beaten, about 1 minute. Still beating, gradually incorporate the olive oil. Sift the flour and salt together, then gradually fold into the egg batter. Continue to beat on medium speed for about 10 to 15 minutes, incorporating air into the batter.

3. Generously oil the popover or muffin tins. Pour the batter in so that it fills each cup about half full. If you have only one popover pan, you can use a nonstick muffin pan for the remaining batter or wait until the first batch is done to reuse the popover pan.

4. Place the pans into the oven and bake the *cavacas* for about 45 minutes, until nicely golden. Do not open the oven door during the entire baking process or the muffins may collapse.

5. When the *cavacas* are done, cool slightly, and then remove them from the tins. Drizzle the topping lightly over the *cavacas* while they are still a little warm. Let the icing dry before serving. Store in an airtight nonmetal container.

FOR THE ICING

1. In a small bowl, whisk together the confectioners' sugar, 1 tablespoon/ 15 ml of the water and the vanilla. It should be smooth, with the consistency of very thick cream. Add more of the remaining water to achieve the right consistency. Please note that if you use milk instead of water, the icing will take longer to dry.

Hood Cookies of Graciosa

Capuxas

MAKES ABOUT 5 DOZEN

Maria Silva's grandchildren turn these sugar cookies upside down and call them mouse ear cookies. However, right side up, they are the shape of the old traditional hooded coverings worn by the women on the island of Graciosa in the Azores. You can see the face in the middle of the long sides. I add a touch of lemon and cinnamon to mine, but you can add orange or lime as well. Maria recommends that if you use large eggs, an additional ¾ to 1 cup/90 to 120 g of flour may be needed. Read the recipe through and have all the ingredients ready.

---

1 —— cup/225 g (2 sticks) butter

4 —— cups/480 g flour or more as needed

2 —— cups/400 g sugar

½ —— teaspoon ground cinnamon

Grated peel of 1 lemon, lime or orange (do not use any flavoring oils)

¼ —— teaspoon table salt

2 —— medium whole eggs

4 —— medium egg yolks

1. Preheat the oven to 350°F/180°C, or gas mark 4.

2. Melt the butter in a saucepan to the point of boiling.

3. Meanwhile, dump the flour, sugar, cinnamon, grated citrus peel and salt into a large bowl. Blend the ingredients, aerating them, for about 1 minute. When the butter is melted and quite hot, pour the butter over the dry ingredients, then thoroughly mix until well blended. Let cool for 15 minutes.

4. In a separate bowl, with an electric hand mixer, beat the whole eggs and yolks together until frothy, about 1 minute. Make a well in the center of the buttered, dry ingredients. Gradually, while mixing, incorporate the beaten eggs, forming a smooth, medium dough. The dough should pull away from the sides of the bowl and be pliable and easily rolled without sticking to your hands. If it is still sticky, add some more flour if necessary, in small increments, up to about ¾ to 1 cup/90 to 120 g more. Turn out the dough onto a floured workspace and knead for about 5 minutes. You will see if it is still sticky.

5. Take a piece of dough about the size of a small walnut and roll it with your hands into a ball. While holding the ball in one palm, spread open the first two fingers of the other hand, forming a narrow "V" and make a slight impression in the dough. With slight pressure and gently rocking the "V" of your fingers back and forth a few times, form a little marble-size ball in the middle of the V. Bring each end down the sides, forming the hood. Looking at it sideways, it will look like the letter *C* with a bump (the face) in the center. Carefully transfer the shaped dough to a parchment-lined sheet pan. Repeat with the remaining dough.

6. Bake for about 15 to 16 minutes, until lightly golden. Some people like to bake them until medium golden, which gives a crunchier texture, but I like a more tender bite with this cookie.

Whiskey Biscuits
Rosquilhos de Aguardente

MAKES 4 TO 5 DOZEN

Mild in flavor and low in sugar, this traditional biscuit is for dunking into hot coffee or tea. This biscuit gets leavening from the *aguardente* (hard liquor). Vodka would be the perfect substitute if you cannot get the *aguardente*. To update these biscuits, add some citrus flavor and/or cinnamon to the dough. You could even drizzle some simple confectioners' sugar icing over the cooled biscuits. A stand mixer works great for this recipe. These could be baked on a sheet pan but direct baking helps them dry quicker. I have broken down the steps to give more detail. Read the recipe through first to understand the process.

12	large eggs
2	tablespoons sugar
¾	cup/180 ml light olive oil
½	cup/120 ml *aguardente* whiskey or vodka
1	teaspoon/6 g table salt
8 to 9	cups/960 to 1080 g all-purpose flour, divided

1. Dump the eggs into the bowl of a stand mixer. Beat the eggs with the whisk on medium speed, until frothy, about 1 minute. Mix in the sugar, then gradually incorporate the olive oil and *aguardente*. Switch to the dough hook of the mixer.

2. Mix the salt with the flour in a separate bowl. In 1-cup/120-g increments, add 8 cups/960 g of the flour, mixing for about 20 seconds between each addition. Keep mixing until the dough pulls away from the sides of the bowl, about 5 minutes. Take a small walnut-size piece of dough to roll in your hands. If it seems too sticky to roll, add another ½ cup/60 g flour and mix again. It should not be too sticky or too dry but should be pliable.

3. Dust a workspace with some flour and dump the dough out onto it. Knead the dough for a few minutes until smooth.

4. Line 2 or 3 sheet pans with a clean kitchen towel and set them nearby. Take walnut-size pieces of dough and roll them into a ball. Then roll them into 5- to 6-inch/12.5- to 15-cm long ropes about ¾ inch/2 cm thick. Bring the two ends together into a ring, overlapping one end onto the other, wrapping and smoothing it onto the second end. The rings will be about 2 to 3 inches/5 to 7.5 cm in diameter. These can be made larger if desired. Place on the kitchen towel. Repeat with the remaining dough, filling the sheet pans.

5. Bring about 4 quarts/3.6 L of water to a boil in a pot. Carefully lift up a ring, keeping its shape, and drop it into the boiling water. Repeat, working in small batches with 6 or 7 of the rings at a time. When the rings rise to the surface, scoop them out and place back onto the kitchen towel to drain. Repeat with the remaining rings. Let the rings air-dry for about 15 minutes.

6. Meanwhile, preheat the oven to 500°F/250°C, or gas mark 10, with a rack set in the middle level.

(continued)

Dough is shaped into rings and simmered in water. A horizontal cut it made around the exterior of the rings before baking directly on the oven rack.

7. Using a very sharp paring knife or razor blade, make a horizontal cut in the middle of the side of each ring, cutting all around the diameter to the middle but without going through the middle.

8. Open the oven door and carefully pull the middle shelf halfway out. Carefully and quickly, place as many rings as the shelf has space for directly on the shelf. Push the shelf back in and bake for 10 minutes. Reduce the heat to 350°F/180°C, or gas mark 4, and bake for 15 minutes, then reduce the heat again to 200°F/100°C and bake for 5 minutes. Open the oven and quickly scoop them onto a sheet pan to cool. Bring the temperature of the oven back up to 500°F/250°C, or gas mark 10, to bake the remaining biscuits. When cool, store in tins. These can also be iced like the Sweet Iced Popovers on page 317.

Orange Cinnamon Cake
Bolo de Canela com Laranja

SERVES 10 TO 12

I first enjoyed this cake at my niece's christening. Her mother, MaryLou, who came from Coimbra, shared this cinnamon-lover's cake with the essence of orange. I have adapted this recipe to include orange juice to give an extra tenderness to the crumb.

---

8 ——— tablespoons/112 g (1 stick) butter

2 ——— cups/400 g granulated sugar

6 ——— large eggs, separated

2 ——— cups/240 g all-purpose flour

4 ——— teaspoons/12 g ground cinnamon

1 ——— teaspoon/3 g baking powder

½ ——— teaspoon table salt

Grated peel of 1 orange

½ ——— cup/120 ml whole milk

½ ——— cup orange juice

Confectioners' sugar, for dusting

1. Preheat the oven to 350°F/180°C, or gas mark 4. Grease and lightly flour a 10-inch/25-cm tube pan.

2. In a medium bowl using an electric mixer on medium speed, cream the butter with the granulated sugar until fluffy, about 2 minutes. Incorporate the egg yolks, beating well after each addition, mixing for 1 minute.

3. In a separate bowl, sift together the flour, cinnamon, baking powder, salt and grated orange peel. With the mixer on medium-low speed, add the dry ingredients in increments to the batter, alternating with the milk and orange juice. Continue to mix for about 2 minutes on medium speed.

4. With clean beaters on high speed in a separate bowl, whip the egg whites until soft peaks form. Fold into the cake batter. Pour the batter into the prepared pan. Bake for about 50 minutes, or until toothpick inserted into the middle comes out clean. Serve this with a dusting of confectioners' sugar. A dollop of whipped cream and perhaps a few raspberries make this an elegant dessert.

Spiced Carrot Cake with Orange

Bolo de Cenoura com Especiarias e Laranja

SERVES 10 TO 12

Freshly harvested carrots help me switch gears with some of my baking. Making use of fresh carrots in savory dishes is easy, but one of my favorite things to bake is this carrot cake.

---

9 —— extra-large eggs, at room temperature, separated

1½ —— cups/300 g granulated sugar

1 —— teaspoon/3 g ground cinnamon

½ —— teaspoon nutmeg

½ —— teaspoon ground Jamaican allspice

1 —— tablespoon/15 ml Beirão or Grand Marnier (see Note)

1 —— pound/454 g carrots, peeled, trimmed and medium grated (do not use a fine grate)

Grated peel of 1 orange

2 —— cups/240 g all-purpose flour

2 —— teaspoons/6 g baking powder

½ —— teaspoon table salt

Confectioners' sugar, for dusting

1. Preheat the oven to 350°F/180°C, or gas mark 4. Grease a 10-inch/25-cm tube pan.

2. Using an electric hand mixer on high speed, beat the egg whites until soft peaks form, about 3 minutes.

3. In a separate large bowl, beat the egg yolks for 1 minute. Gradually, by spoonfuls, incorporate the granulated sugar and continue beating on medium speed for 1 minute, then gradually mix in the spices, Beirão, carrots and grated orange peel.

4. Sift the flour with the baking powder and salt into a separate bowl. In small increments, using a spatula, fold the flour into the batter by hand, incorporating air as you do. When the flour is fully incorporated, gently fold in the beaten egg whites.

5. Pour into the prepared pan. Bake for 45 to 50 minutes, until a toothpick inserted into the middle comes out clean. Cool slightly, then loosen around the edges. Invert onto a plate and invert back onto a serving dish so that it stands upright. Dust with confectioners' sugar when completely cool.

Note: Beirão is a Portuguese liquor that has the flavors of orange and anise. Grand Marnier can be substituted.

Fluffy Bread

Pão de Ló

SERVES 10 TO 12

It has been said "Bread of the Lord" is the actual name of this cake, as *Ló* is the abbreviated form of "Lord." This particular version, which happens to be my favorite, is different from the usual ones because the eggs are not separated and there isn't any lemon or orange zest. You can add them if you wish. This cake is less fluffy than other versions but very moist. Dolores Chaves is known in our community for her version of *Pão de Ló*. The cake is versatile. It can be served as is, cut up to use in other recipes, dressed up with a fruit sauce or wherever your creativity takes you.

10-inch/25-cm angel food pan

9 or 10 — jumbo eggs (2½ cups/550 g), room temperature

2¾ —— cups/550 g sugar

1½ —— cups/225 g all-purpose flour

1. Preheat the oven to 350°F/180°C, or gas mark 4. Generously grease and flour the angel food pan.

2. Whip the eggs in a large bowl with an electric mixer, until frothy. Spoonful by spoonful, beat in the sugar until the batter is pale yellow and fluffy. Gradually sifting the flour over the batter, fold in the flour by hand, mixing for 2 to 3 minutes.

3. Pour the batter into the prepared pan. Bake for 55 minutes. Serve with a glass of port.

Madeiran Carrot Pineapple Cake with Coconut
Bolo de Cenoura com Ananás e Coco

SERVES 10 TO 12

The unusual combination of carrots, walnuts, pineapple and coconut, embodied with the essence of orange and lemon, gives this wonderfully moist cake an almost tropical feel. Arcenia Texeira, who lived on the island of Madeira, shared this wonderfully moist cake. I have adapted her recipe measurements, converting them from *chávena* measurements (6-ounce/168-g teacup) to a standardized 8-ounce/225-g cup. Teaspoon measurements have been standardized as well. This perfect cake needs no icing and is just enjoyable with a cup of tea, coffee or simply alone. Make sure you use a solid-bottom angel food or tube pan.

10-inch/25-cm tube pan

4 —— large eggs

1½ —— cups/300 g granulated sugar

2 —— cups/240 g loosely packed, finely shredded, peeled carrots

2 —— cups/290 g coarsely chopped walnuts

2 —— cups/330 g crushed pineapple, well-drained

1½ —— cups/150 g coconut flakes

2 —— teaspoons/10 ml vanilla extract

Grated peel of 1 lemon

Grated peel of 1 orange

2 —— cups/240 g all-purpose flour

2 —— teaspoons/6 g baking soda

½ —— cup/120 ml vegetable or corn oil

Confectioners' sugar, for dusting

1. Preheat the oven to 350°F/180°C, or gas mark 4. Grease and flour a tube pan well.

2. Beat the eggs on high speed with an electric mixer until frothy, about 1 minute.

3. Gradually beat in the granulated sugar, ½ cup/100 g at a time, then beat for 3 minutes.

4. Beating well after each addition, add the carrots, walnuts, well-drained pineapple, coconut, vanilla and grated lemon and orange peels, about 1 minute.

5. Mix the flour with the baking soda and fold into the cake batter.

6. Slowly incorporate the oil into the batter, mixing well for 1 minute.

7. Scrape the batter into the prepared pan.

8. Bake for at least 1 hour, or until the toothpick inserted near the center comes out clean. Do not overbake.

9. Remove from the oven. Cool for 5 minutes. Insert a knife or spatula around the sides and funnel to loosen the cake. Invert onto a plate and invert back to have the cake upright. Sprinkle with confectioners' sugar when cool.

Toasted Almond Crusted Caramel Cake
Bolo de Caramelo

SERVES 10 TO 12

Caramel lovers will enjoy this moist, intensely caramel-flavored cake. This unusual but familiar family cake found in Cousin Evelina's personal recipe book is made in three parts. The sauce, the cake itself and the topping/filling are easy-to-make components of this luscious cake.

MAKE THE SAUCE

¾ ——— cup/150 g sugar

1 ——— cup/235 ml heavy cream

FOR THE CAKE

1 ——— cup/225 g butter, softened

1 ——— cup/200 g sugar

4 ——— large eggs, separated

1½ ——— cups/180 g all-purpose flour

2 ——— teaspoons/6 g baking powder

½ ——— teaspoon table salt

MAKE THE SAUCE

1. Heat the sugar in a small saucepan until it is melted and becomes a light amber color, about 10 minutes. Remove the pan from the heat. Gradually, to avoid spattering and burning yourself, stir constantly while you mix in the cream, forming a sauce. Set aside and allow to cool.

FOR THE CAKE

1. Preheat the oven 350°F/180°C, or gas mark 4. Grease and lightly flour two 8-inch/20-cm or one 10-inch/25-cm cake pan (without tube).

2. In a bowl with an electric mixer on medium-high speed, cream the butter with the sugar until light pale yellow and fluffy, about 3 minutes.

3. Mix in the egg yolks, beating well after each addition.

4. Incorporate the caramel sauce, blending thoroughly.

5. In a bowl, sift together the flour, baking powder and salt. Add to the batter, mixing on medium speed for 1 minute.

6. In a separate bowl, with the mixer on high speed and clean beaters, beat the egg whites until soft peaks form. Fold the whites, by hand with a spatula, into the cake batter, folding until the whites are no longer visible, about 1 to 2 minutes.

7. Pour the batter into the prepared pan(s), spreading gently to even it out. Bake for about 35 minutes, until a toothpick inserted in the center comes out clean and the edges start to pull away from the sides of the pan.

8. Let cool 5 minutes and remove from the pan. Cool completely.

FOR THE FILLING/TOPPING

½ ——— cup/100 g sugar

½ ——— cup/120 ml whole milk

8 ——— tablespoons/112 g butter

2 ——— cups/290 g toasted almonds or walnuts, finely chopped

FOR THE FILLING/TOPPING

1. While the cake is cooling, caramelize the sugar as in the first step of the caramel sauce, until honey colored. Gradually, while stirring, pour in the milk. Stir in the butter and the chopped nuts. Keep a little warm so that it will spread easily.

2. To form a layer cake, slice the larger cake horizontally so that you have 3 even layers, or use the 2 smaller cakes for a 2-layer cake. Place one layer on a serving dish. Spread some of the filling on the layer, leaving a 1-inch/ 2.5-cm border around the edges, and then top it with the next layer. Repeat and top it with the last layer. Ice the cake with the remaining filling/topping. Chill slightly before serving as the topping tends to be a little soft. (If the topping is too warm it will drip down the sides.)

Azorean Pineapple Upside-Down Cake
Bolo de Ananás Açoreano

SERVES 10 TO 12

One of the best things Portuguese sailors transplanted to the Azores was the pineapple, which now grows plentifully on the island of São Miguel. I first enjoyed this cake on a visit to Graciosa in the Azores. Adapted some years ago from one baked by the mayor's wife of the town of Luz on the island of Graciosa, this luscious fruitful cake, which has a heavenly moist texture and just the right amount of sweetness, continues to please. This cake is baked upside down by starting with the top going into the bottom of the pan first. Using canned instead of fresh pineapple is doable, but you will miss out on the fresh taste.

FOR THE TOP

½ ———— cup/120 ml water

1 ———— cup/200 g sugar

1 ———— fresh pineapple, cored, cut crosswise into ½-inch/1.3-cm rings

Fresh stemmed and pitted cherries, plums or figs (optional)

FOR THE TOP

1. Generously butter and flour a 9-inch/23-cm round cake pan with 2-inch/5-cm sides. Separately, in a heavy-bottomed 1-quart/1-L saucepan, stir the water and sugar together and set over medium-high heat. Bring the sugar water to a boil, about 5 minutes. Reduce the heat to medium and continue to simmer, without stirring, for 15 more minutes, until you see it turning amber. Give the pan a little swirl. It should turn a medium amber in 5 minutes more. Watch carefully as it will turn quickly. Reduce the heat to low and cook until it takes on a rich golden amber color, 1 more minute. Total time is about 25 minutes.

2. Use a potholder or heavy dishcloth to hold the cake pan with one hand. As you pour the caramel into the pan with your other hand, tilt the pan back and forth to coat the bottom and sides until there is very little movement of the caramel. Set the pan aside to allow the caramel to cool. It will make crackling sounds as it cools.

3. While the caramel is cooling, prepare the pineapple, and other optional fruits, cutting the plums and figs into quarters lengthwise, discarding the stems and pits, if necessary. Arrange 4 or 5 pineapple rings on top of the firm caramel-coated bottom of the pan. You can fit more rings if they are small. Place the cherries, plums or fig quarters in the remaining spaces. You don't have to fill every space.

(continued)

FOR THE CAKE

8 —————— tablespoons/112 g (1 stick) butter, softened

1 —————— cup/200 g sugar

3 —————— large eggs

2 —————— cups/240 g all-purpose flour

1 —————— tablespoon/8 g baking powder

¼ —————— teaspoon table salt

⅔ —————— cup/180 ml pineapple juice made from remaining fresh pineapple rings, crushed, puréed and strained

½ —————— cup/120 ml whole milk

Toasted almond slices, for garnish

FOR THE CAKE

1. Preheat the oven to 350°F/180°C, or gas mark 4.

2. In a large bowl with an electric mixer on high speed, cream the butter and sugar together until fluffy, about 2½ minutes. Beat in the eggs, one at a time, mixing well after each addition.

3. Sift together the flour, baking powder and salt in a separate bowl. With the mixer on medium speed, incorporate the dry ingredients in increments, alternating with the pineapple juice and milk. Mix for 1 minute until the batter is fluffy.

4. Scrape the batter into the pan, covering the fruit and caramel evenly. Bake for about 45 to 50 minutes, until golden and a toothpick inserted into the middle comes out clean.

5. Cool slightly and then invert the cake onto a serving plate while still fairly hot. Should a piece of fruit stick to the pan, remove it and just place it in its proper place on the cake. Garnish the cake with the toasted almond slices.

Bread Pudding with Beirão Liquor

Pudim de Pão com Licor Beirão

SERVES 12

I have had requests for Portuguese bread pudding. This is a spin of my Aunt Leibia's bread pudding, which she frequently delivered to our door.

FOR THE BREAD PUDDING

2 ——— cups/470 ml whole milk

2 ——— cups/470 ml light cream

2 ——— cups/400 g plus 2 tablespoons/25 g sugar, divided

½ ——— cup/112 g butter

½ ——— teaspoon ground cinnamon

Grated peel of 1 orange

5 ——— large eggs

½ ——— cup/70 g raisins

2 ——— tablespoons/30 ml Beirão liquor (Grand Marnier can be substituted)

Day-old Portuguese bread (substitute Italian, European or artisan bread), heavy crusts removed, torn into 2-inch/5-cm pieces, about 12 cups/ 1200 g (leftover Portuguese sweet bread is especially perfect)

1 ——— cup/135 g slivered almonds (optional)

FOR THE BREAD PUDDING

1. Preheat the oven to 350°F/180°C, or gas mark 4. Butter an 8 x 12–inch/ 20 x 30.5–cm or 9 x 13-inch/23 x 33–cm pan.

2. In a saucepan over medium heat, warm the milk and cream with 2 cups/ 400 g of the sugar, butter, cinnamon and grated orange peel until you see tiny bubbles form around the edges and a bit of steam rising from the milk, about 5 minutes. Now that the milk is scalded, remove from the heat.

3. Lightly whisk the eggs in a large bowl until frothy. Gradually, while still whisking, pour in the warm milk in a steady stream. Mix in the raisins and liquor.

4. Toss in the bread, turning it in the custard. Let it stand for about 15 minutes to absorb the custard. Pour the bread mix into a generously buttered pan. Sprinkle the remaining 2 tablespoons/25 g sugar over the top, then scatter the slivered almonds over all.

5. Bake for 45 to 55 minutes, until a knife inserted into the center comes out fairly clean. The top will be golden. Serve warm or at room temperature, drizzled with the Beirão sauce. It can be chilled and reheated.

(continued)

EQUIPMENT

Candy thermometer

FOR THE BEIRÃO SAUCE

1 ———— cup/200 g sugar

3 ———— tablespoons/45 ml water

½ ———— cup/112 g butter, softened

1 ———— egg

3 ———— tablespoons/45 ml Beirão liquor
or Grand Marnier

Pinch of cinnamon

FOR THE BEIRÃO SAUCE

1. In a small saucepan over medium heat, heat the sugar and water until the sugar is dissolved and a syrup forms. When the candy thermometer registers 165°F/74°C, remove the syrup from the heat.

2. Add the butter and stir until the butter is melted into the syrup.

3. Lightly whisk the egg in a medium bowl. While whisking, drizzle in the hot butter and sugar syrup. Stir in the liquor and cinnamon, blending well. Serve warm over warm or room temperature bread pudding.

Variation:

Caramel Upside-Down Bread Pudding: In a saucepan, combine 1 cup/200 g sugar with ½ cup/120 ml water and 1 tablespoon/15 ml Beirão liquor or Grand Marnier. Place over medium heat, stirring, until lightly golden, about 25 minutes (see page 333). Pour into the well-buttered baking pan or baking dish and tilt the pan back and forth to coat the bottom. Sprinkle almonds on the caramel coating. Let cool. Make the bread pudding as directed above but cut the amount of sugar to 1 cup/200 g. Pour the bread mixture into the coated baking dish. Bake as directed but in a water bath. When done, cool slightly and turn out, upside down, onto a large serving dish with sloped sides to serve.

Maria Cookie Pudding Cake with Orange
Bolo de Bolacha Maria com Laranja

SERVES 12 TO 16

After enjoying a similar version of this dessert at a local Portuguese restaurant, my friend asked me to dissect it. This is my version of a popular modern dessert that seems to have elevated the basic layered pudding of the Maria cookies into a lovely elegant cake, for any occasion. Even if you have a heavy meal, there is room for this light dessert. Maria cookies taste just like tea cookies or animal crackers, but are easier to use for this dessert. Make sure you make the cake a day ahead to allow it to firm up and be well chilled. Read the recipe through before beginning.

EQUIPMENT

9-inch/23-cm springform pan or round cake pan (not a tube pan) with removable bottom

8-inch/20-cm cardboard round (optional, see Note)

Double boiler

PREPARE THE PAN USING METHOD A OR B

A. Trace the bottom of the springform or disk of the removable pan onto parchment paper. Cut out the circle and set aside. If you are using the springform pan, with the bottom in place, lay a large piece of plastic wrap centered over the pan. Place a second one, centered across the first piece. Place the 8-inch/20-cm cardboard round on the plastic wrap, pushing the cardboard down into the bottom of the pan. Top the cardboard round with the equal size piece of parchment paper. The plastic wrap should be under the cardboard but come up the inside of the pan and drape over the sides.

B. If you are using a removable-bottom pan, remove the bottom disk of the pan and line the ring with plastic wrap as above. Then take the removable disk and place it back into the bottom of the pan, so that the plastic comes up the sides to the top and drapes over as for the springform pan. Place the cardboard round on top if using, followed by parchment paper, onto the disk.

(continued)

> *Note:* For transporting, I usually line the pan with plastic wrap, place a cardboard round on top of the plastic and then line the top of the cardboard with parchment, cut to fit. Then I start to assemble. This method removes the risk of losing the bottom part of the pan. For serving at home, I simply use the bottom of the pan as my base, lining the pan only with parchment paper and covering it with plastic wrap to chill.

FOR THE CUSTARD

5 ——— gelatin sheets

4 ——— large egg yolks

1 ——— cup/200 g sugar

1 ——— cup/235 ml whole milk

Grated peel of 1 orange or 1 teaspoon/5 ml orange extract

¼ ——— teaspoon ground cinnamon

8 ——— ounces/225 g whipped cream cheese, softened at room temperature

2 ——— cups/470 ml heavy cream

TO ASSEMBLE

2 ——— 7½-ounce/210-g packages Bolacha Maria cookies (about 32)

2 ——— cups/470 ml strong decaffeinated or regular coffee, at room temperature

½ ——— cup/65 g toasted almond slices, for garnish (optional)

Variation: You can dress up this using your favorite chocolate ganache sauce and lightly drizzle it in between two layers and then give a fancy drizzle over the final top layer.

FOR THE CUSTARD

1. Place the gelatin sheets in a bowl and cover with cold water. Let stand for about 5 minutes.

2. In the top of a double boiler, whisk together the yolks with the sugar, then gradually stir in the milk. Toss in the orange peel and cinnamon. Heat the ingredients, stirring to thoroughly blend, over medium heat. When the milk is steaming hot but not boiling, about 3 minutes, lift the gelatin from the water, using your hands to squeeze out excess water. Add the gelatin to the heated milk, stirring just until the gelatin is dissolved and well blended, about 30 seconds. Remove the pan from the heat.

3. Using a fine sieve, strain the custard into a bowl and then whisk in the softened cream cheese, whisking until it is dissolved into the custard. Place the bowl in a large container surrounded by a bath of ice to cool quicker. Stir occasionally until the custard is cooled. Remove from the ice bath, cover and chill in the refrigerator for about 15 to 20 minutes.

4. Remove the custard from the refrigerator.

5. Separately, whip the heavy cream in a chilled bowl until soft peaks form. Carefully fold the whipped cream into the cooled custard filling, folding gently until any traces of cheese and cream are no longer visible.

TO ASSEMBLE

1. Putting aside 2 cookies, take the remaining cookies and, working in layers, lightly dip each cookie in the coffee and place them side by side on the bottom of the pan. (Just dip, don't soak the cookies or they will fall apart before you get them in the pan.) Repeat with a second layer, placing the cookies over the seams of the first layer.

2. Spread some custard over the cookies, forming a ½-inch/1.3-cm layer. Repeat with the cookies and coffee but with only a single layer of cookies and then spread some more custard. Repeat the process, ending with the custard on top. There should be 3 or 4 layers of filling depending on how much you put on each layer. If you end up with 3 layers, it is okay. It still works.

3. Crush the reserved 2 cookies into fine crumbs and sprinkle over the top. Wrap the plastic over and chill for several hours or overnight to firm up. To serve, unwrap and slide the cardboard round onto a serving plate. Garnish with the toasted almonds. Drizzle your favorite chocolate over the top if desired.

Ana's Maria Cookie Cake with Pineapple
Bolo de Bolacha Maria com Ananás

SERVES 12 TO 16

The coolness of pineapple makes this version a refreshing treat. This cake should be chilled for several hours before serving. The variations can keep growing, as I think of using fresh raspberries, strawberries or blackberries for this dessert. I know you will come up with other ideas, too. Tea cookies or actually animal crackers, laid side by side, can be a good substitute for the Maria cookies. As always, read the recipe through. This is slightly different than the previous one.

EQUIPMENT

9-inch/23-cm springform pan or other tubeless pan with removable bottom

8-inch/20-cm cardboard round

Double boiler

FOR THE CUSTARD

5	———	gelatin sheets
4	———	large egg yolks
1	———	cup/235 ml whole milk
½	———	cup/100 g sugar
1	———	8-ounce/225-g container whipped cream cheese, softened at room temperature
2	———	cups/470 ml heavy cream

FOR THE CUSTARD

1. Line the bottom of the pan as in the previous recipe (see page 339). Set aside.

2. Place the gelatin in a bowl and pour in enough cool water to cover. Set aside and let stand for about 5 minutes.

3. In the top of a double boiler, whisk together the egg yolks, milk and sugar. Set the pan over medium heat and, while stirring constantly, bring the custard to a simmer, about 3 minutes. Do not allow to boil.

4. Remove the gelatin from the water, squeezing off excess water. Whisk the gelatin into the warm custard, cooking it and whisking until the gelatin has dissolved and blended into the custard, about 30 seconds. Remove from the heat. Using a fine sieve, strain the custard into a bowl and whisk in the cream cheese, whisking until dissolved into the custard. Place the bowl in a large container surrounded by a bath of ice to cool quicker. Stir occasionally until the custard is cooled. Remove from the ice bath, cover and chill in the refrigerator for about 15 to 20 minutes.

5. Remove the custard from the refrigerator.

6. Whip the heavy cream in a chilled bowl until soft peaks form, about 2 minutes, then fold into the custard, folding until any trace of cheese and cream are no longer visible.

(continued)

TO ASSEMBLE

1 ———— 16-ounce/454-g can crushed pineapple

2 ———— 7½-ounce/210-g packages Bolacha Maria cookies (about 32)

1 ———— cup/235 ml reserved pineapple juice or additional milk for cookie dipping

1 ———— cup/100 g shredded sweetened coconut flakes, toasted in a dry skillet until light golden

TO ASSEMBLE

1. Using a fine sieve set over a small bowl, drain the pineapple, pressing on it slightly, reserving the juices. Set aside.

2. Quickly dip the cookies, one at a time, into the juice and make a layer on the bottom of the lined pan. (Just dip, don't soak the cookies or they will fall apart before you get them in the pan.) For the bottom, make two layers of cookies, the second layer overlapping the seams of the first layer. Don't worry about the small negative spaces. Spread a scant ½-inch/1.3-cm layer of filling over the cookies. Repeat a single layer of cookies over the custard. Repeat the custard. On the third level of cookies, spread the very well-drained crushed pineapple over the cookies. Top with another layer of cookies followed by the remaining filling. Sprinkle the top with the toasted sweetened coconut flakes. Cover the top with plastic and chill overnight.

3. Remove from the pan, and unwrap the plastic. Gently slide onto a serving plate. If using the cardboard, slide the cake off the metal cake bottom as you slide it onto the serving plate. Additional whipped cream can be served on the side.

Mariana's Sweet Rice Pudding

Arroz Doce à Moda da Mariana

SERVES 6 TO 8

When it comes to making sweet rice for the Feast of the Holy Ghost, Mariana Morais, who is from the Azore islands, has earned her badge in heaven. Her method requires less thought than the traditional method. Her added touches are butter and lime, not usually found in other versions of this sweet dessert. The creamy texture is denser than its mainland counterparts. When completely cool, it can firm up enough so that you could almost lift up a slice like pizza.

1½ —— cups/270 g short-grain rice, such as Arborio

4 —— tablespoons/56 g butter

7 —— cups/1645 ml whole milk

1½ —— cups/300 g sugar

Peel of ½ lime

¼ —— teaspoon table salt

2 —— large egg yolks, lightly beaten

Ground cinnamon, for sprinkling

1. Combine the rice, butter, milk , sugar, lime peel and salt in a 3-quart/2.7-L saucepot. Place the pan over medium-high heat and bring to the edge of a boil. Reduce the heat to medium-low and, while constantly stirring, simmer the pudding slowly until it becomes the consistency of medium oatmeal and the rice is fully tender, without any bite, about 25 to 30 minutes.

2. In small increments, briskly whisk about 1 cup/235 ml of the hot pudding into the yolks to warm them and prevent curdling. Transfer the warm milky yolks to the pot of pudding, whisking quickly to blend them into pudding. Simmer and stir for another minute. Remove the lime peel.

3. Pour the pudding into shallow serving platters or individual dessert dishes and garnish with a sprinkling of cinnamon, or rub a pinch of cinnamon between your thumb and forefinger as you release the cinnamon closely over the surface of the pudding into a design. Repeat the pinching and rubbing action until the design is complete. Chill, covered, until needed. Remove from the refrigerator about 15 minutes before serving.

Baked Silk Custard Cake with Poached Plum

Sericaia

SERVES 6

When I traveled to the Alentejo, on my way to the westerly town of Elvas, near the border of Spain, I stopped at Adega do Cachete in Monsaraz, not just for the great meals but also for the *sericaia*, a specialty. This luscious custard-like cake, almost like a soufflé, has a moist texture and is traditionally accompanied with a poached plum, simmered in a sugar syrup. If you don't have the plum, feel free to skip it, or make it contemporary and substitute another fruit or use a fruit compote. This recipe, adapted from Blandina Pereira, is easy to prepare; you simply cook the custard, then bake it topped with a dusting of cinnamon. Be careful not to overbake or it will be dry. The dessert is usually baked in a shallow clay tart pan or pie plate–like dish and sliced into wedges. However, it can easily be made in 6 individual ramekins, each served with a slice of plum or fruit on top or on the side, if desired.

FOR THE PLUMS

5 ——— cups/1175 ml white wine

½ ——— cup/100 g sugar

½ ——— cup/120 ml orange juice

½ ——— cup/120 ml water

Peel of 2 oranges

1 ——— cinnamon stick

3 ——— red or black plums (or other fruit as desired)

FOR THE PLUMS

1. Combine the wine, sugar, orange juice, water, orange peels and cinnamon stick in a 3-quart/2.7-L pot. Stir and bring to a boil over high heat, then reduce the heat to medium and simmer, stirring occasionally, until the sugar is dissolved. Add the plums, submerging them, and simmer for 15 to 20 minutes over medium-high heat, until fork-tender. Transfer with a slotted spoon to a dish to cool completely. Cut the plums in half lengthwise, then remove the pits and stems. Continue to simmer the syrup until slightly reduced, about 5 minutes. Cool completely and reserve.

2. Remove the orange peel and cinnamon stick. Cool. Drizzle the syrup over the plums to coat. Reserve until needed.

(continued)

EQUIPMENT

Flat-edged wooden spoon

10-inch/25-cm Pyrex or ceramic pie plate or six to eight 1-cup/235-ml ramekins

Double boiler (optional)

FOR THE CUSTARD

1⅓ —— cups/265 g plus 1 tablespoon/12 g sugar, divided

1 —— cup/120 g all-purpose flour

6 —— medium eggs, separated

2 —— cups/470 ml whole milk

1 —— cinnamon stick

Peels of 2 lemons

¼ —— teaspoon table salt

Ground cinnamon, for dusting

FOR THE CUSTARD

1. Preheat the oven to 400°F/200°C, or gas mark 6.

2. Lightly butter the pie plate or ramekins and set aside.

3. In the top of a double boiler or a heavy-bottomed 3-quart/2.7-L pot, combine 1⅓ cups/265 g of the sugar with the flour, mixing thoroughly until well blended, about 1 minute. Make a well in the middle, dump in the yolks and lightly whisk the egg yolks into the sugar-flour mixture. While whisking, gradually, in a steady stream, pour in the milk, forming a slurry and completely blending into a cream-like consistency. Toss in the cinnamon stick, lemon peels and salt.

4. Here is where you need to be patient. Stirring constantly with a wooden spoon, cook the custard over medium heat until it reaches a thick pudding consistency and is steaming, about 20 to 25 minutes. If you let it thicken too quickly over too high a heat, it will be lumpy. Stir well and constantly to avoid burning on the bottom. Remove from the heat. Discard the peels and cinnamon stick, then set aside to cool a little.

5. Separately, in a medium bowl, beat the egg whites to soft peaks and incorporate the remaining 1 tablespoon/12 g sugar, about 2 minutes. Gently fold tablespoons of beaten egg whites into the cooled custard, being careful not to deflate or break the fullness of the meringue. Fold until there are barely any egg whites showing. Do not worry about getting every bump out. Spoon, do not pour, the meringue gently into the pie plate, being fairly even without trying to spread it out. The puffed meringue whites give the custard lift.

6. Sift a light to medium coat of cinnamon over the top, enough so you do not see any custard. Bake for 15 minutes if using the ramekins, adjusting to 18 to 20 minutes for the 10-inch/25-cm pie plate. The texture should be almost like soft custard soufflé cake, not a firm cake. It will start to crack around the puffed-up edges as it becomes done. It will also deflate a little and firm up slightly as it cools down. *Sericaia* can be served warm or cold garnished with the sweet poached plums.

Heavenly Cream
Natas do Céu

SERVES 6

This simple dessert is so light in texture it almost floats in your mouth. Other versions use condensed milk and gelatin. If you can't find these cookies, tea biscuits and animal crackers make a good substitute, but you will need extra cookies because they are smaller in size. Though it is not traditional, I prefer to poach the meringue because it reduces the risk of salmonella; plus, poaching will prevent the whites from weeping. Just be sure to drain them well in a sieve.

EQUIPMENT
Candy thermometer

FOR THE SWEET EGG TOPPING
2 —— tablespoons/30 ml water
½ —— cup/100 g sugar
12—— large egg yolks (save the whites for the meringue, below)
2 —— teaspoons/10 ml whole milk
Peel of 1 lemon

FOR THE MERINGUE LAYER
12—— large egg whites, at room temperature
3 —— tablespoons/36 g sugar
1½ —— cups/355 ml whole milk, divided

FOR THE SWEET EGG TOPPING

1. Combine the water and sugar in a small saucepan. Stir. Heat the sugar water over medium-high heat until it reaches 230°F/110°C and forms a light thread-like syrup, about 10 minutes. Do not boil or allow the syrup to become golden. Set aside.

2. Separately, whisk the yolks in a small bowl with the milk. Add the lemon peel. Gradually, while still whisking, drizzle in the sugar syrup, incorporating it thoroughly into the yolks. Transfer the sweetened yolks back into the syrup pan. Set the pan over low heat and cook, stirring, until thickened like pudding and just starting to spit. Remove from the heat and set aside.

FOR THE MERINGUE LAYER

1. In a medium bowl, using an electric mixer on high speed, beat the egg whites until foamy, about 30 seconds. Continue to beat on high speed while gradually adding the sugar, spoonful by spoonful. Beat until soft meringue peaks form, about 1 minute. Set aside.

2. Heat 1 cup/235 ml of the milk in a 2-quart/1.8-L pot. Simmer the milk to the edge of boiling, about 2 minutes. Using a large spoon, place two or three large spoonfuls of the beaten egg whites into the simmering milk to poach. When they start to rise up to the top, flip them over with a spoon and cook for about 1 minute more, until they start to rise again. Transfer with a slotted spoon to a colander set over a bowl to drain off the excess milk. Return the milk to the pot. Repeat with the remaining meringue, adding the remaining ½ cup/120 ml milk to the pot as needed. Set aside.

(continued)

FOR THE CREAM

1 ——— pint/470 ml heavy cream

¼ ——— cup/50 g sugar

TO ASSEMBLE

2 ——— 7½-ounce/210-g packages Bolacha Maria cookies (about 32)

Ground cinnamon, for sprinkling

FOR THE CREAM

1. Whip the cream with the sugar in a chilled bowl until soft peaks form, about 1 minute. Cover and keep chilled until needed.

TO ASSEMBLE

1. Use a rolling pin to roll the cookies into fine crumbs, or use a food processor.

2. In an 8 x 12–inch/20 x 30.5–cm or a 10-inch/25-cm shallow round serving bowl, layer some of the cookie crumbs on the bottom. Add a layer of meringue followed by a layer of half of the cream. Start again with cookie crumbs, then meringue and the remaining cream. Top it all off with the sweet egg topping drizzled over all. Sprinkle with cinnamon. Chill before serving.

Note: You can also assemble this in individual serving ramekins.

Cheese Pastries Vila Franca Style
Queijadas à Moda de Vila Franca do Campo

MAKES ABOUT 24

On the island of São Miguel in the Azores archipelago, the recipe for perhaps the most well-known delicate pastry of the island is a well-kept secret. It is a recipe held by one very tight-lipped family and one can only dissect it so far. After having enjoyed these dainty treats, this is my interpretation based on what I remember. Here I use vanilla or orange for flavoring and found that cream cheese is not only easier to use but also gives a creamier texture. Kitchen shops sell miniature cupcake tins that have twenty-four 2-inch/5-cm molds in each tray. Though the use of lard was very common in pastry dough and added flavor, here I give the option of all butter or equal amounts of butter and lard.

EQUIPMENT

Rolling pin or dough roller like a ravioli machine

2 miniature cupcake mold trays

Miniature paper cupcake liners

FOR THE FILLING

12	ounces/336 g cream cheese
1	cup/120 g confectioners' sugar, sifted
½	teaspoon vanilla or orange extract
1	large egg yolk, stirred
¼	cup/60 ml egg whites, slightly beaten

FOR THE PASTRY

2	tablespoons/28 g butter, at room temperature
2	tablespoons/28 g lard, at room temperature
¼	cup/50 g granulated sugar
1	large egg yolk
1¼	cups/150 g all-purpose flour, plus extra for rolling
½	cup/120 ml ice cold water or as needed
1	cup/120 g confectioners' sugar, sifted, or as needed

FOR THE FILLING

1. Using the medium-high speed of an electric hand mixer, beat the cream cheese with the sugar and vanilla until thoroughly combined. Add the yolk and egg whites, then continue to beat until smooth but do not whip any air into the filling, about 2 minutes.

2. Cover with plastic pressed against the filling and keep chilled until needed. Makes about 2½ cups/588 ml.

FOR THE PASTRY

1. Cream the butter and lard together in a bowl until fluffy and pale yellow, about 1 minute.

2. Incorporate the granulated sugar and then beat in the egg yolk.

3. Using a fork, cut the flour into the butter and sugar until it looks like tiny pebbles. Drizzle just enough ice water, about ¼ cup/60 ml to start, into the mix to form a smooth, pliable dough. Lightly knead, without overworking the dough, for a minute until smooth. Wrap in plastic wrap and chill for 1 hour.

4. Remove the dough from the refrigerator and turn out onto a lightly floured surface. Roll to 1⁄16 inch/1.5 mm thin. The pasta dough sheeter is perfect for rolling this. Lay the sheets of dough out in front of you. Use a 4-inch/10-cm biscuit cutter to cut rounds of dough.

(continued)

The pastry dough is pulled up and pleated around the filling. Baked in paper liners then cooled, the pastries are ready to be dusted with confectioner's sugar.

5. Place a scant 2 teaspoons/10 g of the filling in the middle of each circle. In small ¼-inch/6-mm increments pinch pleats one at a time, bring up the pastry edges over the top of the filling and gently pleat the dough around the filling, pinching each pleat and gently pressing against the filling. Pinch again the very tip of all the pleats to completely encase the filling, then give it a little twist, forming a little peak. The pastry will support the filling and have a mound. Repeat with the remaining dough and filling.

6. Preheat the oven 300°F/150°C, or gas mark 2. Prick the tops of each pastry with a toothpick to allow any air or steam to escape. Sometimes if there is too much air it may burst at a seam. Place each in a mini paper liner set in the cups of the baking tin. Bake the pastry until lightly golden, about 20 to 25 minutes. Remove from the trays and allow the pastries to cool completely. Should some of the filling burst at a seam, just trim it off. Chill for a couple of hours. To serve, sift a heavy coating of confectioners' sugar over each one.

Cream-Filled Jesuit Puff Pastry

Jesuitas

MAKES ABOUT 16

Jesuitas are a pastry that can be looked at as a pizza-shaped slice of a flaky Portuguese-style, Danish puff pastry, filled with sweetened egg yolks and topped with a coating of meringue or icing before it is baked. Here I have updated the old classic using premade delicate puff pastry found in the freezer section of your supermarket and the lighter filling of pastry cream, which is quicker to make and has less sugar than the sweet egg filling. Check out different brands of puff pastry because some are made with butter and some are not. The butter ones are the best in flavor. The pastry sheets come in various sizes depending on the brand, which makes it difficult to say the amount of filling will be perfect, too much or too little. If there is any filling left over, scoop it into a cup and get a spoon.

The old method is to spread the icing on top of the pastry before it is baked, which weighs down the pastry and results in the traditional flatter slice with a nice caramelized sugar glaze. You can still do this and then dress it up with a drizzle of extra icing after it has cooled. This version uses the icing after baking, which not only allows the puff pastry to puff up into wonderful flakiness, as puff pastry dough is meant to do, but also leaves the icing whiter. Instead of pastry cream, you can use the traditional Sweet Egg Filling on page 305.

FOR THE CREAM FILLING

3 ——— large egg yolks

Pinch of table salt

6 ——— tablespoons/72 g sugar, divided

3 ——— tablespoons/24 g flour

1 ——— cup/235 ml whole milk

2 ——— tablespoons/30 ml heavy cream

Peel of 1 lemon or orange

1 ——— cinnamon stick, about 3 inches/7.5 cm long

1 ——— tablespoon/14 g butter

FOR THE CREAM FILLING

A day ahead or several hours earlier, make the cream filling

1. In a bowl, whisk together the yolks, salt and 3 tablespoons/36 g of the sugar until pale yellow, and then gradually incorporate the flour.

2. In a small pan over medium heat, warm the milk, cream and remaining 3 tablespoons/36 g sugar until scalded, not boiling, about 3 to 4 minutes. Whisking constantly, slowly stream some of the hot milk into the eggs to temper them. Transfer the warmed eggs back into the pan of milk and cook, stirring, for 1 minute. Toss in the citrus peels and cinnamon stick.

3. Set the pan over medium heat. Stirring constantly with a wooden spoon, cook the filling until it is like thick pudding and sputters, about 4 to 5 minutes. Remove from the heat immediately.

4. Whisk in the butter. Remove the lemon peel and cinnamon stick.

5. Set a mesh strainer over a bowl and pour the custard into it, pushing it through to strain out any lumps or solidified egg white that didn't break down. Place a sheet of plastic wrap or wax paper over the custard, pressing it onto the surface of the custard to prevent condensation, which will water down your filling. Chill for several hours or overnight in the fridge. It will thicken more as it cools. Makes about 1 cup/225 g of pastry cream for 1 pound/454 g of pastry dough.

(continued)

FOR THE PASTRY

1 ——— 1-pound/454-g package puff pastry dough (see Note)

Parchment paper

FOR THE PASTRY

1. Preheat the oven to 450°F/230°C, or gas mark 8.

2. Remove the dough from the refrigerator about 15 minutes before using. When it is time to bake, make sure the custard as well as the pastry are well chilled. The dough should not be so cold that it is too stiff to roll but not as warm as room temperature. Otherwise, it will be difficult to work with. If it gets compressed it will be difficult to unfold. If the pastry is overworked or loses its chill, it will not puff up as much. You can re-chill the dough for 10 to 15 minutes if it gets soft and difficult to work with.

3. Lightly flour your workspace. Roll out one sheet of dough into a rectangle a scant ⅛ inch/3 mm thick. Some dough may end up 6 x 12 inches/15 x 30.5 cm, some nearly 18 x 11 inches/45.7 x 28 cm. Slide the dough onto a piece of parchment paper so the long side of the dough is facing you. Prick the dough all over with the tines of a fork. Spread about ½ cup/112 g of filling lengthwise along the long side closest to you, leaving a ¾-inch/2-cm edge on three sides. Bring the far edge of the long side over toward you, over the filling side. Fold the pastry over the filling, and press or pinch to seal the three sides.

4. You can skip this step and continue with step 5, or if you wish to make it a little more traditional, top with a meringue coating of 3 egg whites beaten with 2 tablespoons/24 g sugar until stiff. Spread thinly over the top of the pastry, then continue with step 5. This will give it a caramelized sugar glaze but less height. They will be almost as thin as a slice of pizza.

5. Make cuts every 3 inches/7.5 cm on the diagonal, alternating sides of the length so that when you cut, front to back, you will cut the pastry on the diagonal from right to left and again diagonally from left to right, the whole length of the pastry, forming triangles. Do not cut down the middle lengthwise. Do not separate them. Don't worry about the filling oozing out. It will seal during the baking. Slide the parchment and pastry onto a sheet pan. Repeat with the second sheet of puff pastry.

6. Place the sheet pan in the oven, reduce the heat to 400°F/200°C, or gas mark 6, and bake until golden, about 35 minutes. Allow to cool completely. Each sheet of pastry makes about 7 or 8 *Jesuitas* depending on the size of your pastry sheets and the size you make them. Keep refrigerated unless you are serving shortly.

After spreading the filling over one half of the dough lengthwise, fold the dough over the filling, pressing to seal. Brush with optional meringue topping, step 4, before cutting.

FOR THE TOPPING

1	——	scant cup/135 g sliced almonds
¼	——	cup/30 g confectioners' sugar
2	——	teaspoons/10 ml milk

FOR THE TOPPING

1. Heat the almonds in a dry nonstick skillet, frequently tossing, until they take on a light golden color. Remove from the pan and set aside.

2. Mix the sugar and milk in a small bowl to make a medium-thin icing. Drizzle over the pastry triangles, and quickly scatter some almond slices over and allow to dry. The icing needs to be wet for the almonds to stick. As an added touch, the icing can be drizzled over the meringue-glazed traditional style.

Note: If you make your own puff pastry or purchase a professional brand, the sheets of dough are larger. An 18 x 11–inch/45.7 x 28–cm sheet will give you about 10 slices per sheet and will fit perfectly in the same size sheet pan. If your sheets are smaller, just roll out to the thickness indicated above and adjust. You can also make the diagonal cuts every 4 inches/10 cm for larger slices.

Custard Tarts Belem Style
Pasteis de Nata

MAKES ABOUT 1 DOZEN

This version of silky custard tart is quicker but no less luscious. Use good-quality store-bought puff pastry sheets made with butter for the best flavor. The filling is a straightforward custard cream that is easy to make. These are delicious no matter what time of day. For a simple, one- or two-bite dessert, you can rewarm them in the oven, sprinkle them with Portuguese Beirão liquor or Grand Marnier and dust with cinnamon. The pastry dough, homemade or store-bought, also can be set up ahead; lining the tins, wrap them individually in plastic, nesting them one inside the other, and freeze until needed. When needed, fill the frozen lined tart tins and bake as directed.

EQUIPMENT

Small unfluted 2¾-inch/7-cm tart tins that have a 1¾-inch/4.5-cm diameter bottom, or closest in size (see Note)

Candy thermometer

FOR THE FILLING

1	——	cup/200 g sugar
3	——	tablespoons/45 ml water
1½	——	tablespoons/12 g cornstarch
2	——	cups/474 ml heavy cream, cold
10	——	egg yolks
¼	——	teaspoon table salt

Peel of 1 lemon

FOR THE DOUGH

1	——	1-pound/454-g package puff pastry dough, chilled
¼	——	cup/56 g Buckeye margarine, softened (see Note)

> *Note:* Disposable aluminum tart tins and unfluted, flared tart shells work best.

> *Note:* Buckeye margarine is a professional baker's margarine. Regular margarine can be used.

FOR THE FILLING

1. Mix the sugar and water together in a small pan and bring to a simmer. When the temperature on a candy thermometer reaches 230°F/110°C, about 2½ minutes, it should be a light syrup. Remove from the heat.

2. Separately, in a 2½-quart/2.3-L pot, combine the cornstarch and the cold cream. Gradually, while whisking, mix in the egg yolks and salt. Add the lemon peel. Still whisking, drizzle in the sugar syrup. Set the pot over medium heat. Stir constantly with a wooden spoon until the custard is lightly thickened, about 15 minutes. Do not boil. Remove from the heat, discard lemon peel, cover with plastic wrap, pressing it against the filling surface, and set aside to cool. When cool, chill in the refrigerator until cold.

FOR THE DOUGH

1. Set the tins out on a sheet pan. On a lightly dusted workspace, preferably stone, roll out the pastry dough into a rectangle about ¼ inch/6 mm thick. Turn the dough so the long end faces you. Spread the soft margarine scantily over the dough's surface. Starting at the long side, roll the dough up tightly, like a long jelly roll, to the diameter of the tart's bottom, about 1¾ inches/4.5 cm or the size you have.

2. Working quickly, cut the roll of dough crosswise into 1-inch/2.5-cm slices. Cover and transfer the slices to a sheet pan and let them rest for about 20 minutes in the refrigerator to relax the dough.

(continued)

3. Remove them from the refrigerator. Place one of the slices in a tin. Moisten your thumb with water and firmly press the center of the slice down into the middle of the tin, making sure the bottom has only a thin (⅛-inch/ 3-mm) covering. As you turn the tin with one hand, use the wet thumb of the other to press the dough against the inside of the tin while sliding it up to the top, forming an edge all around. Moisten your thumb again and repeat from the center out, making sure the tin is evenly and thinly lined all around. Repeat with remaining tins. Cover the sheet pan and then let them for rest another 20 minutes in the refrigerator to chill while the oven is heating up. You do not want the dough to get warm or it won't puff.

TO ASSEMBLE

1. Preheat the oven to 500°F/250°C, or gas mark 10.

2. Fill the lined tins with the cooled filling to a scant three-fourths full, about 2½ tablespoons/37 ml without any of the filling touching the edge of the pastry.

3. Bake immediately on the middle shelf of the oven for 15 to 20 minutes, until pastry is golden. The crust should be crisp and flaky. Remove from the oven and cool for about 1 minute, then remove from the pastry tins. If they are allowed to cool too long, they will stick to the tins. These can be served, chilled, warm or at room temperature, dusted with cinnamon. Store covered and chilled.

Caramel Hard Candy

Rebuçados

YIELDS 2½ DOZEN

On special occasions like the *Festa do Espirito Santo* and holidays, for those who like caramel, this old recipe is the perfect ending. The trick is to not burn the caramel but to cook it so that it is light to medium golden amber in color. This recipe can be a little tricky to do by yourself, so I recommend having a second pair of hands if possible. Once the caramel is ready, you must move quickly, almost in a frenzy, before the caramel cools and hardens into an unworkable mass. Be careful not to burn yourself with the hot caramel. Rolling in sugar is a regional variation.

EQUIPMENT

3 to 4 — large flat 12-inch/30-cm platters

Kitchen scissors

Knife

Frilled tissue paper squares (optional)

Any color tissue paper that is used for gift wrapping (optional)

FOR THE PLATES

Softened butter as needed

2 ——— cups/120 g powdered sugar, for coating (optional)

FOR THE CANDY

2 ——— cups/400 g granulated sugar

1 ——— cup/240 ml water

Peel of 1 lemon or lime

1 ——— teaspoon/5 ml white vinegar

FOR THE PLATES

1. Generously butter three flat plates, the knife and the blades of the scissors. Pour the sugar onto the fourth plate.

FOR THE CANDY

1. In a 3-quart/2.7-L saucepan, mix together the sugar, water, lemon peel and vinegar. Bring to a full boil over medium-high heat. Reduce the heat and simmer over medium heat until the color becomes light to medium amber, about 15 to 20 minutes. Don't let it get too dark unless you like a heavier caramel, almost burnt, flavor. Remove the peel. The timing really depends on how it looks. Your idea of medium heat may be different from mine.

2. Quickly pour the molten caramelized candy onto the two generously buttered plates in a narrow strip, if you can. If you wait too long, it will harden. Frequently re-butter the scissors and knife. You must work from the outside of the plate in. Use the buttered scissors and knife to immediately start cutting 1- to 2-inch/2.5- to 5-cm pieces, a thumb's diameter, away and set onto a third buttered plate without the pieces touching each other. Toss the pieces into the powdered sugar then roll and toss in your hands to round any edges. Return pieces to the sugar platter to finish cooling. Repeat until all the candies have been rolled in the sugar. Wrap each candy in frilled tissue paper when completely cooled, if desired. Customarily, rolling in the sugar is not done when tissue paper is used.

To frill the tissue paper

Method #1: Cut 4-inch/10-cm squares of tissue paper. Fold in half. Fold in half again. Take the scissors and make cuts about ⅟₁₆ inch/1.5 mm apart all along the edges. Open up and place a candy in the middle. Fold over and twist to close.

Method #2: Fold a square of tissue paper around the candy and, with the scissors, make skinny cuts along the top edges of the paper.

Preparations

The recipes in this chapter are for seasonings, marinades, dressings and sauces that exude the essence of traditional Portuguese flavors.

A Few Words on Preparations, Some Spices and Other Ingredients

It's helpful to have an idea of what spices and other ingredients one might find in a Portuguese pantry beyond the standard items. As Portuguese ingredients go, there isn't much that is hard to get. My father would say, "In a Portuguese house you can always find onions to make *refogado*," the base of many Portuguese dishes. Most Portuguese cooks use what we have on hand and the more perishable ingredients are purchased as needed. While the freshest ingredients are at the top of my list, there are moments for many cooks, Portuguese included, when having alternative backups in the pantry is helpful. The days of mothers cooking at the stove all day are all but gone. Not everyone has the time or space for a backyard garden. So, if really good flavorful tomatoes are not available, especially in winter, good-quality tomato paste or canned chopped tomatoes are good alternatives. When cooks like myself find we are almost out of Sweet Pepper Paste (*massa de pimentão*), page 367, or Chile Pepper Paste (*massa de malagueta*), page 365, then we know we need to make more or keep a commercial backup. While nothing tastes as good as homemade, using frozen or canned versions is acceptable. So feel free to do so as well, especially if there is very little notable difference in flavor. Always check the sodium amounts in canned items, then drain and rinse if you need to. Is my pantry exact every day? No. It varies on demand, depending on what I am making, what I purchase fresh (like leafy greens) and what I am out of, but that goes with any pantry. Online Portuguese markets are great for the few specialty items. For more information on ingredients and spices, see the resource guide on my website, www.portuguesecooking.com.

Mortars and Pestles

There is something to be said for using a mortar and pestle, one of the oldest kitchen tools used to prepare meals in a Portuguese kitchen. Growing up I watched as my father used a mortar and pestle to grind, mash and blend garlic, spices and aromatic herbs into heady concoctions of aromatic seasoning pastes. I learned by watching. Obviously, times have changed, but I still prefer to use my mortar and pestle, and I do quite often. My first one, a wedding gift from my father, was made of wood. However, if you don't have one, use your food processor to pulsate the paste. The result will be close, but in my opinion, food processors cut the spices and herbs, where grinding and pounding with the mortar and pestle fully releases individual oils and the essences of spices and herbs, melding their flavors.

Dry Spice Rub

Pasta Seca dos Temperos

MAKES ABOUT 2 OUNCES/56 G

This aromatic spice mix, which includes the heady spices of paprika, black pepper and cumin blended with aromatic garlic, can be made ahead and stored in a tin or jar, provided all the components are dried, not fresh. Use this with your choice of meats. You can add salt to this mix if desired or add when ready to apply the rub onto meats.

---

4 —— teaspoons/12 g paprika

2 —— teaspoons/6 g onion powder

2 —— teaspoons/6 g ground garlic or 1 or 2 fresh garlic cloves, finely chopped (see Note)

1 —— bay leaf, crumbled

1 —— teaspoon/3 g ground cumin

1 —— teaspoon/3 g ground black pepper

1 —— teaspoon/2 g granulated dried orange peel

½ —— teaspoon crushed dried chile peppers or cayenne pepper (optional)

1. Mix all the ingredients together and store. When needed, take a spoonful or two to use dry. Feel free to adjust individual amounts to your taste, keeping in mind that cumin is a strong flavor that can be an acquired taste.

Note: Only use fresh garlic if the mix is being used immediately.

Spice and Herb Seasoning Paste
Massa dos Temperos

MAKES ABOUT ½ CUP/112 G

Taught to me at a young age, this was my father's concoction for many pork dishes. At that point it then became *our* "go to" seasoning. In this wet seasoning paste, fresh aromatics of cilantro or parsley and fresh garlic are added just before seasoning an ingredient. This is not a premixed "allspice." At times, I omit the salt and use 1 to 2 tablespoons/12 to 24 g of Sweet Pepper Paste (*massa de pimentão*), which you can make yourself (page 367), purchase online or find at markets that sell Portuguese ingredients. As you combine the ingredients, the heady aroma will fill the senses. I love to use it for roast chicken, chicken wings, pork and potatoes. The paste will have some texture to it.

1 ——— tablespoon/18 g coarse kosher salt or Sweet Pepper Paste (page 367)

2 ——— garlic cloves, peeled, cut in half

1 ——— tablespoon/8 g paprika

1 ——— bay leaf, crumbled

1 ——— tablespoon/4 g finely chopped fresh parsley or cilantro

½ ——— teaspoon freshly ground pepper

½ ——— teaspoon turmeric (optional)

½ ——— teaspoon hot chile pepper sauce (optional)

¼ ——— teaspoon ground cumin (optional)

2 to 4 — tablespoons/30 to 60 ml olive oil

1. Use a mortar and pestle to grind the salt and garlic together, forming a paste. Mash in the paprika, bay leaf, parsley, pepper, turmeric, chile pepper and cumin, mixing well after each addition. Stir in the olive oil.

2. Spread the paste over meats before cooking or place the seasoned meats in a nonreactive bowl and add enough white wine to just cover. Marinate for several hours or overnight.

Basic Chile Oil

Molho de Piri-piri

MAKES ABOUT 1 PINT/470 ML

While piri-piri sauce can be purchased ready-made in Portuguese and Brazilian markets, there is something special about homemade, especially if you have the time. If you cannot get the tiny bird's beak chiltepin chiles, this recipe can be adapted using other small chile peppers like Thai chiles and ghost chiles (if you can handle that heat). Crushed dried or fresh, the tiny chiles are also used, as this recipe shows, to simply infuse a flavor medium to create a chile oil. The measurements of this most simple recipe depend on the size of the jar you plan to fill. I suggest storing it refrigerated. A little zip in the dish can go a long way on the taste buds. As I stated in the past, be sure not to touch your eyes after handling these peppers. A splash of cold milk is the best remedy for what I call chile burns.

EQUIPMENT:

1 —— pint/450 ml or desired size jar with tight-fitting lid, sterilized and air-dried

Sufficient amount of tiny chile peppers to fill your jar loosely, rinsed, dried, stems and caps removed

2 —— parts olive oil, divided

1 —— part cider vinegar, divided

1 —— tablespoon/18 g coarse kosher salt or to taste

1 to 2 — tablespoons/15 to 30 ml whiskey or brandy (optional)

1. Fill the jar with the prepared peppers. Working in small increments, start with combining ½ cup/120 ml olive oil and ¼ cup/60 ml vinegar and pour into the jar. If you need more, continue in the 2-to-1 ratio until the jar is filled.

2. Add the salt and whiskey, then cover the top with some wax paper and screw the cover on and shake. Let stand for about 2 weeks, in the refrigerator, to extract the chile heat, shaking the jar from time to time because the oil and vinegar do separate.

3. To use, hold back the chiles and pour out the amount of hot sauce you need to flavor soups and stews, basting sauces, marinades or even as a simple condiment. Serve some of the fiery gems on the side with soup. Take a bite and soften the fire with a spoonful of soup. Store for up to 2 months in the refrigerator.

Note: Though some cooks may add garlic, I suggest adding garlic at the time you are preparing a recipe. You will be better able to control the amount of garlic flavor you give a dish and it's better for food safety, because garlic can promote botulism bacteria when stored in oil.

Chile Marinade

Vinho d'Alhos com Piri-piri

MAKES ABOUT ½ CUP/120 ML

This is just one version of many marinades for grilling. You can cut some of the heat by excluding the seeds.
Use your favorite chile pepper for this marinade, which also makes a great basting sauce, or *molho*.
The tang of vinegar is a flavorful counterpoint to the chiles.

---

1 —— teaspoon/6 g coarse kosher salt or to taste

2 or 3 — garlic cloves, finely chopped

2 or 3 — tiny chile peppers, stemmed, finely chopped (about 1 to 2 teaspoons/ 3 to 6 g)

1 —— tablespoon/8 g sweet paprika

½ —— cup/120 ml lemon juice, cider vinegar, white wine or brandy

½ —— cup/120 ml olive oil

1. In the bowl of a mortar, grind the salt and garlic together with the pestle to form a paste. Grind in the chile peppers and paprika.

2. Blending, drizzle in the lemon juice, followed by the olive oil. Mix well and let stand for 30 minutes in a bowl with a cover. Pour over meats set in a bowl, turning to coat evenly, and marinate for several hours or overnight. Alternatively, use it to baste meats while grilling.

Note: Chile Pepper Paste (*massa de malagueta*) is a hot salty preparation. Mix 1 pound/454 g fine chopped chiles of choice, stems and caps removed, with ½ cup/145 g coarse kosher salt. Stirring daily, refigerate for one week. Pack in jars, top off with olive oil. Store in refrigerator and use as needed. Alternatives are hot sauce, crushed diced chiles and commercial brands of hot chopped peppers.

Sweet Pepper Paste
Massa de Pimentão

MAKES ABOUT 2 CUPS/450 G

Massa de pimentão is a characteristic ingredient, especially in the Alentejo.
It stores easily in the refrigerator until needed. Add a spoonful or two to seasonings, rubs or braises to
ramp up the flavor. This recipe is adapted from my book *Portuguese Homestyle Cooking*.

EQUIPMENT:

Free-standing stainless steel, footed colander with small holes or mesh (a cheesecloth can be used to line a colander that has large holes) or a 10 x 12 x 2–inch/25 x 30 x 5–cm wooden box with ¼-inch/6-mm spaces between bottom slats

2 ——— sterilized 8-ounce/225-g jelly jars with tight-fitting lids

Wax paper as needed

4 ——— very large red bell peppers, cored, seeded and quartered

5 ——— pounds/2270 g coarse kosher salt (not pickling salt, which is too fine)

½ ——— cup/120 ml olive oil (Portuguese, Spanish or Italian extra virgin)

Note: When stored in the refrigerator, *massa de pimentão* and *massa de malagueta* will last for at least 6 months. Do not add fresh garlic to this preparation.

1. Set a rectangular, fine-mesh colander or box on the bottom of a large, nonreactive pan or dish with 1-inch/2.5-cm sides. Make sure it sits directly on the pan.

2. Pour a ¾- to 1-inch/2- to 2.5-cm layer of salt into the bottom of the box or colander to create the salt base. Do not move the container once you have set it in place and added the salt.

3. Arrange a layer of peppers on the salt, cut side down, pressing them into the salt. Be sure to cut any curled piece of pepper, or mold can grow in the curl.

4. Pour a ½-inch/1.3-cm layer of salt over the layer of peppers; repeat with the remaining peppers and top off with a final ½-inch/1.3-cm layer of salt. Cover with wax paper, then top with a heavy plate or two to weight it down. Place a small item under the pan to tilt it so the pepper juices will run away from the box or colander. Set the pan aside on your counter for up to 4 days to allow the juices to drain from the peppers and run into the bottom pan. After the third day, the peppers will be thinner, about ¼ inch/6 mm or even less. The amount of water draining will have stopped.

5. Wipe off the excess salt (do not rinse) and place them in the bowl of a food processor. Pulse for about 15 to 20 seconds to a medium texture, not a smooth purée. (A meat grinder can also be used.)

6. Fill the sterilized jars, leaving about 1 inch/2.5 cm of headspace at the top. Pour ½ inch/1.3 cm of olive oil over the ground peppers. Place a piece of wax paper over the opening. Close the jar tightly over the wax paper and refrigerate.

7. To use, simply scrape aside the solidified olive oil, scoop out a tablespoon or two of the paste and add a tablespoon/15 ml of olive oil on top of the jarred peppers before recovering.

Sauces and Vinaigrettes

Molhos e Molhangas

The word *molho* normally indicates a pan sauce or gravy from a stew, braise or sauté. However, it is used loosely enough to also mean simply seasoned vinaigrettes that are used to drizzle over fresh cheese, fried fish and mini omelets. *Molho cru* (*cru* meaning "raw sauce") and *escabeche* (as it's known on the mainland) are simply uncooked vinaigrettes. Most of the vinaigrettes are raw, while others, such as the Vinegar Sauce with Tomato/*Tomatada*, from *Portuguese Homestyle Cooking*, and the version in this book on page 377, are lightly simmered and then removed from the heat before adding the vinegar. We refer to these as *molhangas* (pronounced *me-yunga* or *mel-yunga* depending on the region). All of these vinaigrettes, which vary from one region to another, add a brightness and tang to the food they are splashed and drizzled over.

Onion and Parsley Vinaigrette

Molho Cru

MAKES ABOUT 2 CUPS/470 ML

Simply drizzling this flavorful vinaigrette over the farmer's-style Fresh Cheese *Requeijão* (recipe in *Portuguese Homestyle Cooking*) or Easy Cream Cheese (page 201) gives it life. Fresh mozzarella can be used as a substitute. Individual taste-bud-grabbing flavors of onion, garlic and chiles meld together with just the right amount of zing from the essence of heat to please the palate. You don't want to make it so spicy, however, that the heat of the peppers overpowers the flavor of the other ingredients. Edelberto Ataide, an excellent and popular Portuguese cook, generously shared his recipe, which calls for parsley. I also like it with fresh cilantro. This can be served over fried or grilled fish, freshly boiled potatoes or as a dipping sauce for your bread.

½ — medium onion, finely chopped (about ½ cup/80 g)

½ — cup/30 g finely chopped parsley or cilantro (6 to 8 large sprigs)

½ — cup/120 ml red wine vinegar or as needed

1 to 2 — rounded tablespoons/15 to 30 g Chile Pepper Paste (page 365)

½ — head garlic, peeled, mashed or finely chopped (about 5 large cloves)

10 — tablespoons/150 ml Portuguese or Italian extra virgin olive oil

1 to 2 — teaspoons/6 to 12 g coarse kosher salt or to taste

1. In a small bowl, combine the onion and parsley. Pour in enough vinegar to just cover them. Stir and mix in the chile pepper paste and garlic. While whisking constantly, drizzle in the olive oil. Season with salt. The sauce should have body to it, not a watery consistency. Let stand for minimum 1 to 1½ hours to meld the flavors.

2. **To serve with fresh cheese:** Blot the cheese with paper towels before serving to prevent any residual whey from weeping into the spicy sauce. Season the cheese with extra salt if needed. Place cut slices of cheese or the whole round of cheese on a serving dish and drizzle the sauce over or around the cheese. Olives and chunks of fresh crusty bread are good accompaniments.

Roasted Garlic Dressing

Molho de Alho Assado

MAKES ABOUT 1 CUP/235 ML

This is a delightfully simple dressing that imparts a garlicky flavor with an interesting touch of sweet pepper to fresh cheese. At Atasca Restaurant in Cambridge, Massachusetts, Chef Jose (Joe) Cerqueira serves this over dishes of sliced fresh Portuguese cheese, tomatoes and red onions. This adapted version is easy to make and easily doubled. Here I have cut the recipe to serve with one 8-ounce/227-g round of fresh cheese. The remaining garlic (if using a whole head) can be mixed with a little extra virgin olive oil and spread on fresh or toasted bread points. If you prefer, wrap just 5 cloves in foil. Add the chile paste in small increments to your taste.

1 ——— small head garlic, unpeeled

¼ ——— cup/60 ml olive oil

¼ ——— cup/60 ml Chile Pepper Paste (page 365) or hot sauce

Coarse kosher salt to taste

¼ ——— cup/40 g coarsely chopped red onion

1 ——— tablespoon/4 g finely chopped parsley

1. Preheat the oven to 400°F/200°C, or gas mark 6.

2. Roast the garlic. Wrap the head of garlic or just 5 large cloves in foil and place on a baking sheet. Roast in the oven for 20 minutes. When cool enough to handle, just squeeze the individual cloves out of their skins into a bowl and mash or use a mortar and pestle.

3. Combine the mashed garlic with the olive oil and chile pepper paste and taste. Season with salt if needed. Add the chopped onion. Spoon some of the dressing over slices of fresh Portuguese farmer's-style cheese or even fresh mozzarella on a serving dish with slices of tomatoes and perhaps some thinly sliced *presunto* ham. Sprinkle with the parsley and serve.

Note: *Presunto* ham is the Portuguese version of the Italian prosciutto, which can be substituted.

Aromatic Cumin Sauce

Molho de Cominhos

MAKES ABOUT 3 CUPS/705 ML

You will not be disappointed if you try this heady sauce drizzled judiciously over boiled soft-shell crab or shelled crabmeat. Cumin's flavor is an acquired taste. It is one spice used more in the Azores islands than the mainland. Keep in mind that cumin is a potent spice. A little bit goes a long way, so gradually adjust the amount to your taste. Cousin Tony Ortins, who is from Graciosa, loves to use it, especially with fresh boiled soft-shell crabs.

---

2 —— cups/470 ml water

¼ —— cup/40 g finely chopped onion

¼ —— cup/60 g tomato paste

2 —— tablespoons/8 g finely chopped parsley or cilantro

1 —— tablespoon/15 ml olive oil

1 —— tablespoon/15 ml hot sauce or Chile Pepper Paste (page 365)

3 —— garlic cloves, coarsely chopped

1½ —— teaspoons/7 ml wine vinegar

¼ —— teaspoon ground cumin or to taste

⅛ —— teaspoon (2 or 3) Jamaican allspice berries

1 —— teaspoon/5 g coarse kosher salt to taste

1. Mix all the ingredients, except the salt, in a medium saucepan. Bring to a boil over medium-high heat, reduce the heat to low and simmer for 5 minutes. Taste for salt and add only if needed, and it is ready to serve.

Butter and Garlic Wine Sauce

Molho de Manteiga, Vinho e Alho

MAKES 2½ CUPS/588 ML

Here is a very quick and easy to make spicy sauce from my friend Ana Craveiro. The essence of cilantro melds with butter, wine and garlic when heated into a sauce that complements the shellfish. You can have this sauce ready and waiting for the shrimp or scallops to come off the grill, the broiler or out of the oven. Shellfish drizzled with this fast sauce can be served as a starter, or simply add a fresh salad to make a light meal.

2 ——— cups/470 ml white wine

½ ——— cup/112 g butter

2 ——— tablespoons/16 g finely chopped garlic

1 ——— tablespoon/15 ml hot sauce

2 to 3 — tablespoons/8 to 12 g finely chopped fresh cilantro or parsley, divided

Pinch of coarse kosher salt to taste

1. Combine the wine, butter, garlic, hot sauce and half of the cilantro in a small pot and bring to a boil. Reduce the heat to medium-low and simmer for 1 minute, until well blended. Add the salt if needed. Garnish with the remaining cilantro.

Garlic Cream Sauce with Cilantro

Molho de Natas com Alho e Coentros

MAKES 1 CUP/235 ML

Serving a dipping sauce on the side of traditionally non-dipped fish cakes and shrimp turnovers works well, especially when it is a creamy garlic one that delightfully pleases the taste buds. So here I blend garlic with cilantro to infuse this smooth, creamy sauce just right. The lemon juice and mustard give a nice counterpoint to the cream. When paired with codfish cakes, croquettes or shrimp turnovers for dipping, this sauce not only matches the strength of their flavor but also brings an already wonderful starter up to a contemporary level.

---

2 — tablespoons/28 g butter

1 — tablespoon/8 g flour

3 — garlic cloves, smashed

1 — cup/235 ml heavy cream

2 — tablespoons/8 g finely chopped cilantro or parsley

1½ — teaspoons/7 g Chile Pepper Paste (page 365) or to taste

1 — teaspoon/5 ml lemon juice or to taste

¼ to ½ — teaspoon Dijon mustard

¼ — teaspoon ground white pepper

¼ — teaspoon ground cumin (optional)

1 — teaspoon/6 g coarse kosher salt or to taste

1. Melt the butter in a small saucepan. Whisk in the flour and stir to make a roux. Cook over low heat for about 1 minute to cook out the starch. Add the garlic and cook just until the garlic is really aromatic but not colored, about 30 seconds.

2. Gradually whisk in the heavy cream and then add the cilantro, chile pepper paste, lemon juice, mustard, pepper and cumin. Simmer over medium-low heat for 10 minutes or so, until slightly reduced. Do not allow to boil. Season the sauce with salt if needed. Let cool. Remove the garlic cloves before using and serve the sauce warm or at room temperature.

Simple Mustard Cream Sauce

Molho de Mustarda Simples com Nata

MAKES ½ CUP/120 ML

This by far is the easiest mustard sauce I have ever made. Equal parts wine and mustard blended with cream, herbs and white pepper give a light kick to pan sauces. The recipe can be doubled for larger uses or cut in half for one serving. Be creative and add your special touches.

¼ ——— cup/60 ml heavy cream

2 ——— tablespoons/30 ml white wine

2 ——— tablespoons/22 g your favorite mustard

½ ——— tablespoon/2 g finely chopped parsley

¼ ——— teaspoon freshly ground white pepper

½ ——— teaspoon coarse kosher salt or to taste

1. Place all the ingredients in a jar or container with a tight-fitting lid. Cover tightly and shake vigorously for 1 to 2 minutes, until well blended. Taste for salt and adjust if needed

2. **To Use:** Blend 1 to 2 tablespoons/15 to 30 ml into pan drippings of sautéed steak or coat a rack of lamb before pressing the meat with bread crumbs.

Wine-Based Tempura Batter
Massa Vinha

MAKES 2 CUPS/470 ML

This is a light batter usually made with wine, but it can be done with beer as an alternative. Commonly used for coating cut vegetables, especially green beans, asparagus and cauliflower, it is also a great batter for coating fish and even oysters for frying. The addition of wine and chile sauce gives the batter a puffy texture with a kick. Water can be used to make it alcohol-free, but the batter texture will be different. According to oral history, it was this method the Portuguese taught to the Japanese for tempura.

---

3 —— eggs, at room temperature, separated

1½ —— tablespoons/23 ml white wine (beer or water can be substituted if desired)

1 —— teaspoon/6 g coarse kosher salt or to taste

Dash or two of hot sauce (optional)

¾ —— cup/90 g all-purpose flour

Corn oil as needed

Assortment of rinsed and parboiled (if necessary) vegetables, cut into serving pieces

1. In a bowl with an electric mixer on high speed, beat the egg whites until soft peaks form, about 1 to 2 minutes. Set aside.

2. Lightly whisk the eggs yolks in a separate bowl, and gradually mix in the wine and salt. Stir in the hot sauce.

3. Sift the flour over the batter and fold in, blending well.

4. Fold in the beaten egg whites until no whites are visible.

5. **To Use:** Pour 4 to 5 inches/10 to 12.5 cm of oil into a deep pot and heat to 350°F/180°C. Dip the prepped ingredients into the batter. Immediately fry the coated vegetables in the hot oil until golden. Drain on paper toweling. Serve as a side or as a starter with Simple Mustard Cream Sauce (page 374) or Garlicky Tomato Sauce with Sweet Pepper Paste (page 377) to dip the fried vegetables into.

Garlicky Tomato Sauce with Sweet Pepper Paste
Tomatada

MAKES ABOUT 2½ TO 3 CUPS/588 TO 705 ML

If you are a gardener, you know that moment when tomatoes are in abundance, ripening all at once. Suddenly you find yourself thinking of things to make. This garlicky sauce is a great way to use up some very ripe freshly harvested tomatoes. Regina Sousa, of Graciosa in the Azores, learned this garlicky sweet pepper version, which has a little kick and tang, during her early culinary lessons from a mainland cook. Use the best very ripe fresh tomatoes you can find or in the middle of winter, use the best-quality canned ones available. This Alentejo-influenced sauce is usually served over boiled potatoes. It can also be served over savory filled crepes. If you cannot make or find sweet pepper paste, substitute 2 teaspoons of paprika or process sweet red peppers with a teaspoon of coarse salt in the food processor until fine textured.

¼ —— cup/60 ml olive oil

10 —— garlic cloves, finely chopped

6 —— cups/1080 g peeled, seeded, finely chopped tomatoes

2 —— teaspoons/10 g Sweet Pepper Paste (page 367)

1 —— teaspoon/5 g Chile Pepper Paste (page 365) or hot sauce or generous pinch of crushed red pepper

½ —— teaspoon coarse kosher salt or to taste

3 —— tablespoons/45 ml cider vinegar

1. Heat the oil in a 2-quart/1.8-L heavy-bottomed pan. Toss in the garlic.

2. When the garlic becomes aromatic but not colored, about 30 seconds, stir in the tomatoes, sweet pepper paste and chile pepper paste, then bring to a boil. Reduce the heat to medium and simmer until the sauce is reduced to the point where you can draw a spoon across the bottom of the pan and the line nearly remains, about 30 to 35 minutes. The amount you yield will depend on how much you reduce the sauce.

3. Season with salt and mix in the vinegar. Serve over boiled potatoes.

Acknowledgments

How does one express enough gratitude and appreciation for the hours of help so many have given me with this book? I was always taught to cherish the knowledge of those who cleared the path, especially those cooks who have been living the Portuguese culture every day for years. For my family, my late father, my mother and grandmother, my aunts, cousins and friends, I cannot thank you enough for your teachings, influence, support and encouragement. Whether you helped me test, shared your personal recipes, gave helpful tidbits, lent me a cooking tool, let me stick a measuring cup under your hand before you tossed an ingredient into a pot, answered my questions or simply taste tested—I am so grateful. As a first-generation Portuguese-American, like many, I cherish my roots. Although I don't know every Portuguese recipe, I have expanded my family recipe box thanks to everyone who has, in some form, shared his or her personal family recipes.

First to my husband, Philip, thank you for being all that you are. Through thick and thin, no matter how many pots, pans and bowls came your way, you rolled with it and kept things operating like a well-oiled machine. Although you don't cook, you tasted and tasted; you weren't shy about critiquing and you were unbelievable. To Nancy, my son-in-law Mike, Marc, my daughter-in-law Sara and my grandchildren, you were always up for a challenge and there is nothing like family support. Thank you!

Thank you to my testers, who came through recipe after recipe, with the positives and negatives that helped me filter through so many dishes. It didn't matter how little or how much you helped, from testing, advising or critiquing—it was invaluable to me. You might have forgotten what you did, but I haven't; thank you to Laureen Andria, David Ankeles, Steve Baker and Teresa Gonçalves Baker, Else and Zizi Bettencourt, Joe and Maria Cerqueira, Amelia Conceição, Ana Matos Craveiro, Valerie Curtiss, Elaine Emmett, Melody Lema, Cecilia Lortscher, Feliz Matsuda, Marc and Sara Ortins, Ezilda Raposo, Renee Oliveira Rogers, Michael and Nancy Savage, Gil Sequeira and Daniel Torres.

To Kim Allen, Michael Amaral, Jose Antonio, Dolores Antunes, Edelberto Ataide, João B., D. Batalha, Michael Benson, John Bettencourt, Sister Kathy Bettencourt, John Borges, Antonio Bragança, Maria Braz, Margarida Bettencourt Carvalho, Delia Case, Maria Cerqueira, Dolores Chavas, Barbara and John Ciman, Maria Coimbra, Teresa Constantino, Maria Cunha, Jay DeFrank, Antonio and Maria dos Santos, Maria Pereira Ellis, "mother" Julia Fernandes, Lili Oliveira Ferreira, Dolores and John Figueiredo, Noreen Galopim, Mary Gil, Amelia Gonçalves, Fatima Lima, Dilia Luz, Duarte and Maria Machado, Dalila Martins, Feliz (Shirly) Matsuda, Fel and Edith Medeiros, Nazare Mendes, Ester and Antonio Mendonca, Marguerite and Joe Mendonca, Angel Micarelli, Mariana Morais, Rui and Lucy Neves, Isaura Nogueira, Maria Elpidia (Pita) Nunes, Antonio and Noelia Ortins, Mary Ortins, Caroline Pacheco, Maria Alice Pais, Virginia Pais, Blandina Pereira, Ezilda Raposo, Lucy Rebelo, Marylou Ribeiro, Clara Santos, Maria Santos, Fred Shaw, Conçeicão Silva, Imelda Silva, Linda Silva, M. Quelmine Silva, Maria Silva, Francine Sousa, Regina Sousa, Arcenia Texeira, Helder Texeira, Roger Texeira, my aunt Ana and uncle Ilidio Valente, Maria Veludo, Anne Marie Viviers and Maria Elena Zanni: to all of you, thank you again for helping make this book possible.

A special thank you to my amazing longtime friend, Chef Joe Cerqueira. Joe has been a great inspiration to me and has been enthusiastic and helpful with recipes and events in both my projects, as well as just a great friend. Christened Jose Antonio Neto Cerqueira, "Joe" Cerqueira came to the United States from Arcos de Valdevez, of the Minho region in northern Portugal, when he was just twenty-three years old. Before he came, he had already begun to build up immense experience in the hospitality business by working and learning in his aunt's restaurant, working in restaurants in France and then traveling to Venezuela, where he learned their formality of hospitality. Arriving here, he found his niche, working his way in the restaurant business and opening his first location with his wife Maria, where we first met him, in Cambridge, Massachusetts. After opening Atasca Restaurant, some years later, he relocated to 50 Hampshire Street in Cambridge, where he and Maria continue to work hard satisfying customers. He has graciously shared some of his recipes for this book.

Again, thank you all for helping me share and preserve the flavors of our heritage. Thank you to Chef Manuel Azevedo for your kind words but especially for giving me the boost I needed to finish this book.

Thank you to Ted Axelrod. Your creativity goes beyond words. It was a wonderful and inspiring learning experience and an utmost pleasure to work with you on the photography. To my publisher, Will Kiester, for believing in this book, and to Marissa Giambelluca, Meghan Baskis and Karen Levy, it has been a pleasure to work with you. The team effort has been unbelievable.

About the Author

Ana Patuleia Ortins was born and raised in Peabody, Massachusetts. In the early 1930s, her father, Rufino, and his family immigrated to the United States from Galveias, a small town in the Alentejo Province of the Portugal mainland. Rufino shared his culinary talent and passion for his Portuguese food with Ana when she was very young, showing her how to gut sardines and cut kale as fine as grass for caldo verde soup. His tutelage, coupled with a zest for traditional dishes inherited from her mother, Filomena, who died when Ana was young, inspired her to learn as much as she could about her culinary roots and eventually, to document the family recipes she was raised on in her first book, *Portuguese Homestyle Cooking*. In *Authentic Portuguese Cooking*, Ana takes a deeper look at the little-known food of her heritage. Included are family recipes shared by family and friends as well as many obtained during trips to Portugal and the Azores, the ancestral home of her husband, Philip. Ana has an associate's degree in culinary arts from the Essex Agricultural and Technical School. She has contributed articles to *Fine Cooking* magazine, *Portugal Magazine, Seabourn Club Herald* and, most recently, the online magazine *The Cook's Cook*. She continues to teach culinary classes and is a member of the Northeast Chapter of Les Dames d'Escoffier. She resides with her husband in Peabody, Massachusetts.

Index

Note: Titles are indexed in both English and Portuguese. Ingredients and general subject entries are indexed in English only, with the exception of some specialty foods/terminology that are indexed in Portuguese as well. Page numbers in italic indicate figures.